Language and Globalization

Language and Globalization explores the effects of language in the processes of globalization. Norman Fairclough adopts the approach of combining critical discourse analysis with cultural political economy to develop a new theory of the relationship between discourse and other dimensions of globalization. Using examples from a variety of countries such as the USA, Britain, Romania, Hungary and Thailand, *Language and Globalization* shows how the analysis of texts can be coherently integrated within political economic analysis. Fairclough incorporates topical issues such as the war on terror and the impact of the media on globalization into his discussion. Areas covered include:

- Globalization and language: review of academic literature
- Discourses of globalization
- The media, mediation and globalization
- Globalization, war and terrorism.

This book will be of interest to students and researchers in applied linguistics, language and politics and discourse analysis.

Norman Fairclough was formerly Professor of Language in Social Life at Lancaster University, and is now an Emeritus Professor. His publications include *Language and Power* (1989), *Discourse and Social Change* (1992), *New Labour, New Language?* (Routledge, 2000) and *Analyzing Discourse* (Routledge, 2003). His current research is focused upon transition, globalization and Europeanization in Eastern Europe.

Language and Globalization

Norman Fairclough

Routledge
Taylor & Francis Group

LONDON AND NEW YORK

First published 2006 by Routledge
2 Park Square, Milton Park, Abingdon, Oxon OX14 4RN

Simultaneously published in the USA and Canada
by Routledge
270 Madison Ave, New York, NY 10016

Transferred to Digital Printing 2008

Routledge is an imprint of the Taylor & Francis Group, an informa business

© 2006 Norman Fairclough

Typeset in Perpetua by BC Typesetting Ltd, Bristol BS31 1NZ
Printed and bound in Great Britain by
TJI Digital, Padstow, Cornwall

British Library Cataloguing in Publication Data
A catalogue record for this book is available from the British Library

Library of Congress Cataloging in Publication Data
Fairclough, Norman, 1941–
    Language and globalization / by Norman Fairclough.
        p.   cm.
    1. Language and languages.   2. Globalization.   3. Mass media.
    4. Terrorism.   I. Title.
    P107.F35 2006
    303.48′2–dc22   2006011412

ISBN10: 0–415–31766–5 (hbk)
ISBN10: 0–415–31765–7 (pbk)
ISBN10: 0–203–59476–6 (ebk)

ISBN13: 978–0–415–31766–5 (hbk)
ISBN13: 978–0–415–31765–8 (pbk)
ISBN13: 978–0–203–59376–9 (ebk)

Contents

Acknowledgements

The publishers and editors would like to thank the following people and organizations for permission to reproduce copyright material:

R. MacDonald, 'Fiddly jobs, undeclared working and the something for nothing society', *Work Employment and Society* 8.4 (1994); Z. Gille, 'Cognitive cartography in a European wasteland: multinational capital and Greens vie for village alliance', in M. Burawoy *et al.* (2000); Greenpeace Australia, *Map Ta Phut: A New Market for Australian Coal*, 2005, http://www.greenpeace.org.au/climate/pdfs/MapTaPhut. briefing.pdf; Greenpeace International, *Stop Climate Killing Coal Plants in Thailand*, 2005, http://www.greenpeace.org/international/press/releases/stop-climate-killing coal-plan; Romanian Ministry of Communications and Information Technology, *'Outsourcingul'* Press release, 22 November 2005; T. Friedman, *The Lexus and the Olive Tree*, New York: First Anchor Books (2000); S. Eizenstat, 'The threat to a more open global system' 1999, http://bogota.usembassy. gov/wwwse909.shtml; Department of Trade and Industry *Our Competitive Future (UK Competitiveness White Paper*, (1998)), http://www.dti.gov.uk/comp/competitive/; ECLAC (UN Economic Commission for Latin America and the Caribbean) *Globalization and Development*, (2002), http://www.eclac.cl/cgi-bin/getProd. asp?xml=/publicaciones/xml/5/10035/P10035.xml&xsl=/tpi-i/p9f.xslebase= /tpl/top-bottom.xslt; Dr Mahathir bin Mohamad *Renewing Asia's Foundations of Growth*, East Asia Economic Summit, (2002), http:www.larouchpub.com/ other/2002/2940.mahathir.html; Coaching and Mentoring Website, *What are Coaching and Mentoring?* (2005) http:www.coachingnetwork.org.uk/Resource-Centre/WhatAreCoachingAndMentoring.htm; Council of the European Union *Presidency Conclusions, Lisbon Council Meeting*, (2000), http://ue.eu.int/ueDocs/ cms_Data/docs/pressData/en/ec/00100–r1.eno.htm; University of Bucharest *Manual of Quality Control*, (2004), http://www.unibuc.ro/ro/; Commission of the European Communities, *Communication from the European Commission on the Social Agenda*, (2005), http://europa.eu.int/comm/employment_social_policy_

agenda/spa-en.pdf; Romanian Ministry of European Integration, National Development Plan 2004–2006, (2002), http://www.mie.ro/Pdr/Romana/mdp_ro/dezvoltare/pnd2004/download/cuprins.htm; Romanian Commission against Poverty and for Promotion of Social Inclusion, *National Action Plan Against Poverty and for Social Inclusion,* (2001), http://www.capsis.ro/pagini/ro/pnainc.php; Cosmopolitan, 'Ghidul Cosmo al marilor decizii (Cosmo guide to big decisions)', *Cosmopolitan (Romanian edition)* April 2005; Bush, *Address to the Nation,* 11 September 2001, http://www.whitehouse.gov/news/releases/2001/09/20010911-16.html; President G.W. Bush, *Address to a Joint Session of Congress and to the American People,* 20 September 2001, http://www.whitehouse.gov/news/releases/2001/09/20010920-8.html; President G.W. Bush (2003) *Remarks in Commencement Address to US Coast Guard Academy,* 21 May 2003, http://www.whitehouse.gov/news/releases/2003/o5/20030521–2.html; Condoleeza Rice, 'The president's national security strategy', (2002) in I. Stelzer (ed.) *Neoconservatism,* London: Atlantic Books; John Ashcroft, Prepared remarks for the US mayors' conference, 25 October 2001, reprinted in R. Jackson *Writing the War on Terrorism. Language, Politics and Counter-terrorism,* Manchester: Manchester University Press, (2005); Tony Blair, *Doctrine of the International Community,* Chicago, 22 April 1999, http://www.number-10.gov.uk/output/Page1297.asp; Tony Blair, Speech in the George Bush Senior Presidential Library, Washington, April 10 2002, http://www.number-10.gov.uk/output/Page1712.asp; Tony Blair, Speech at the Foreign Office Conference, London, 21 January 2003, http:www.number-10.gov.uk/output/Page1765.asp; Václav Havel, Fulbright Prize Address (1997), http://www.fulbrightalumni.org/olc/pub/FBA/fulbright_prize/havel_address.html.

I am grateful to members of the Discourse Analysis Research Group in Bucharest for discussions on aspects of 're-scaling' in Romania, to Ruth Wodak for our collaboration on the impact of the Bologna Declaration on higher education in Austria and Romania, to Bob Jessop and Andrew Sayer for our collaboration on the place of semiosis in critical realism and for many discussions and ideas, and above all to my wife Isabela Ieţcu for her help with Romanian material in the book, our discussions about aspects of change in Romania, and her love and support throughout the period when I was working on the book.

Introduction

This is a book about globalization, but with a particular focus on language. It is also partly about war, because I see the so-called 'war on terror' as closely linked to the more recent history of globalization. Later in the Introduction I shall explain how. But I'll begin with the question: why approach globalization with a focus on language?

Let's take a concrete example, a statement by the Romanian Minister of Communications and Information Technology at a National Conference on 'Outsourcing' in November 2005 (Ministry of Communications and Information Technology 2005).

> Outsourcing is an area of success for Romanian Information and Communications Technologies. Competition in this market has become intense, with Romania having to compete in the global village not only with European countries but also with countries in the Far East and Latin America. Only a marketing and branding strategy which is well structured and envisaged for the medium term will help us to situate ourselves in a leading position in this global competition.

This sort of business discourse (we might be tempted to say 'jargon') is very familiar in the West, but it has only begun to appear in Romania and other 'post-communist' countries of Central and Eastern Europe over the past few years. This is my translation of the Romanian original below, and I think readers will recognize most of the words I have italicized.

> *Outsourcingul* este un domeniu de *succes* al *IT&C – ului romanesc. Competitia* pe aceasta piata a devenit una foarte stransa, Romania fiind nevoita sa concureze in *satul global* nu doar cu tarile europene, ci si cu cele din Orientul Indepartat sau America Latina. Doar o *strategie* de *marketing* si de *branding* bine structurata si gandita pe termen mediu ne va ajuta sa ne situam pe un loc fruntas in aceasta *competitie globala.*

We can take this official statement as indicative of one area of contemporary globalization – Romania, which had a socialist economy and a one-party state until 1989, is now operating economically in the capitalist 'global economy', and has become something approaching a 'western democracy'. We can also see that this change for Romania includes a change in the Romanian language: some of the italicized vocabulary is recent direct borrowing from English ('marketing', 'branding', 'outsourcing' – the suffix '-ul' in the Romanian is the definite article, like 'the' in English), while some other words ('succes', 'competitia', 'global', 'strategie') previously existed in Romanian and are historically the same as words familiar to us in English (with differences in spelling, pronunciation and morphology due to the difference between the languages), but are used here in the ways and with the meanings of contemporary business English, which is new in Romanian. And we have one direct translation of an English expression which has become a cliché associated with globalization – 'global village' ('satul global'). But this modern and, for Romania, novel business discourse is combined with one expression which now sounds rather archaic: 'un loc fruntas', which I translated as 'a leading position'. This was itself something of a cliché in socialist times, before 1989.

So the new business discourse in Romania is expressed in a Romanian language which is strongly influenced by the English language – and more specifically the discourse of business in English. But the relationship between economic globalization as it affects Romania and the new business discourse goes deeper. The economic globalization is real enough in some sectors of the economy. Real people are engaged in real economic processes on a global scale; their economic practices have changed, and so have their identities – some economic agents (e.g. people in management and marketing) in Romania now are in a meaningful sense different sorts of people from economic agents before 1989. But this could not have happened without the change in discourse – indeed the change in discourse is an inherent element of the economic change. One can see the relationship between the two in historical terms: it was only after the discourse began to circulate and be disseminated in Romania that the new economic practices, institutions, organizations and agents which it predicted and prescribed for Romania (we might say 'imagined' for Romania) began to become real. Economic change began to occur when the discourse was operationalized, implemented, put into practice. Some of the terms and categories in this discourse (particularly 'outsourcing', 'a marketing and branding strategy') are on one level ideas, but ideas that only have an impact when they are operationalized through changes in organizational practices and structures. But the one archaic Romanian expression I referred to ('un loc fruntas') is a small illustration of a major theme in the book: globalization, and social change more generally, do not simply dispense with the past – on the contrary, change coexists with continuity, and the ways in which things change in particular places depend upon the social and historical context. But let me move on from the example and discuss the question 'why approach globalization with a focus on language?' in more general terms.

Language in processes of globalization

Here are two very general formulations of the complex sets of changes which have been widely referred to as 'globalization': 'a process (or set of processes) which embodies a transformation in the spatial organization of social relations and transactions . . . generating transcontinental or interregional flows and networks of activity, interaction, and the exercise of power' (Held *et al.* 1999: 16); 'complex connectivity . . . the rapidly developing and ever-densening network of interconnections and interdependencies that characterize modern social life' (Tomlinson 1999: 2). These 'flows', 'networks' and 'interconnections' are generally seen as very diverse in character, and including for instance: flows of goods and money, and international financial and trading networks, in the economic field; intergovernmental networks, and interdependencies and interactions and interconnections between international agencies such as the United Nations, the International Monetary Fund and the World Trade Organization and government agencies at national and regional levels; the mobility of people as migrants, tourists, or members of commercial or governmental organizations; flows of images and representations and interactions through contemporary media and communications technologies; and so forth.

Let me make three initial points about language in processes of globalization, understood in this sort of way.

First, the networks, connectivities and interactions which cut across spatial boundaries and borders crucially include, and we might say depend upon, particular forms (or what I shall call *genres*) of communication which are specialized for trans-national and interregional interaction. And the 'flows' include flows of representations, narratives and *discourses*. In that sense, it is partly language that is globalizing and globalized. ('Genres' and 'discourses' will be important categories in the book, which I explain more fully below. In essence, a genre is a way of communicating or interacting, and a discourse is a way of representing some part or aspect of the world.) The genres of communication I am referring to include for instance the genres of trans-national news media, such as CNN news programmes, which are organized to communicate news in a distinctive (though widely imitated) way which is familiar and easily recognized all over the world. Another example is the genres or formats of the websites of international organizations such as the United Nations, the European Union, or international corporations like IBM, or campaigning organizations like Greenpeace – although there are variations, the design and organization of websites involve genres of communication which are internationally used and recognized. An example of the discourses which I am referring to is 'neo-liberal' economic discourse, which claims amongst other things that markets are 'self-regulating', and presents the role of states and governments as 'facilitating' the working of markets but not seeking to 'interfere' with them. Another example is discourses of popular culture (e.g. popular music), which are widely disseminated across the globe on the websites and in the magazines which young people use.

Second, it is important to make a distinction between actual processes and tendencies of globalization, and discourses of globalization. We cannot get away from the fact that although 'globalization' is a set of changes which are actually happening in the world (though what the set includes is highly controversial), it is also a *word* which has quite recently become prominent in the ways in which such changes are represented. But this is a simplification, because the word 'globalization' is used in various senses within more complex discourses, which are partly characterized by distinctive vocabularies in which 'globalization' is related in particular (and differing) ways from other 'keywords' such as 'modernization', 'democracy', 'markets', 'free trade', 'flexibility', 'liberalization', 'security', 'terrorism', 'culture', 'cosmopolitanism' and so forth. And these discourses are more than vocabularies – they also differ in grammatical features (e.g. in some discourses but not others, 'globalization' is represented as an agent which itself causes changes in the world, as in 'globalization opens up new markets'), as well as forms of narrative, forms of argumentation and so forth.

Third, having made this distinction, it is equally important to consider what the *relationship* is between actual processes of globalization and discourses of globalization. In broad terms, we can say that discourses of globalization do not merely represent processes and tendencies of globalization which are happening independently. They can under certain conditions also contribute to creating and shaping actual processes of globalization. For example, the neo-liberal economic discourse I referred to above has been highly influential in giving a particular shape to global economic processes and relations. Globalization as a set of actual processes of change is, as I have indicated above, very complex and multi-faceted (e.g. it has economic, political, cultural, environmental and military aspects), and too 'big' a phenomenon to be controlled by any particular agency. But particular agencies (e.g. powerful governments and corporations, and international agencies like the IMF) do attempt, with some success, to push and inflect aspects of globalization in particular directions, and discourses such as neo-liberal economic discourse are an important part of the strategies they develop to do this.

I should just briefly mention a thorny epistemological problem which arises in what I have been saying. I have argued that we need to distinguish actual processes of globalization from discourses of globalization, but then argued that discourses contribute to creating and shaping actual processes of globalization. Notice also that as soon as we start discussing the latter, we inevitably represent them in particular ways, drawing upon particular discourses. So I would seem to be saying two contradictory things: we need to make the distinction between actual processes and discourses – but we can't actually separate them. Actually my position is rather that (a) there *are* real processes of (e.g. economic) globalization, independently of whether people recognize them or not, and of how they represent them; (b) but as soon as we begin to reflect upon and discuss these real processes, we *have* to represent them, and the ways in which we represent them inevitably draw upon certain discourses rather than others. So we might say that the problem turns into that of how we decide *which* discourses to draw upon in reflecting upon and discussing these real processes – how we determine whether and to what extent particular discourses provide us with representations which are adequate for these processes.

To put it another way, how do we evaluate different discourses in terms of what Sayer (2000) calls their relative 'practical adequacy'? This would include whether they are reliable guides to action, whether what they suggest or imply about what will happen if we act in certain ways actually *does* happen. And we can support such judgements with various sorts of social scientific evidence. On the other hand, certain discourses (which arguably include the neo-liberal economic discourse I have referred to) which can be shown to be *not* adequate for real processes, which lack 'practical adequacy', can also be shown to be used to create and sustain unjust or undemocratic positions and relations of power, and can in that sense be regarded as *ideologies* (Eagleton 1991, Larrain 1979, Ricoeur 1986, Thompson 1984). So, I am suggesting that we *can* distinguish between actual processes and discourses, but that it is a rather more complex matter than it might appear to be.

Voices on globalization

A vast amount has been said and written about globalization, and this in itself makes it a difficult and sometimes confusing issue to write about. It is made more confusing if we do not distinguish what has been said or written by *whom*, and differentiate the main sources of all this talk and writing. I shall distinguish five main agencies and sets of agents:

- Academic analysis
- Governmental agencies
- Non-governmental agencies
- The media
- People in everyday life

Academic analysis differs from the others in that its orientation to globalization is primarily theoretical and analytical (the production of descriptions, interpretations, explanations and theories), whereas the others have a broadly practical orientation towards globalization as it impinges upon the practical conduct of social life, an orientation to action and strategies for action. This is not to say that academic analysis cannot incorporate a practical orientation – academics too are in some cases pursuing strategies to push globalization in particular directions, and their theory and analysis sometimes serves strategic ends. There is also a difference between media and the other practical agencies in that media in part represent the actions and strategies of the latter, which again does not preclude media agencies from having their own practical orientations and strategies, or being used as vehicles for those of others.

I am using 'governmental agencies' in a broad sense to include for instance national governments, political leaders, agencies which are a part of national governments (ministries, committees and so forth), local government, agencies of what we might call international government such as the United Nations or the World Bank or World Trade Organization. 'Non-governmental agencies' is used in an equally broad sense which includes for instance business corporations, political parties, charities such as Oxfam, and campaigning or monitoring organizations such as Greenpeace or CorpWatch. The media includes the press, radio, television and the internet, and in general terms all those entities which contribute to the socially important process of 'mediation'. We can understand mediation as partly a matter of overcoming distance in communication, communicating with 'distant others'. But when people communicate with 'distant others' they use particular 'media' (as the plural of 'medium') such as television, which have their own codes, conventions, formats, genres and so forth, and which affect the character of the communication in particular ways (Silverstone 1999, Tomlinson 1999). Mediation is socially important in the sense that, wherever people live and whatever they do in life, their experience is now a complex mixture of direct unmediated experience (e.g. in face-to-face interactions with others) and mediated experience (e.g. through watching television). 'People in everyday life' is an important corrective to the *public* character of the other sources: people have their own experiences of globalization in their ordinary lives and the various communities they are a part of (this includes what they watch on television), and they react to it in particular (and very diverse) ways, act in response to it, and in so doing produce representations which are also a significant part of all the talk and writing about globalization.

There are two points to note about this classification of sources. First, they are not fully discrete. There are flows between the different sources – for instance, academic analysis directly or indirectly contributes to the language of governmental and non-governmental agencies and the media, and may even be absorbed and appropriated in popular representations of globalization (for instance, McLuhan's concept of the 'global village' has been very widely disseminated, McLuhan and Fiore 1967). And in some cases academic analysis itself draws from other sources, e.g. from management literature on globalization. Second, differentiating just five major sources is inevitably a simplifying generalization, given that there are so many different 'voices' in the ongoing 'conversation' about globalization, but it will at least help us keep in mind the important question, '*who* is saying this?'

The structure of the book

The seven main chapters of the book partly correspond to these diverse voices. Chapter 1 reviews positions taken in the academic literature on discourse as an aspect or element of globalization. Chapter 2 sets out the approach I shall adopt to the topic of globalization and language, which is a version of critical discourse analysis embedded within a 'cultural' approach to political economy (I shall introduce this approach briefly below). In Chapter 3 I discuss strategies and discourses of globalization of governmental and non-governmental agencies, focusing on the internationally dominant strategy and discourse of 'globalism' or neo-liberal globalization (see below). In Chapter 4, I discuss how processes of globalization impact upon specific spatial 'entities' (nation-states, cities, regions, etc.) in terms of the idea of 're-scaling', i.e. changing relations between local, national, and international (including 'global') scales of social activity and interaction. I focus upon a national entity (Romania) and its repositioning in relation to the global scale and the 'macro-regional' scale of the European Union, drawing on material from governmental agencies. In Chapter 5 I deal with the media and mediation, which I do not refer to in Chapter 4, but which are clearly a significant aspect of and influence on processes of re-scaling. Up to this point, the focus will be on public agencies, but in Chapter 6 I shall discuss the strategies which people leading their ordinary lives in specific localities (cities, towns, villages) develop for coping with and acting upon a globalizing world, and the effects of these strategies on globalization – what we might call 'globalization from below' (Falk 1999).

Chapter 7 deals with war and terrorism, and the examples I discuss come from governmental agencies. I mentioned above my view of the 'war on terror' as closely linked to the recent history of globalization. A discussion of this issue may seem surprising in a book about globalization, so let me briefly explain it, and in so doing clarify the particular stance I am taking on globalization and its language facet. This book, like any treatment of such a vast theme as globalization is bound to be, is selective – it includes certain things and excludes others, highlights certain things and backgrounds others. A major theme will be what Steger (2005) has called 'globalism' (see also Saul 2005), which is the strategy and discourse of globalization which has become most influential, has had most effect on actual processes of change, and is associated with the most powerful countries, international agencies and corporations. The key feature of 'globalism' is that it interprets globalization in a neo-liberal way as primarily the liberalization and global integration of markets, linked to the spread of a particular version of '(western) democracy', and the strategies it is associated with are aimed at shifting or inflecting globalization in a neo-liberal direction. To put the point in a more contentious way, it is a strategy for *hijacking* globalization in the service of particular national and corporate interests.

People often portray the 'war on terror' as having been sparked by the attacks on the World Trade Center and the Pentagon in September 2001, and there is clearly some truth in that. But it can also be interpreted in a broader frame as the centrepiece of a longer-term shift on the part of the USA, with the support of a number of allies (especially Britain), from 'soft power' to 'hard power', in response to pressures on 'globalism' which began to build up from the mid-1990s (Steger 2005). These included economic crises in Asia and Latin America which led to widespread doubt about whether globalization in its globalist form could 'deliver the goods', coupled with growing concern about the negative effects of this form of globalization (including the increasing gap between rich and poor, the international debt crisis, the inequities of world trade), and an emerging international movement in opposition to it. The shift from 'soft' to 'hard' power is a shift from persuasion and relatively discrete and indirect pressures to change, to the open use of economic and military power.

The 'enemy' in the 'war on terror' is not just terrorist groups and organizations but also nation-states ('rogue states', 'failed states') which fail to accommodate to the globalist agenda. The American 'neo-conservatism' which is associated with this shift combines open and if need be unilateral use of US military superiority to achieve its national interests, and a continuing commitment to neo-liberalism and the core of the earlier globalist agenda. The Iraq War and other military interventions are partly justified as spreading 'freedom' (which means 'economic liberty' as well as political freedom or democracy) and 'open markets'. So the 'war on terror' can be interpreted as an element of the USA's strategy to preserve its own hegemonic position, partly by responding aggressively to threats to globalization in its globalist form, which it sees as according with its interests. Although we can say that these threats do include what most people would agree is terrorism, and morally indefensible as such, terrorism is only a relatively small part of them. Let me note also that recent use of the word 'terrorism' is highly controversial: it is used by advocates of the 'war on terror' to lump together forms of violence which others see as morally different (e.g. the Palestinian 'intifada', and the planting of bombs on public transport in Madrid and London, see Honderich 2003), while excluding state violence (e.g. the violence of the Israeli government against Palestinian civilians).

The book includes a considerable number of specific examples and texts, representing the five main 'voices' I identified above, and as befits a book on globalization representing various countries and trans-national agencies: the European Union, the United Nations, the USA, Britain, Romania, Hungary, Malaysia, Austria and Denmark.

Critical discourse analysis

I approach 'globalization and language' as a research topic through a version of 'critical discourse analysis'. Critical discourse analysis (abbreviated as CDA) is an area of interdisciplinary research and analysis which began to develop as a distinct academic area some twenty-five years ago (around 1980) and now includes a number of different approaches (Fairclough and Wodak 1997). What they have in common is a concern to ensure more satisfactory attention in critical social research to 'discourse' as a facet of social life, and to its relation to other facets of social life, than they have received in the past. 'Discourse' is associated with a particular way of conceptualizing and researching language, as well as other semiotic forms such as visual images or 'body language' (facial expressions, gestures and so forth). Critical analysts of 'discourse' approach language as one facet of social life which is closely (I would say 'dialectically', see below) interconnected with other facets of social life, and is therefore a significant (though generally somewhat neglected) aspect of all the major issues in social scientific research – economic systems, social relations, power and ideology, institutions, social change, social identity and so on.

Like other socially oriented approaches to language study, CDA includes analysis of instances of language use (be it in speech, in writing, or on television or the internet) – let's call these 'texts' in an extended sense (extended, because 'texts' are conventionally just written). Let's take a short extract from one text as an example:

> The driving idea behind globalization is free market capitalism – the more you let market forces rule and the more you open your economy to free trade and competition, the more efficient your economy will be. Globalization means the spread of free-market capitalism to virtually every country in the world. Therefore globalization also has its own set of economic rules – rules that revolve around opening, deregulating and privatizing your economy, in order to make it more competitive and attractive to foreign investment.
>
> (Friedman 2000)

This extract illustrates some features of the 'globalist' discourse I've been referring to. It explicitly defines globalization as 'the spread of free-market capitalism to virtually every country in the world' (though one might ask what exceptions 'virtually' implies). It assumes or presupposes – simply takes for granted – that globalization is 'driven' by an 'idea' ('free market capitalism'). Most serious literature on globalization represents it as so complex and multi-faceted that it seems odd to see it as somehow the effect of a single idea. But this is what 'globalist' discourse does: it represents the highly complex phenomenon of globalization reductively as purely economic, as a particular form of capitalism and a particular view of what capitalism should – must – be like. So globalization is governed by 'rules' (which seems highly implausible in itself), which are simply the precepts and prescriptions of economic neo-liberalism ('opening, deregulating and privatizing your economy, in order to make it more competitive and attractive to foreign investment'). Notice that the extract is vague about agency and responsibility at points where it would seem important to be clear: whose 'idea' is this, where does it come from? Who or what 'spreads' free-market capitalism? Who produces and enforces the 'rules'? Globalization is represented as a process without agents, yet as I have indicated above the 'globalist' strategy to push globalization into the form it is here claimed to simply *have* is very clearly the strategy of certain powerful agents. There is more to be said about the extract, but this is enough for my present purposes.

But CDA (and I am now talking specifically about the version I use in the book, see Chouliaraki and Fairclough 1999, Fairclough 2000a, Fairclough 2003) does not stop at such analysis of individual texts. It is also concerned as we have seen with discourses and genres, which transcend individual texts, and involve 'intertextual' relations within large sets of texts. We can see features of 'globalist' discourse in this text, but this discourse (indeed any discourse, or genre) can only be identified on the basis of features which are recurrent across a substantial number of texts, and which show a measure of stability over time. The categories of 'discourse' and 'genre' don't belong at the level of individual texts but at the level of 'social practices', ways of acting associated with particular areas of social life which are relatively stable and durable (e.g. the social practices of organizations such as schools or private companies). And CDA is also crucially concerned with *relations between* discourse (in the abstract sense, as a general facet of social life) at these different levels and other elements of social events and practices, with how these other elements are shaped by discourse and vice versa. In this case, for instance, with relations between 'globalist' discourse, 'globalist' strategies for pushing globalization in a particular direction, and 'operationalizations' of 'globalist' discourse (putting it into operation, or into practice) as material changes in the world, new ways of acting and interacting, new identities and so forth.

So the approach is very much *relational*, not just concerned with discourse (or texts) in their own right but with the relations between discourse and other elements of social life. And the focus is on process and change over time, on relations between discourse and other social elements in processes of globalization as they take place over time. The approach is also relational here: social change can be conceived as change in relations between social elements of all sorts, as a 're-articulation' of social elements which brings them into new relations. For example, one effect of globalism is a re-articulation of relations between business, government, the media and other major fields of social life. And this change in relations includes a change in relations between the sorts of discourse associated with these fields – think of how governments are tending to communicate with the public as consumers rather than just citizens, in a 'business' sort of way, or how business corporations and governments have embraced public relations and increasingly produce media discourse 'for' the media through their 'communications' departments. Moreover, in some cases at least the re-articulation of relations between these different fields seems to take place first in discourse, with changes in discourse then being operationalized in more general change. A final point is that relations between discourse and other elements of social life are *dialectical* (Fairclough 2001). What this means is that although the elements are different and one cannot be reduced to another, they are not discrete, the boundaries between them are fluid. When changes in discourse are 'operationalized' in more general social change, discourse so to speak 'turns into other things' – a neo-liberal representation of a country's economy for instance 'turns into' neo-liberal economic practices, which affect amongst other things how flows of finance and investment are regulated. The discourse is we might say 'internalized' in the practice (Harvey 1996), just as designs for a new automobile engine are internalized and materialized in the engine itself. This condensed summary of aspects of CDA will be elaborated on in Chapter 2.

The term 'discourse' will be used in this book, as it is generally used, in two different senses, and this can be confusing. I have used both above. 'Discourse' is used as an 'abstract noun' (which can't be made plural, and which occurs without definite and indefinite articles, '*the*', '*a/n*') to refer to what we might call 'the semiotic' (language and other semiotic forms) as one part or facet of 'the social' – the abstract noun is used in a very abstract way. It is also used as a 'concrete noun' (which can occur with an indefinite article and in the plural – 'a discourse', different 'discourses') in the sense of particular ways of representing aspects of the world (e.g. different political discourses – Liberal, Social-Democratic, Marxist, etc).

Methodology

Let me say a little about the methodology I shall use in analysing aspects of globalization from a language perspective. By 'methodology' I understand the way in which we approach a topic of research such as 'globalization', or 'globalization and language', in order to arrive at 'objects of research' (Bourdieu and Wacquant 1992), ways of tackling the topic in a theoretically coherent and systematic way – ways of making the topic researchable, as we might put it. There are many different ways of doing this for any particular research topic, so it is a matter of developing an approach which suits your particular theoretical and practical concerns and objectives. This involves bringing a particular range of theoretical perspectives and categories and methods of analysis to bear on the research topic – selecting from those available in the light of broader concerns and objectives. There are no right answers here. It is up to our academic colleagues and students and perhaps people operating in the practical world (e.g. politicians or campaigners) to tell us how fruitful or useful our particular methodologies are – in the terms I used earlier, how 'practically adequate' they are.

CDA has a central position in my own methodology, as I have indicated. But CDA itself has developed (differently in different versions) as a synthesis of theoretical perspectives, categories and methods from different academic disciplines – Linguistics, Sociology, Political Theory, Philosophy and so forth (Fairclough and Wodak 1997, Chouliaraki and Fairclough 1999), so the approach of any particular version of CDA towards language is already oriented towards certain theoretical positions and concerns and analytical methods within the social sciences. I take a 'transdisciplinary' approach to research (Fairclough 2003), which is one view of interdisciplinarity, and which sees research as a process of bringing different disciplines and theories to bear together on a research topic, setting up a dialogue between them through which each is liable to change. So the version of CDA I bring to this book is a particular synthesis which bears the marks of earlier research, which has assimilated ideas and categories from disciplines and theories drawn upon in that research. And in this book further synthesis will take place. This will include approaching the topic of 'globalization and language' with a synthesis of CDA and a version of 'political economy'. Political economy differs from conventional economics in insisting that there are political preconditions for economic processes, relations and systems. The version I work with is now being called 'cultural political economy' (Jessop 2004, Jessop and Sum 2001), and it extends the general point that economies are necessarily embedded in (and conditional upon) other social fields including culture and discourse. This includes the claim that discourses can (under certain conditions) have causal effects upon political economies as material realities, i.e. contribute to their social constitution. I give a fuller explanation of 'cultural political economy' and my reasons for choosing to work with it in Chapter 2. A general methodological concern is with achieving a more satisfactory treatment of discourse within a cultural political economy approach to globalization.

Having said a little about methodology, let me clarify even more briefly my ontological and epistemological positions. Ontologically, I adopt a version of critical realism (Fairclough *et al.* 2004) which claims that social relations and 'objects' (e.g. economic systems, states, practices of management or governance) have a materiality which is not conditional upon the fact or the nature of human knowledge of them, but that they are nevertheless socially constructed, that social objects and social subjects are co-constructed, and that discourse contributes to their construction. Epistemologically, I reject equally positivist accounts of economic and social facts which exclude their social and discursive construction, and voluntarist forms of discourse analysis which fail to recognize that the socially constructive effects of discourse are subject to certain non-discursive conditions, in favour of an approach to research which emphasizes the dialectical character of relations between different elements of the social including discourse.

Conclusion

The gist of what I have said in the Introduction is summed up in the following points:

- Globalization is in part a discursive process, involving genres and discourses.
- It is easy to confuse actual processes of globalization with discourses of globalization, and it is important to distinguish the two.
- Yet because globalization has a significantly discursive character, it is equally important to analyse the relations between discourse and other elements of the changes associated with globalization, including the constructive effects of discourse on material changes.
- Critical discourse analysis (CDA) constitutes a valuable resource for researching these relations between discourse and other social elements, seeing them as dialectical relations. One advantage is that it allows us to incorporate textual analysis within social analysis of globalization.
- I take a transdisciplinary approach to researching globalization which combines CDA with 'cultural political economy', with the aim of achieving a more satisfactory treatment of discourse within a cultural political economy approach to globalization.
- It is useful to draw broad distinctions between the main 'voices' in debates on globalization. I distinguish academic analysis, governmental agencies, non-governmental agencies, the media and people in everyday life.

1 Globalization and language: review of academic literature

There is a vast and ever-growing academic literature on globalization. I shall begin this chapter by differentiating in broad terms four positions within this literature on discourse as an element or facet of globalization: objectivist, rhetoricist, ideologist and social constructivist. The *objectivist* position treats globalization as simply objective fact, which discourse may either illuminate or obscure, represent or misrepresent. The *rhetoricist* position focuses on how various discourses of globalization are used for instance by politicians to persuade publics to accept certain (sometimes unpalatable) policies. The *ideologist* position focuses upon how particular discourses of globalization systematically contribute to the legitimation of a particular global order which incorporates asymmetrical relations of power such as those between and within countries. Finally the *social constructivist* position recognizes the socially constructed character of social life in general and forms of globalization in particular, and sees discourse as potentially having significant causal effects in processes of social construction.

I shall then discuss in more detail a selection of work which adopts the social constructivist position, which I have already committed myself to in the Introduction. I shall on the one hand be using the existing literature as a source for ideas on and approaches to discourse, as well as discussing how it has added to the range of contemporary discourses of globalization, and on the other hand arguing that the significance of discourse as a facet of globalization has generally not been adequately appreciated and needs to be addressed more systematically. This will lead into the presentation of my own approach in Chapter 2.

Discourse in globalization: four positions

One can find various classifications of approaches within the academic literature on globalization (Held *et al.* 1999, Hay and Marsh 2000, Cameron and Palan 2004). Since my own is specifically concerned with orientations to discourse, I shall begin this section by briefly summarizing the three approaches distinguished on broader grounds by Held *et al.* (1999): 'hyperglobalist', 'sceptical' and 'transformationalist'. Hyperglobalists see globalization as the emergence of a single global market which is supplanting the nation-state as the primary economic and political unit. Some (neo-liberals) see this positively as human progress, others (radicals and neo-Marxists) see it negatively as the triumph of global capitalism. Sceptics on the other hand argue that contemporary levels of economic independence are not new, that the level of global economic integration was higher in the late nineteenth century, and that the contemporary evidence indicates regionalization (with Europe, East Asia and North America as the main ('triadic') economic blocs) rather than globalization, and the continuing economic power of nation-states. Transformationalists agree with hyperglobalists that contemporary globalization is unprecedented though they argue that it is much more complex and multidimensional than the emergence of a global market (it has for instance political, cultural, military, as well as economic dimensions), that the character of nation-states (and much else) is radically transformed but they are not being supplanted, and that the outcomes of globalization are contingent and unpredictable.

This very generalized classification of a highly diverse literature indicates some of the main points of controversy. One is whether globalization spells the end of the nation-state as the primary economic and political unit. Another is whether globalization is a phenomenon specific to the last few decades, or a cyclical phenomenon over several centuries. A third is whether globalization is a primarily economic phenomenon, or a diverse set of phenomena (economic, political, cultural, military, ecological) which are substantially autonomous, though certainly interconnected. A fourth is whether globalization amounts to homogenization, or whether on the contrary, globalization is consistent with diversity within all the different phenomena it encompasses.

There is no direct match between the four positions on discourse as a facet of globalization I distinguished above (objectivist, rhetoricist, ideologist and social constructionist) and the hyperglobalist, sceptical and transformationalist approaches. But there is a tendency for hyperglobalists to be objectivists; sceptics tend towards the rhetoricist or ideologist positions, and the social constructionist position tends to be more prominent amongst transformationalists. But these are, let me emphasize, very rough correlations.

Objectivist position

I use the term 'objectivist' (Bourdieu and Wacquant 1992: 7–9) because those adopting this position treat globalization as simply objective processes in the real world which it is the social scientist's task to describe. They do not see globalization as also having a significant 'subjective' aspect, in contrast for instance to Robertson (1992: 8) for whom globalization is 'both the compression of the world' ('objective') and 'the intensification of consciousness of the world as a whole' ('subjective'). Recognition of discourse as a facet of globalization is one way of addressing its 'subjective' aspect – consciousness of the world, after all, implies representations of the world, and therefore discourse.

A sophisticated example of objectivism is the influential work of Held *et al.* (1999) which I have already referred to. It is not that discourse is entirely absent from their account of globalization: they refer for instance (1999: 1) to 'the popular rhetoric of globalization', and to globalization as an 'analytical construct' and 'historical narratives' of globalization in academic literature (both of which imply the discursive character of academic theorizing and analysis). Yet when they set out their analytical framework (14–16), discourse is not referred to as a facet of globalization, and the book as a whole does not recognize discourse as a significant aspect of globalization.

Here for instance is the way they define globalization (1999: 16):

> a process (or set of processes) which embodies a transformation in the spatial organization of social relations and transactions – assessed in terms of their extensity, intensity, velocity and impact – generating transcontinental or interregional flows and networks of activity, interaction, and the exercise of power.

Globalization is defined in an objectivist way as (just) a 'set of processes', and the opening comments on page 1 of their Introduction suggest if anything that discourse is likely to get in the way of social scientific analysis of them: globalization is 'in danger of becoming a cliché: the big idea which encompasses everything', and 'although the popular rhetoric of globalization may capture aspects of the contemporary zeitgeist, there is burgeoning academic debate as to whether globalization, as an analytical construct, delivers any added value in the search for a coherent understanding of the historical forces which . . . are shaping the socio-political realities of everyday life'. Where for Robertson 'consciousness of the world as a whole' is an irreducible part of globalization, we find a clear divide here between 'popular rhetoric' and the 'zeitgeist' (which presumably subsumes 'consciousness of the world as a whole') on the one hand, and the social scientist's 'analytical concepts' for understanding what are represented as real (objective) processes.

Rhetoricist position

Generally speaking, those who focus on rhetoric are concerned with how representations of globalization are used to support and legitimize actions and policies within particular arguments. An example is Hay and Rosamond (2002), who claim that 'there is plenty of evidence . . . of actors deploying particular rhetorics of globalization in the attempt to justify often unpalatable social and economic reform'. For instance, globalization is often invoked 'as non-negotiable external economic constraint' which imposes 'market-conforming deregulation' on individual states, as in Tony Blair's statement that 'the key to New Labour economics is the recognition that Britain . . . (has) to compete in an increasingly international market place' (speech to the Confederation of German Industry, 1996). The 'international market place' is presupposed, taken as fact, as is also the consequent policy priority for states of making their countries (Britain in this case) competitive in this 'market place'. The 'unpalatable' reforms which follow from this include reducing the 'safety net' of the welfare system.

Hay and Rosamond actually draw a distinction between 'globalization as discourses' and 'globalization rhetoric'. The former refers to the 'way in which globalization has come to provide a cognitive filter, frame or conceptual lens or paradigm through which social, political and economic developments might be ordered and rendered intelligible'. What is in focus here is the effect of globalization on the 'repertoire of discursive resources' available to people. 'Globalization as rhetoric' by contrast refers to 'the strategic and persuasive deployment of such discourses . . . to legitimate particular courses of action'. The authors go on to show interesting differences between major EU countries (France, Germany and the UK) in their globalization rhetoric, as well as differences in the case of the UK between domestic and European contexts (where globalization is presented as inexorable) and international contexts (where globalization is presented as contingent, and in need of defending from its detractors).

Notice that they view 'globalization as discourses' in terms of the effects of globalization in delimiting (and changing) the repertoire of available discourses. There is a discussion of the difference between the 'effects of globalization itself' and the 'effects of having internalized popular constructions of globalization', and the authors suggest that policy-makers 'may well serve . . . to bring about outcomes' consistent with the discourses they have internalized, 'irrespective of their veracity'. This points to the social constructionist position that discourse can be implicated in causal processes producing the real processes of globalization, but the position is not clarified, and it is not the main focus of the paper.

Ideologist position

Those who focus on ideology are concerned at a more systemic level with how discourses contribute to achieving and sustaining the dominance or hegemony of particular strategies and practices, and the social forces who advocate them and whose interests they serve. An example is Steger (2005).

Steger sees globalization as both a set of material processes and 'a system of ideas circulating in the public realm as more or less coherent stories that attempt to define, describe and evaluate these very processes'. The most influential of these 'stories' is what he calls 'globalism' (which I referred to briefly in the Introduction). This is a neo-liberal story which represents globalization as, and reduces it to, the global spread of the 'free market' which neo-liberals advocate. (I discuss globalism more fully in Chapter 3 as a discourse which constitutes part of the strategy pursued by powerful governmental and non-governmental agencies.) This is an ideology in Ricoeur's (1986) sense of this highly controversial term – it distorts reality (globalization cannot be reduced to the 'free market'), legitimizes the action and policies of powerful social agents, and contributes to the integrative effect of 'integrating and holding together individual and collective identity'. It is (some would argue rather that it has been, because it is now increasingly challenged, Gray 1999, Saul 2005) in Gramscian terms (Gramsci 1971) a hegemonic ideology, an ideology which has achieved a measure of consent or at least acquiescence across social groups and social fields and international boundaries.

Those who focus on the ideological character of discourse as a facet of globalization differ, in accordance with different understandings of ideology, on whether they see ideology as a significant aspect of social construction. For some, it is the distorting effects of ideology which are highlighted, and ideologies produce a 'false consciousness' of the reality of globalization, without any sense that they change that reality. Steger however does see the hegemonic position of globalism as producing real effects and changes in the character of globalization. He refers to Butler's observation that the constant repetition, public recitation and 'performance' of an ideology's core claims frequently have the capacity to produce what they name (Butler 1996: 112).

Social constructivist position

Finally, the *social constructivist* position places a more explicit emphasis on the socially constructed character of social realities, and the significance of discourse in their social construction. I should make it clear that I am not discussing here 'social constructionism' (Gergen 1999) as a particular philosophy of science which 'in its strong form claims that objects or referents of knowledge are nothing more than social constructions' (Sayer 2000), implying that reality does not have properties which exist independently of our knowledge of them (of whether we know of them, or how we represent them). Recognition of the socially constructed character of social realities is common across many positions within social science, and it is often consistent with realism (Sayer 2000) – as I explained in the Introduction, I adopt a version of realism in this book.

As I have indicated, there is some recognition of the significance of discourse in the social construction of globalization amongst those who primarily adopt other positions on discourse as a facet of globalization, which indicates that one sometimes finds a combination of the positions in academic work. Indeed Cameron and

Palan (2004) argue that there is a covert acknowledgement of globalization as discursively constructed even in some of the 'objectivist' literature, in the sense that academic narratives which purport to merely describe the reality of globalization are used to ground advocacy for changes in globalization – for 'cosmopolitan democracy' in the cases of Held *et al.* (1999). I shall focus here however on researchers who see discourse as primarily significant in the social construction of globalization.

Discourse in the social construction of globalization: a selective review

Cameron and Palan (2004) themselves argue that narratives of globalization have constructive effects on the real processes and institutions of globalization. Narratives which are plausible for enough people and which they can come to believe in lead them to invest (their time, energy, money and other resources) in the imaginary futures which these narratives project, and through their commitment to an investment in them ('investment' in the widest sense), they can bring them into being. (This is reminiscent of the claim of Bourdieu and Wacquant (2001) that neo-liberal discourse is 'endowed with the performative power to bring into being the very realities it claims to describe'.) There are two important provisos. First, not every narrative will be plausible for people, and narratives are subject to a 'reality check' (Cameron and Palan 2004: 8). Cameron and Palan don't really clarify their position on this matter, but what is suggested is that to be seen as plausible and to be taken up and invested in, narratives need to resonate with (Fairclough *et al.* 2004) people's experience of the world as it actually is. This is a corrective to strong forms of social constructionism, for it suggests that 'intransitive' properties of the real world (that is, properties which exist independently of our theories or narratives or discourses) as they are experienced through the practical engagements of ordinary life, as well as narratives, have causal effects on real changes in the world.

The second proviso is that 'the "reality" that eventually arises from . . . attempts to enact a theory may bear little resemblance to what (people) actually predicted and prepared for', though nevertheless 'theories and perceptions must be considered important causal factors in the changes that we witness' (2004: 4). Again, the authors do not elaborate on or clarify this point, though it is an important one. We can clarify it if we view causality as a complex relationship which excludes mono-causality – that is, changes are always the effect of a multiplicity of causes (Fairclough *et al.* 2004). Causal factors may include narratives embedded within strategies to direct change in certain ways, but rejection of mono-causality entails that such strategies may have unintended consequences. Intransitive properties of the real world are also causal factors in how it changes, including its structural characteristics, the inertia of structures and institutions, the existing identities of individual and collective social actors and so forth. In these comments on Cameron and Palan, I am pre-empting aspects in my own approach which I shall elaborate on later.

Cameron and Palan make a point that is similar to what I said in the Introduction about the importance of distinguishing different agencies and agents involved in or with globalization. Specifically, they argue that narratives of globalization which hold little plausibility for academics may be highly plausible for businessmen and politicians and other practical agents and agencies involved in processes of globalization. Thus the most influential narratives amongst the latter have been what Held *et al.* call 'hyperglobalist' narratives which are in my terms 'objectivist', particularly in forms which are impossibly crude for most academics. 'Globalism' in Steger's sense is the most influential of them all. Moreover, it is these narratives and discourses which have had most influence on real changes.

Cameron and Palan offer their own narrative of globalization as the interconnection between three different 'imagined' (and in part realized, institutionalized) economies and 'spatialities': the 'offshore', 'private', and 'anti' economies. These are hierarchized, in that the 'offshore' (or 'global') economy 'has a strongly normative content' for the other two. The 'private economy' is also designated the 'competition state', and the 'anti-economy' is a space of 'social exclusion' which, in contrast to the other two, lies outside the emergent global order. These 'imagined economies' originate separately in their own narratives, yet this 'dominant imagery' or 'cartography' of globalization is 'paradoxically hidden' – in fact the narrative of the interconnection between the three is Cameron and Palan's own. The connection they are suggesting between (the narratives of) globalization and 'social exclusion' is interesting, and we can sum up how the three 'economies' are interrelated as follows: the necessity for the state to 'go private', curtail its public responsibilities for its citizens, and become the 'competition state' follows from the 'inevitability' of globalization in a neo-liberal form, and therefore of a competitive struggle for survival between national economies in the 'offshore' economy; the 'inability' of the state to address poverty except in the limited and inadequate guise of 'social exclusion' and policies for 'inclusion' follows from the priorities of the competition state (which include producing a competitive labour force but exclude all but limited care for the victims of globalization).

Jessop (1999, 2002) views globalization as 'a supercomplex series of multicentric, multiscalar, multitemporal, multiform and multicausal processes', with both structural and strategic moments. Structurally, globalization is increasing global interdependence (increasing in spatial extension and/or velocity) among actions, organizations and institutions within different 'functional sub-systems' (economy, law, politics, education and so forth) or spheres of the 'lifeworld' (in the sense of those parts of social life which are outside systems). Strategically, globalization is various actors' attempts to globally coordinate their activities in particular sub-systems of the lifeworld. The effects of discourse in the social construction of globalization are built into Jessop's view of 'strategies'. There is a dialectic between structures and strategies (or, more abstractly, structure and agency) within his theory: structures constrain but do not determine strategies; structures are produced and reproduced through strategies; structures can be transformed through strategies. Groups of agencies and agents develop alternative and often competing strategies, especially in times of instability or crisis, for structural change. But strategies 'are always elaborated in and through discourses', different 'narratives that seek to give meaning to current problems by construing them in terms of past failures and future possibilities'.

Discourses and narratives 'simplify' ('translate' and 'condense' in the terms of Harvey 1996, see Fairclough and Thomas 2004) economic and political relations – the latter are so complex that any action oriented towards them requires 'discursive simplification', a selectivity in terms of what is included and excluded, hence the constitution of discourses as 'imaginaries'. Which competing discourses (narratives, imaginaries), which strategies, succeed in establishing themselves and achieving dominance or hegemony depends upon a number of factors. First, 'structural selectivities': structures are more open to some strategies than to others. Second, the scope and 'reach' of the discourse (narrative) – for instance, the discourses of 'globalization' or 'knowledge-based economy' might be seen as 'nodal discourses' which articulate many other discourses (e.g. those we can sum up with the labels 'lifelong learning', 'social exclusion', 'flexibility'). Third, there are the differential capacities and power of the social agents whose strategy it is 'to get their messages across', e.g. their access to and control over mass media and other channels and networks for diffusion. Fourth, there is the 'resonance' of discourses with people's experience of the world, and their capacity to mobilize people.

Discourses (and narratives) have non-discursive effects. Thus 'the economy as an object of regulation is viewed as an imaginatively narrated system', and 'the state system is treated as an imagined political entity', and discourses 'have a key role in the always tendential constitution and consolidation of the economic, political and other systems, shaping the forms of their institutional separation and subsequent articulation'. This does not imply that either economies or states are 'just discourse', for discourses 'help modify their institutional materiality'. On the other hand, it does imply that regimes of accumulation and types of state are 'co-constituted' (alongside other, non-discursive, constitutive factors) by discourses (narratives, imaginaries). Discourses also work as rhetoric – for instance, neo-liberal narratives of globalization whose imaginaries are used to legitimize unpopular policies such as cuts in the 'social wage'.

Globalization is interpreted as changes in the 'scales' on which social activity and interaction take place, and in relationships between scales. It is associated with the emergence of new scales, not only the 'global' scale, but also for instance the scale of international regional economic blocs (notably the 'triadic' regions of North America, Europe and East Asia) and cross-border regions which combine regions in different nation-states. The institutionalization, regulation and governance of emergent scales is conditional upon specific technologies of power. Globalization is not exclusively to do with the global scale, but with new sets of relations between the global scale and other scales and the 're-scaling' of particular spatial entities (nation-states, regions within them, cities, etc.) with respect to particular sub-systems (economy, law, etc.) or a combination of sub-systems. The global scale is 'an ultimate horizon for action' and 'a means to orient actions' on lesser scales. Actual changes in scale and scalar relations can be seen as the operationalization, the putting into operation or practice, of the imaginaries associated with successful strategies, and therefore discourses and narratives. Scales are not naturally given; they are socially constituted.

Jessop's analysis foregrounds the structural contradictions of globalization, referring particularly to neo-liberal economic globalization as the dominant form, as particular forms of contradictions which are inherent in capitalism, and the strategic dilemmas which agencies and agents are consequentially faced with. One theme I shall take up in later chapters is how these strategic dilemmas appear as paradoxes and contradictions in texts.

Harvey's (1996) view of globalization is based upon conceiving space and time as social constructs, and in that they are *co*-constructed we can speak in an aggregating way of 'space-times'. The social construction of 'space-times' is moreover a cartography, a mapping, in which different space-times are constructed with particular relations between them. The construction of a cartography of space-times is simultaneous with the construction of a repertoire of social practices, social relationships, power relationships, social (e.g. gender) identities and values, which are distributed across different space-times and differentiated along with space-times. Thus the social construction of time and space is a fundamental facet of the construction of the social life of a community. Therefore changes in the construction of space-times is an equally fundamental facet of social change, be it the transition from feudalism to capitalism, or contemporary processes of globalization.

Harvey's account of the social construction of space and time is grounded in a dialectical theory of relations between discourse and other 'moments' or elements of the social process. His theorization of discourse (1996: 77–95) is quite exceptional for its explicitness and sophistication in the literature of globalization. He views discourse as one of six distinctive and dialectically related moments of the social process: discourse, power, beliefs and values and desires, social relations, institutions and rituals, and material practices. The relations are dialectical in the sense that 'each moment is constituted as an internal relation of the others' – thus for instance discourses 'internalize in some sense everything that occurs as other moments', and 'discursive effects suffuse and saturate all other moments'. But 'internalization is always a translation or metamorphosis . . . rather than an exact replica or perfect mimesis', a 'gap' always exists between different moments – which is why no totalitarian attempt to 'sew up' social life can fully succeed. Moreover, each moment 'internalizes heterogeneity' in translating other moments – diversity in beliefs, values and desires for instance translate into heterogeneity in discourses, and the co-existence of contrasting and sometimes conflicting discourses. Harvey's dialectical theory gives primacy to processes and flows and relations, yet he recognizes that flows crystallize into relative 'permanences', which one can see as relatively stabilized conjunctures of the six elements, be it nation-states, or urban landscapes, or social institutions, which can seem eternal and immovable to those who inhabit them. Such permanences can easily lead (and have often led) to the misguided impression that there are simple mono-causal relations between what seem to be fixed entities, which are expressed in such claims as 'globalization leads to a widespread sense of insecurity', or 'neo-liberal discourse has made states subservient to markets'.

Discourses of space-time are an essential moment or facet of the social construction and re-construction of space-times. But the discourses which are a part of these processes don't come out of nowhere. We can construe space and time in all sorts of fanciful ways, but discourses which are effective within their ('re')construction are subject to what I referred to earlier as a 'reality test' – they 'translate' and (being inherently selective) 'condense' other moments of the social process so that the 'imaginaries' they project for space-time cartographies are grounded in actual constructions of space and time as they are practically experienced through people's engagement in the world. New constructions of space-times and their interconnections inherently have a discursive moment which is however translated into other moments, enacted in social relations and forms of power, institutionalized, materialized, internalized in beliefs and values and desires. Discourse is constitutive, but not in a determinative sense. In Williams' words (1977: 37–8):

> We find then not a reified 'language' or 'society' but an active social language. Nor is this language simply a 'reflection' or 'expression' of 'material reality'. What we have rather is a grasping of this reality through language, which as practical consciousness is saturated by and saturates all social activity, including productive activity.

Other relevant literature on globalization

There remains a substantial amount of literature on globalization, some of it influential, generally 'transformationalist' in the terms of Held *et al.* (1999) and oriented to the socially constructed character of social life, which however says little about discourse. An example is Tomlinson (1999), which is a study of globalization and culture. Tomlinson's approach to the cultural facet of globalization centres upon the concept of 'deterritorialization', a weakening of the ties between culture and place, a process of 'globalizing culture' which does not however at all amount to the emergence of a homogeneous 'global culture'. Global events 'may add to the extension of the individuals's "phenomenal world"': people probably come to include distant events and processes more routinely in their perceptions of what is significant for their own personal lives' with an 'ever-broadening horizon of relevance in people's routine experience' to which their exposure to the media contributes substantially. Deterritorialization has 'ambivalent effects' on self-identity, on the one hand freeing self-identity from the limiting constraints of particular places, but on the other hand undermining the security and certainties of being tied to a particular place. Deterritorialization is often associated with cultural 'hybridity', the 'mingling of cultures from different territorial locations' (a banal example is changes in 'food culture' with the increasing availability and familiarity of foods and dishes from all parts of the world). An objection to specifically tying hybridity to globalization is that it sometimes implies a prior stage of 'pure' cultures, though there is a case for claiming that cultures are never 'pure', they have always been subject to 'mingling' and hybridity 'goes all the way down'. However, the current pace and scale of hybridity is arguably something new. Nevertheless, there are two provisos: first, that deterritorialization is dialectically linked to 'reterritorialization': cultural mixtures can stabilize; second, that power relations can structure such mixtures in ways which give certain cultural elements salience over others.

Tomlinson develops this argument with virtually no mention of discourse. Yet it seems clear that discourse is an important facet of deterritorialization and reterritorialization of culture. In discussing 'mediation' and the combination of mediated and direct experience in the deterritorialization of particular 'local' places, he comments that 'televisual experience . . . is highly mediated not only in terms of the technical determinants of the form . . . but in terms of the complex set of semiotic codes, conventions, formats and production values it employs', and refers to the 'textual characteristics of the medium: its modes of address, its narrative strategies and so on'. Discourse is alluded to at this point, but in general terms and without development. Yet deterritorialization (including the impact of television) surely changes what we might call the 'repertoire' of discursive resources available to people in local contexts – the range of discourses (people experience new ways of representing aspects of the world, including aspects of their own direct experience of it), genres (new ways of interacting and communication, some of which – telephone conversations, emailing, text messaging, etc. – may become routine), and styles (new forms of identity and ways of communicating identity). One can draw two conclusions. First, that there is a great deal more to be said about deterritorialization, and cultural aspects of globalization more generally, with respect to discourse. Second, in so far as Tomlinson's book contains insights about cultural aspects of globalization which have significant discursive implications (even though these are not explored in his book), his contribution to the literature on globalization does have interest and value for a study of discourse as a facet of globalization. For instance, the category of 'interdiscursive hybridity' (the combination of different discourses, and/or genres, and/or styles in texts) has been prominent within CDA (Fairclough 1992, Chouliaraki and Fairclough 1999), and it is suggestive for how Tomlinson's insights could be put to work in discourse analysis.

The general point here is that it is not necessarily only academic literature on globalization which incorporates discourse in a reasonably systematic way into its theorizing and analysis that is of value in developing a more satisfactory treatment of discourse as a facet of globalization – other literature contains ideas and categories which might be 'translated' into discourse analytical terms. Another example is Bauman (1998). Bauman begins by commenting on 'globalization' as a 'vogue word' ('the more experiences they pretend to make transparent, the more they themselves become opaque'), and sets himself the task of trying to 'disperse some of the mist which surrounds the term'. But the main emphasis in his book is on new forms of social division associated with globalization, between 'globals' on the one hand, who have the freedom to roam the world with a diminishing sense of obligation to their places (and countries) of origin, who can enjoy all the creative possibilities of 'hybridity', and 'locals' on the other who are confined to (sometimes effectively imprisoned within) particular localities, and whose 'mobility' if they have it is the mobility of 'vagabonds'. The book does contain quite a lot of critical commentary on the dominant discourse of globalization (on terms such as 'mobility' and 'flexibility', for instance). But there are many insights which are formulated with little or no reference to discourse which could fruitfully be 'translated' into questions for discourse analysis. If 'globals' and 'locals' have different relationships to place (and space) and time as Bauman suggests, can we show this through changes in, and new variations in, representations of space and time in texts? If 'mobility' means very different things to 'globals' and 'locals' (and those who are 'in between'), what can we say about representations of different categories of people 'on the move' – business and other elites, migrant workers, refugees? If 'globals' are increasingly isolated from 'locals', how do forms of communication between them change, and where are the 'gaps' in communication? What is happening for instance to communication in the 'public sphere'? How is the increasing pre-occupation with 'security' and 'crime' which Bauman identifies manifest in public and media discourse? And so forth.

Discourse in globalization: summary

Let me sum up the main claims about the relationship of discourse to other facets of globalization which I have identified in the academic literature:

- Discourse can represent globalization, giving people information about it and contributing to their understanding of it.
- Discourse can misrepresent and mystify globalization, giving a confusing and misleading impression of it.
- Discourse can be used rhetorically to project a particular view of globalization which can justify or legitimize the actions, policies or strategies of particular (usually powerful) social agencies and agents.
- Discourse can contribute to the constitution, dissemination and reproduction of ideologies, which can also be seen as forms of mystification, but have a crucial systemic function in sustaining a particular form of globalization and the (unequal and unjust) power relations which are built into it.
- Discourse can generate imaginary representations of how the world will be or should be within strategies for change which, if they achieve hegemony, can be operationalized to transform these imaginaries into realities.

We are not forced to choose between these claims; on the contrary, there is truth in all of them. What is generally lacking in the existing literature however is a systematic approach to theorizing and analysing discourse as a facet of globalization which can show these various effects of discourse and the relationship between them, and help explain them. In Chapter 2 I shall sketch out an approach which will I hope help to fill that gap.

2 My approach to globalization and language

I have already said a little about my approach in the Introduction, in the sections on CDA (critical discourse analysis) and methodology. I shall now give a more detailed and systematic explanation of the approach. As I indicated in the Introduction, I think it is fruitful in researching discourse as a facet of globalization to work with a form of 'cultural' political economy (Jessop 2004, Jessop and Sum 2001) which incorporates the version of CDA I describe below. Since cultural political economy is the wider framework in this approach within which CDA is embedded, I shall begin with the former and then move on to the latter.

Cultural political economy

Political economy differs from classical economics in asserting that economic systems and economic changes are politically conditioned and embedded – that they depend upon and are closely interconnected with political forms and systems (Polanyi 1944). Cultural political economy asserts that economic and political 'objects', using this term in a very wide sense, are socially constructed. These 'objects' include economic systems, economic organizations, the division of labour, the state, forms of management and governance and so forth. It also emphasizes that there is a 'subjective' side to this construction of 'objects' – that the processes of socially constructing them construct not only the 'objects' themselves but also the social 'subjects' associated with them, that they are 'co-constructions' of subjects and objects. Bringing people into the process also brings in culture: economic and political 'objects' are also culturally conditioned and embedded – so for instance particular economic systems or forms of state depend upon and are closely interconnected with particular meanings, interpretations, narratives, values, attitudes, identities and so forth. Furthermore, these processes of social construction inherently involve discourse – they have a partly discursive character, and the 'objects' and 'subjects' that are constructed are in part what we can call *effects* of discourse.

What I have referred to as the actual, real processes and tendencies of global-ization – what is actually happening as opposed to what is represented as happen-ing – are highly complex, diverse, uneven and multidimensional (economic, political, social, cultural, ecological and so forth). They are much too complex to be fully controlled by any human intervention. Nevertheless, as in any situation of major social change, various groups of people develop strategies to try to regu-late, direct and control elements of these real processes, and if these strategies are successful they may inflect and partly redirect the trajectory of actual global-ization. Such strategies have an inherently discursive character: they include discourses, which represent and narrate what has happened in the past and is happening in the present, including why previous systems have failed, and imagine and advocate possible alternatives for the future, possible economic (social, poli-tical, cultural) orders which might overcome existing problems and offer better futures. Even if as in the case of globalism the primary objectives of the strategy are economic, the non-economic conditioning and embedding of economic systems, objects and processes which I have alluded to means that a strategy is only likely to succeed if it aims for general social and cultural change.

In situations of disorientation and crisis, one finds a proliferation of discourses imagining alternative forms of organization for economy, state and society. This is what happened in the case of the crisis which began in the 1970s, which put in question both the 'Fordist' economic system which had been dominant since the Second World War and the 'Keynesian' welfare state (named after the econ-omist John Maynard Keynes) which was strongly associated with it (Jessop 2002). It was this crisis that preceded and in a sense set the stage for the emergence of neo-liberalism and globalism. One central question for cultural political economy is about the variation, selection and retention of discourses, that is, how certain of the many discourses which are circulating in a time of crisis are selected, and how they come to be retained (or institutionalized), and thereby come to be capable of having constitutive effects on real economic, political and social processes. The point is that the mere existence of alternative discourses means little. It is only those which pass through the mechanisms and processes of selection and retention that can contribute to social (re)construction. This is a question one can ask about the discourse of globalism – how did it come to be selected from a range of alter-natives and retained (institutionalized)?

We also need to ask of course how it came to shape actual processes and ten-dencies of globalization, or in other words how it came to be 'operationalized' and implemented. Operationalization points us to the dialectical character of relations within discourse and between discourse and other elements or moments of the social. A discourse is operationalized through being enacted in ways of acting and interacting which themselves have a partially discursive character in that they include genres (ways of interacting communicatively), for instance in ways of working, managing, governing, or conducting politics; through being inculcated in ways of being, social and personal identities, which also have a partly discursive character in that they include styles (ways of being in their specifically communicative or discursive aspect, as opposed to their bodily or somatic aspects), for instance the identities of workers, entrepreneurs, managers, politicians, teachers; and through being materialized physically in technologies, infrastructures, architectures and so forth. From a discourse analytical perspective a successfully operationalized strategy constitutes a new order of discourse (Fairclough 1992), i.e. a new structured (though flexibly structured) configuration of discourses, genres and styles. Globalism, neo-liberal globalization, is in part an order of discourse in this sense. It is important to add however that the dominance or hegemony of such a successfully operationalized strategy can never be complete or final – because actual processes always exceed even successfully constructed construals of them, because there are always alternative and even counter strategies and discourses, and because any successfully reconstituted reality is a contradictory and crisis-prone reality (Jessop 2004).

The advantage of framing CDA within cultural political economy is that it simultaneously allows us to approach the theme of globalization in a way which can ensure systematic attention to discourse as a facet of globalization, and helps avert the danger of a de-contextualized focus on discourse which overlooks the fact that discourse can only be effective in the social construction of globalization subject to certain conditions. These conditions are not purely discursive in character. They include structural characteristics of particular societies, features of their institutions, aspects of their history, as well as factors to do with the beliefs, attitudes and values of their people. In short, it helps avoid the real danger that in placing a necessary emphasis on often neglected discursive aspects of economic, political and social systems and processes, we throw the baby out with the bath water, and end up overstating the causal effects of discourse, or even treating processes such as globalization as if they were purely discursive.

Discourse as a moment of the social process

Although I shall be framing CDA within cultural political economy, my focus in the book is of course on discourse, and my aim will be to show the value of a particular version of CDA for the analysis of globalization. The book will I hope also contribute to cultural political economy by developing a version of CDA which strikes me as particularly fruitful for it, and applying it analytically. I shall now present the version of CDA (see Chouliaraki and Fairclough 1999, Fairclough 2000a, 2000b, Fairclough 2003, Fairclough *et al.* 2004, Fairclough 2005a, 2005b) in a more detailed and systematic way than I have done so far. I have already drawn upon certain elements in discussing cultural political economy and in the Introduction, so some of it will be familiar.

Like Harvey (1996) I regard discourse as one element or 'moment' of the social process which is dialectically related to other moments ('moment' is used precisely for elements whose relations are dialectical). To say that the relations between moments is dialectical means that although they are different from one another and one cannot be reduced to another, they are not discrete, i.e. the boundaries between them are fluid – they 'flow into' each other. As Harvey puts it, discourses 'internalize in some sense everything that occurs as other moments', and 'discursive effects suffuse and saturate all other moments'. So for instance when changes in discourse are operationalized, discourse so to speak 'turns into other things' – a neo-liberal representation of or imaginary for a country, for example, 'turns into' a neo-liberal political economy, new practices of various sorts, new identities, new material realities.

I shall distinguish three levels of abstraction within social analysis: social structures, social practices and social events. Let us begin at the most concrete level, social events. I use 'events' in a general sense to include all the 'goings-on' of social life, all the actions and happenings which constitute, in Harvey's term, the 'social process'. Discourse is a moment of social events which is dialectically interconnected with other moments. We can use the term 'text' for the discourse moment of social events, meaning not just written texts (the everyday sense of 'text') but also speech as an element or moment of events, and the complex 'multimodal' texts of television and the internet, where language is used in combination with other semiotic forms (visual images including film and photographs, sound effects, 'body language' including facial expression and gestures and so forth). 'Text' is not a perfect term because it has been so closely associated with the medium of writing, but it is widely used in this extended sense, and it is difficult to think of a better term.

At the most abstract level, social structures are the most general and most enduring (but still only relatively enduring) characteristics of societies, such as capitalism as a mode of production or the class structure or the system of gender relations. Again, there is what we can broadly call a semiotic aspect: particular languages can be regarded as social structures of a special sort. We can say that while social structures delimit what is possible (e.g. in the case of the English language, what is and is not an English sentence), social events constitute what is actual – these are different things, because not everything that is possible actually happens. But the relationship between structures and events, the possible and the actual, is not direct. It is *mediated*, and mediated by 'social practices'.

If social structures limit what can be done or happen, and social events are what actually is done or happens, social practices are the way things are generally done or happen in particular areas of social life. Social practices are habitual, ritual or institutionalized ways of 'going on', which are associated with particular institutions (such as the law or education) and, at a more concrete level, particular organizations (such as a school or a business). Examples of individual social practices are interviewing, teaching or shopping. Actually any institution and organization will not be limited to a single social practice; it will be characterized by a specific *network* of social practices. For instance, a school is not simply an organization where teaching goes on, but also examining, curriculum planning and other managerial practices. Institutions and organizations as networks of social practices can be seen as an intermediate level of social structuring, less abstract than what I am calling 'social structures', and closer to actual events. Social practices also have their semiotic (or discourse) moments, which I shall call 'orders of discourse'. We can characterize the order of discourse of an organization such as a school as the semiotic or discourse moment of the school (of the network of social practices that constitutes it), which is dialectically related to other moments.

Orders of discourse are combinations of three sorts of entity: discourses, genres and styles. I have already briefly distinguished between the first two in the Introduction. A discourse is a particular way of representing some aspect or area of social life. A genre on the other hand is a particular way of acting (which amounts to people *inter*acting) communicatively. A style is the discourse moment of a 'way of being', that is, of a social or personal identity. A particular order of discourse will include a number of different discourses, different genres and different styles. These may be complementary to each other (e.g. the various separate practices which make up the network of practices may have their own genres), or they may be alternative and sometimes conflicting possibilities (e.g. a particular school may include different teaching genres, which may in some cases be the focus of conflict). Let's stick with the example of a school: the order of discourse of a particular school will typically include a range of different discourses (associated with the various subjects taught, the social behaviour expected of its members, the management of the school and so forth), a range of different genres (associated with teaching, with school assemblies, with staff meetings, with extra-curricular activities and so forth), and a range of different styles (those of students, teaching staff, administrative and ancillary staff, managers). Since this is an 'order' of discourse, not just a repertoire, these different discourses, genres and styles are articulated together in particular relations – for instance, where there are (conflicting) alternatives, there will be a tendency for one to be the dominant one, the officially recognized and approved one.

So discourses, genres and styles are categories at the level of social practices and orders of discourse. Yet as I suggested in the Introduction, there is also a sense in which they are categories in texts at the level of social events – we can generally identify particular discourses, genres and styles in particular texts. Let us go back to my description of social practices as the way things are generally done or happen in the institution or organization concerned, and social events as what is actually done or happens. There is clearly no simple relationship between what actually happens in a concrete event and what generally happens in an institution or organization, even if the event concerned can be squarely located in a particular institution or organization (and many events cannot). People have a capacity for agency and for acting in ways that are not expected or conventional (though sometimes they act in perfectly conventional ways). Focusing on discourse, this means that there is no simple relationship between texts and orders of discourse, that texts are not merely instantiations of orders of discourse. This doesn't mean that anything goes. Texts draw upon orders of discourse, so we can generally recognize habitual or institutionalized discourses, genres and styles, but they may do so in complex and unconventional ways – for instance by mixing discourses, genres or styles from different orders of discourse, or mixing different and conventionally incompatible discourses, genres or styles from the same order of discourse (e.g. a student may on occasion mix student talk and teacher talk). This is what I call the 'interdiscursive hybridity' of texts.

One particular contribution that CDA can make to cultural political economy, and indeed to social scientific analysis in general, is detailed analysis of texts. Although as we have seen some of the literature on globalization addresses the question of discourse as a facet of globalization in interesting and sophisticated ways, there is a general absence of textual analysis as there is in most social scientific treatments of discourse. Yet we can only fully appreciate how discourse figures as a moment of processes of globalization if we have methods for analysing the concrete forms in which discourse appears within these processes – that is, texts in the broad sense in which I used this term above. This book will therefore include quite a lot of analysis of specific texts. Textual analysis is a field of study in its own right, and it is beyond the scope of the book to provide a systematic introduction to it. Readers are referred to Fairclough (2003), which is an introduction to textual analysis as an element of CDA for social researchers, and to the references it contains to other work in textual analysis. There are a great many features of texts at various levels (from that of the whole text, to that of major sections, to paragraphs, to sentences, to phrases, to individual words) that can be subjected to analysis, and any particular analysis has to be highly selective. I shall be focusing upon those features which are most relevant to the general topic of globalization and the specific issues and questions which arise in approaching this topic from the perspective of cultural political economy and CDA. I shall italicize analytical categories when they are first introduced and in some subsequent uses, and give references mainly to Fairclough (2003), and I shall include a summary of the types of analysis I have used in the conclusion to each chapter, and an overall summary in the Conclusion to the book.

Discourse and social change

Now let us bring time and history into the picture. Social change includes change in the character of social events, in social practices and the networking of social practices and (in the long run) social structures; and in so doing it includes change in the character of texts, in orders of discourse and (in the long run) in languages. Let's leave social structures (and 'the long run') out of the picture for the moment, and think of the other levels with globalization in mind, focusing on social practices.

When a particular social entity (e.g. a particular nation-state) is subject to globalization processes, we can expect change in its institutions and organizations, i.e. change in its social practices, change in how they are networked together, change in orders of discourse, in discourses, in genres and in styles. New institutions, practices, discourses and so forth emerge. Let us take the case of discourses. New discourses are constantly emerging, though they do not emerge out of nowhere; they 'translate' and selectively 'condense' other moments of the social process as people experience them in their practical engagement with the world. They are, in Williams' expression, 'a grasping of reality through language', or rather so many attempts at grasping reality, which may prove more or less 'practically adequate' (Sayer 2000) for reality.

But I want to adopt an approach which is firmly relational. That is, I see what is crucial as change in the *relations* between institutions, organizations, practices, orders of discourses, discourses, genres and styles. This does not mean that these entities do not change internally, nor as I have just said that new entities do not emerge. It means that changes within these sets of entities can be interpreted as effects of changes in relations between them. Let's think of a particular aspect of globalization, the tendency of Western management techniques and models to be globalized, and let's focus on 'new public management'. New public management is the application of certain private sphere management models in public sphere organizations, and includes the treatment of such organizations as if they were operating like private companies in markets, and the treatment of the public as consumers. The 'recontextualization' of such a model in some social entity is actually a complex process whose outcomes are less than predictable, as I argue below. But let us for the moment oversimplify. New public management inherently involves a change in relations between social fields – government on the one hand, private business on the other. Government organizations start to be more like private business organizations in certain ways. We can predict changes in the network of social practices in government organizations – perhaps some new articulation between (and maybe compromise between) bureaucratic ways of doing things and market ways. In part, these will be changes in orders of discourse: relations between new market discourses (maybe representing citizens as 'consumers' of services, for instance) and existing discourses, new market genres (associated with 'branding' the organization, for instance) and old ones, new market styles (e.g. new styles for managers and 'leaders') and old ones. New institutions, organizations, practices, discourse and so forth will emerge within what is fundamentally a change in relations between social fields, institutions, organizations, orders of discourse, discourses, genres and styles. I have given the example in a highly schematic form with the limited purpose of making the theoretical point more concrete.

Let me come back to 'recontextualization'. When processes of globalization affect a particular social entity such as a nation-state, a relationship is set up between the 'outside' and the 'inside' of that entity. This includes practices, networks of practices, orders of discourse, discourses, genres and/or styles which already exist 'outside' the entity (e.g. in other states or regions) coming into contact with the 'inside'. The relationship between outside and inside can be seen as a relationship of recontextualization – external entities are recontextualized, relocated within a new context. But there is an important proviso. Recontextualization can be seen as a dialectical relation which is simultaneously a relation of colonization and a relation of appropriation. On the one hand, the external entity may expand into a new space, but on the other this is a pre-constituted space with its own existing practices, orders of discourse and so forth, and recontextualization can be an active process of appropriating the external entity. Reception of external entities may, depending on circumstances, be more or less passive or more or less active. Moreover, external entities do not just flow into new spaces; they are so to speak 'carried' there. More precisely, external entities are recontextualized in so far as they are appropriated within successful strategies of 'internal' social agencies and agents within the recontextualizing context. This takes us back to Jessop's view of discourses as elements of strategies, and locates recontextualization within strategic struggles and power relations within the recontextualizing social entity.

In many cases, the recontextualization of social practices is in its initial phase the recontextualization of a discourse or discourses which project(s) imaginaries for wider social change. In so far as such discourses are appropriated within successful strategies, they may be operationalized, enacted in new ways of acting and interacting, inculcated in new 'ways of being' and personal and social identities, and materialized in the physical world. We can see these processes in terms of dialectical relations between discourse and other moments of the social process envisaged by Harvey. Discourses are 'translated' into social relations, forms of power, rituals and institutions, beliefs and values and desires, and material practices. But let me stress the contingency of these processes of recontextualization. Social changes are not mono-causal; they involve complex interactions between diverse causal factors and forces. And the effects of discourses as causal forces in social change are contingent upon various factors: whether or not they are appropriated in successful strategies, how well entrenched existing social practices and orders of discourse are, how well they resonate with people's practical experience of social life, whether certain economic, political and cultural preconditions exist (Fairclough *et al.* 2004).

We can extend these observations about discourse to globalization in general. Globalization should not be conceived as a process of homogenization, a gradual dissemination of (essentially Western) social practices, as well as economic and political structures, across the globe. As Jessop suggests, globalization can be conceived of as changes in scales and relationships between scales, and socio-spatial entities such as nation-states are subject to processes of 're-scaling' in which the global scale may be 'an ultimate horizon for action'. We can argue that re-scaling does involve processes of recontextualization, of 'outside' entities coming 'inside', but what is involved is an active and dynamic internal reaction and response to external discourses or other elements. Part of the problem is the powerful discourse of 'globalism', which construes globalization as a progressive harmonization especially with respect to a neo-liberal free market. In fact, a more realistic assumption is that the outcomes of re-scaling may be very diverse, that there are many possible ways of adjusting to the global scale as a 'horizon for action'. Recontextualization may result in various forms of 'syncretism' (Robertson 1992: 93–4), in social practices and orders of discourse which are mixed, hybrid, local adjustments to or variants of dominant external practices.

Let me briefly refer, in a highly schematic way, to an example to make this rather abstract discussion more concrete. Cameron and Palan suggest as we have seen that globalization involves a new imagined/institutionalized set of spatial relations between offshore, private and 'anti-' economies, the latter being the space of 'social exclusion'. This would suggest that countries like Romania which are seeking to connect with the global scale (especially the 'global economy') through re-scaling will have to engage with this new spatialization as it adjusts to the global scale as a 'horizon'. And indeed the external entities which Romania is currently recontextualizing (largely in the context of its accession to the EU) include the privatized competition state (as an alternative to the public welfare-oriented state) and the conversion of problems of poverty into problems of social exclusion. The discourse of 'social exclusion' has been appropriated into government strategy and is now a presence in government and beyond, and it has been translated into policies. But in a country whose active workforce has been steadily declining for over a decade, 20 per cent of whose workforce are migrant workers, which has a hugely inflated agricultural workforce (42 per cent of the working population in 2001), the competitiveness of whose economy upon accession to the EU (anticipated for 2007) is very much in doubt, and 30 per cent of whose people are according to official standards living in poverty, the preconditions for the operationalization of the strategy and discourse of dealing with poverty and social deprivation through combating 'social exclusion' and achieving 'social inclusion' would seem to be absent. And the strategy and discourse have been dismissed in some quarters as inadequate for the nature of the social problems which exist in the country (Stănculescu and Berevoescu 2004). The contradiction between the obligations of government to ensure a reasonable if minimal standard of well-being for the population and its obligation to prioritize the economic competitiveness of the country confront it with massive dilemmas. It is far from clear how the problems of re-scaling will be resolved in this case, but what is clear is that the recontextualization of the strategy and discourse of social exclusion/inclusion is anything but a simple process. I return to this example in more detail in Chapter 4.

Conclusion: summary of the rest of the book

I briefly described the structure of the book in the Introduction, but I want to finish this chapter with a summary which shows how the approach which I have set out above is applied in the rest of the book to the topic of globalization.

In Chapter 3 I shall take up the issue of strategies of globalization and discourses associated with them, focusing upon the strategies of public agencies, including both governmental and non-governmental agencies. One objective will be to identify some of the range of discourses which are associated with different strategies, and to analyse texts which draw upon these discourses. I shall give most attention to the discourse of globalism, given the dominant international position it has achieved. But I shall use textual analysis of a speech by a senior member of the US government to show how the powerful social agents and agencies which back this discourse respond to changing events and circumstances which pose a challenge to it. The dominance of a discourse (and a strategy) is always contingent and precarious, and constantly has to be maintained or re-established, and textual analysis can contribute to showing how this is achieved. Moreover, neither strategies nor discourses stand still: while they may have enough continuity over time to be regarded as the same strategy or discourse, they also change over time and in response to events and problems. A discourse like the discourse of globalism can be seen as a sort of node around which various different discourses cluster, and I shall discuss change in the cluster over time with reference to the emerging connection between the discourse of globalism and the discourse of the 'knowledge-based economy' (KBE). I shall also come back to the issue of variation, selection and retention of discourses, to the mechanisms and processes through which the conjunction between the discourses of globalism and the KBE has been selected over others and retained and institutionalized.

In Chapter 4 my focus shifts from a general discussion of strategies for globalization to processes of globalization as they affect a particular special entity: Romania, one of the 'post-communist' countries of Eastern Europe. The globalization of particular spatial entities (be they countries, cities, regions, etc.) can be seen as a matter of 're-scaling' (Jessop 2002), the re-location of those entities within changing relations between 'scales' (e.g. the national, regional and local) which include the emergence of new scales (such as the global and the 'macro-regional', eg the European Union or the North American Free Trade Area). The re-scaling of Romania involves the recontextualization of a particular set of strategies and discourses, including the discourses of globalism and the KBE, but also many more focused strategies and discourses most of which originate at the scale of the European Union. A central claim of this chapter is that the re-scaling of a country such as Romania, the recontextualization of strategies and discourses and their institutionalization, operationalization and implementation, are inherently problematic and fraught processes. Their outcome depends upon specific structural, institutional, social and cultural characteristics of Romania as a recontextualizing context. It cannot be accurately predicted, and it cannot be managed with any precision. In addition to a general discussion of globalism and the KBE, I shall focus specifically upon two particular recontextualizations of strategy and discourse which relate to the 'Europeanization' of Romania (its incorporation into a European scale): the reform of higher education associated with the 'Bologna process', and EU strategy for combating 'social exclusion' and achieving 'social inclusion'.

Chapter 5 will deal with the media and mediation. The mass media are now the main purveyors of knowledge, information, news, beliefs, values and attitudes, and the political process and processes of political legitimization largely take place through the media. Changes in the international political economy of communication, especially the emergence of a global communications industry dominated by powerful transnational corporations such as Rupert Murdoch's News Corporation, have been an important factor for the relative success of globalist strategy and discourse. Through their direct or indirect influence, these corporations dominate the media internationally. They contribute to the dissemination of globalist discourse, claims and assumptions, and of values, attitudes and identities which are amongst the cultural conditions for the successful implementation of globalism, on the basis of their intimate relationship with other sectors of business, the public relations industry, governments and other agencies. In this chapter I shall first continue with the concerns of Chapter 4 by discussing and illustrating the importance of the media and mediation in processes of re-scaling at the national level, again referring to the case of Romania. I shall then discuss how the media contribute to the construction of a global scale specifically through their constructing, or perhaps rather positing, of a global public sphere, referring to international coverage of the attacks on New York and Washington on 11 September 2001, and including an analysis of a speech by President G.W. Bush.

In Chapter 6 I focus on 'globalization from below' (Falk 1999). As in previous chapters I shall be concerned with strategies, but now with the strategies of individuals or groups in specific places (cities, towns, villages, regions) to adapt to or gain from social change, or defend themselves against its negative effects, using new resources for local action and strategy made available by globalization, which include discourses (as well as genres and styles). I discuss how contemporary globalization affects the forms taken by what we can call the dialectic between the particular and the general (Harvey 1996). This includes how situated action and struggle in particular places increasingly draw upon general resources (techniques, skills, etc. and also discourses) which are used at higher scales (are for instance European, or global) and are now more readily accessible on the local scale, which help in the development and pursuit of strategies but can also obscure the particular local character of social struggles; and how local action on for instance environmental issues (as in my two main examples) increasingly involves alliances or coalitions of agencies and organizations on different scales, including global organizations involved in the new 'transnational activism' (Tarrow 2005) such as Greenpeace.

Chapter 7 will take up from Chapter 3 the view of the discourse of globalism as a node around which other discourses cluster, with changes in the cluster over time. Specifically, I shall focus on the combination of the discourse of globalism with the discourse of the 'war on terror', which one can see as constituting a significant shift in the strategy and discourse of globalism. I shall show this shift through a textual analysis of a speech on the USA's National Security Strategy by Condoleeza Rice, National Security Advisor and then Secretary of State in G.W. Bush's administration. I shall also discuss the discourse of the 'war on terror', identifying salient features of it. I shall argue, in terms of the different relationships of discourse to other facets of globalization I identified in the literature on globalization (see Chapter 1), that this discourse is primarily ideological in the sense that it legitimizes a strategy to preserve and extend US global – and globalist – hegemony. It is also effective rhetorically in persuading many people to accept restrictions on civil liberties. And it also has constructive effects, including an international restructuring of regimes and apparatuses of security, and the convergence of policies on development with security policies (Duffield 2001).

3 Discourses of globalization

In this chapter I shall discuss discourses of globalization associated with strategies for globalization, focusing upon the strategies and discourses of public agencies, including both governmental and non-governmental agencies. My approach is based upon the theorization of strategies within cultural political economy, the view that strategies 'are always elaborated in and through discourses' (Jessop 2002), which I discussed in Chapters 1 and 2. I shall identify some of the range of discourses which are associated with different strategies, and analyse texts which draw upon these discourses. But I shall start from and give most attention to the globalist discourse of globalization, given the dominant international position which the strategy of globalism has achieved. I shall discuss the latter with particular reference to a speech by US under-secretary of State Stuart Eizenstat delivered in 1999 to the Democratic Leadership Council, in the wake of the economic collapse which began in East Asia in the late 1990s. This will allow me to address the question of how the dominant or hegemonic position of this discourse is reasserted and largely successfully sustained in the face of events and circumstances that pose serious challenges to it – the question, to put it differently, of the resilience of this discourse.

It is helpful for understanding the resilience and adaptability of discourses of such scope and power to see them as 'nodal discourses' around which many other discourses cluster (see Jessop 2004 for the similar concept of 'master narratives'). The resilience of the globalist discourse can then be seen as a matter of it being capable of being sustained through changes in the cluster of discourses in response to new circumstances and challenges. This way of viewing discourses of this sort also helps in understanding another important change which I shall discuss, the convergence between globalist strategy and discourse on the one hand and the strategy for constructing a 'knowledge-based economy' (KBE) and the discourse of the KBE on the other. I shall also go back to an issue raised with respect to cultural political economy in Chapter 2, the variation, selection and retention of discourses (Fairclough et al. 2004, Jessop 2004), with respect to mechanisms and processes through which the discourse of globalism and the conjunction between the discourses of globalism and the KBE has been selected over others and retained and institutionalized.

Globalist discourse of globalization

'Globalism' is a discourse of globalization which represents it in reductive neo-liberal economic terms within a strategy to inflect and re-direct actual processes of globalization in that direction. Steger (2005) identifies six core claims of 'globalism':

- Globalization is about the liberalization and global integration of markets.
- Globalization is inevitable and irreversible.
- Nobody is in charge of globalization.
- Globalization benefits everyone.
- Globalization furthers the spread of democracy in the world.
- Globalization requires a war on terror.

These claims are sometimes explicitly asserted in globalist texts, and sometimes supported with an established and recurrent set of arguments, but they also sometimes occur as assumptions or presuppositions (Fairclough 2003), i.e. they are simply taken for granted. The first claim is the most crucial one, and most central to the question of how this particular discourse came to be selected and retained from the range of alternatives. It is associated with another claim that is commonly asserted or presupposed in globalist texts: that the most effective form of capitalist economy is one based upon 'liberalized' markets, where trade and the movement and investment of capital, prices, employment and so forth are subject only to market forces, without the 'interference' of state regulation. This justifies a strategy to extend free market capitalism based on neo-liberal tenets to virtually all the countries of the world.

The plausibility and resonance of this claim rest upon what have been pretty successfully established by advocates of neo-liberalism as 'facts' about the post-Second World War socio-economic order, and especially the 'fact' that markets are self-regulating (based on the highly contentious thesis of the 'invisible hand', the claim that market forces drive the economy to efficient outcomes as if by an invisible hand, Stiglitz 2002), and interference by states (as this history is claimed to have shown) is economically counter-productive and damaging. There is of course the contrary 'fact' that unregulated markets have been shown to produce chaotic and disastrous effects (Polanyi 1944), but in the aftermath of the economic troubles of the 1970s powerful agents and agencies were unreceptive to it. For in addition to a perceived objective plausibility in real experience, market liberalization gained the support of the most powerful states (the USA and Britain were forerunners, under the presidency of Ronald Reagan and the premiership of

Margaret Thatcher) and influential politicians, international agencies which these states effectively control (the World Bank, IMF, WTO, OECD, etc.), private corporations, and many other agents and agencies. This backing was crucial to the selection, retention and operationalization of the globalist discourse of globalization (Falk 1999, DeMartino 2000, Harvey 2005).

Steger describes globalism as a 'story' (or narrative), a discourse and an ideology. The term 'ideology' is not inappropriate: globalism can be seen as having created a space for unconstrained and highly profitable action on the part of the corporations of the most powerful countries on earth, especially the USA, on the basis of the claim that markets work benignly without external regulation which the crises of the late 1990s (in East Asia, Latin America and Russia) have shown to be false. So globalism can be seen as ideological in the sense that it has provided legitimacy and cover for the consolidation and extension of asymmetries of power and wealth. And although some would argue that its heyday was the mid-1990s and it has been in decline since then (Saul 2005), the strategy and discourse have proved relatively resilient and capable of accommodating certain concessions to regulation without major change. It has also gained influence within the European Union despite continuing commitment to some form (if a 'modernized' and arguably weakened one) of the European Social Model.

Epistemologically, discourses are abstract entities (elements of orders of discourse within networks of social practices, see Chapter 2) which are established on the basis of repetition and recurrence over time and in diverse social sites, but ontologically they appear in the concrete form of particular texts (Fairclough *et al.* 2004). One contribution that CDA can make to (cultural) political economic analysis, as I argued in Chapter 2, is methods for analysing texts which illuminate their contribution to strategies, discourses, and their operationalization and implementation, as well as their recontextualization in different places (e.g. countries, regions) and different fields of social life, and their adaptation to changing events and circumstances (Fairclough 1992, 2003). CDA in itself cannot however tell us which texts are significant in terms of the constitutive effects of discourse on social life – that requires institutional and historical forms of analysis.

I shall illustrate the contribution that textual analysis can make in the case of a speech (Eizenstat 1999) whose significance and impact arose from the standing of the speaker (US under-secretary of State Stuart Eizenstat) and the context of crisis for globalism within which it was delivered and to which it addressed (it was delivered in the wake of the economic collapse of the late 1990s), constituting a response by the US government to a crisis which threatened the strategy they supported, as Eizenstat concedes.

The text I shall refer to is a press release which contains a summary of the speech followed by a transcript of the full text. The main genres are *epistemic argumentation* (argumentation for epistemic claims about what is or is not the case – what has happened, what the situation is, etc.) and *normative argumentation*

(argumentation for normative claims about what should (not) happen or what should (not) be done), and the speech is basically structured as a move from epistemic to normative argumentation. The gist of the overall argument is that the crises have shaken confidence in 'economic liberalization' and in that sense posed a threat to US strategy, that the 'undeniable risks' of 'globalization' must be recognized and policies must be developed to avert or mitigate them, but countries must '"stay the course" on economic reform and trade liberalization' – in other words, the globalist strategy must be sustained. Eizenstat argues that the crisis 'did not occur because of these policies' ('pro-growth, trade liberalization and free-market orientation') but because of failures and weaknesses in the countries worst affected.

This is a globalist speech, and I shall begin by showing that. Eizenstat begins with the assertion that US foreign policy has 'diametrically reoriented', from 'containing the spread of communism' towards 'harnessing the forces of globalization in order to sustain international support for democratic, free-market capitalism across the globe'. This is a strikingly frank formulation of globalist strategy to steer globalization in the direction of global free-market capitalism. In this quotation a distinction is implicitly drawn between globalization as a set of 'forces' and the strategy and policies to 'harness' them. But there is a confusion between the two throughout the speech, which is an illustration of the globalist tendency to reduce globalization to globalism. For example, to arrive at a coherent reading of the following paragraph in the transcript we need to take 'globalization' and 'economic liberalization' as equivalent to each other (I have added the italics):

> In short, the financial crisis has exacerbated fears in developing countries and could fuel a backlash against *globalization*. Indeed, the optimistic notion only two years ago that the world was adopting dramatic *economic liberalization* as a model for economic and political development is under challenge.

We can say that the two expressions are 'textured', textually constructed, in a *relation of equivalence*, an example of *classification* as a textual process (Fairclough 2003). Yet the feared 'backlash' is clearly not against (the 'forces' of) 'globalization' as such but against the strategy for 'economic liberalization'.

This confusion is also evident in the following sentence:

> The world must neither resort to protectionist measures in a fruitless attempt to stop globalization nor should we ignore its undeniable risks.

There are two normative claims here ('the world must not resort to protectionist measures', 'we should not ignore its undeniable risks') within an argument which includes implied premises which ground the claims (in the case of the first, 'the world may resort to protectionist measures' and 'any attempt to stop globalization would be fruitless'; in the case of the second, 'the risks of globalization are undeniable'). Furthermore, the argument is *dialogical* in the sense that it responds to the assumed argument of an antagonist (along the lines of: 'the world should resort to protectionist measures to stop globalization, because globalization is dangerous'), refuting its main claim while conceding the premise that globalization is dangerous. But it is a *fallacious* argument (van Eemeren and Grootendorst 1992, 2004) because the standpoint it implicitly attributes to antagonists ('the world should resort to protectionist measures to stop globalization') is not the real standpoint of those who oppose globalism: it is against the strategy and policies of globalism, not globalization, that people advocate protectionist measures, and it is globalism, not globalization, that the crisis has showed to be dangerous. While it would be 'fruitless' to attempt to stop the 'forces' of globalization, 'globalism' is merely a strategy and not a 'force' and it can be stopped. It is worth noting that elsewhere in the speech it is implied that the 'risks' do indeed come from globalism: 'The Clinton Administration is . . . supporting economic openness and liberalization . . . while working to minimize its harshest elements.' In short, what we have in the speech is a confusion and reduction, and one might say obfuscation, that is typical of globalist discourse.

The speech also includes more of the globalist claims identified by Steger: that 'globalization' benefits everyone ('By any measure, globalization is a net benefit to the United States and the world. In an increasingly globalized and interdependent economy, the quest for prosperity is the opposite of a zero sum game'), that it is inevitable and irreversible ('Globalization is an inevitable element of our lives. We cannot stop it anymore than we can stop the waves from crashing on the shore'), and that it strengthens democracy. Given the confusion between globalization and globalism, these ostensible claims about globalization are fallaciously used as claims for globalism.

Let me turn to Eizenstat's account of the Asian crisis:

> However, today's current global economic crisis provides compelling evidence that the same global forces transforming nations and peoples are also posing real challenges to the gains we've made.
>
> The rapid influx of capital, which helped to spur high growth rates in Asia, reversed when domestic and foreign markets lost confidence, contributing to painful recessions. In Indonesia, real GDP last year was down about 15 percent, in Thailand it fell more than 8 percent and in South Korea it fell 7 percent from 1997 levels.
>
> Many of the countries most gravely affected by the crisis lacked well-developed financial systems, with the legal and regulatory frameworks needed to ensure that capital flowed to its most productive user.

Excessive private short-term borrowing of foreign currencies increased the economies' vulnerability to shifts in sentiment. Cronyism, corruption, and a lack of financial transparency contributed to a series of bad investments and weakened banks. The crisis exposed weaknesses and changed perceptions of future growth prospects and fed investors' uncertainty and panic, leading to financial instability and eventually recession.

What began as a currency crisis in Thailand quickly became an economic and political crisis, and the crisis spread to the rest of East Asia and then on to Russia and now Latin America.

This is a *narrative* of the crisis and an *explanation* of it – a mixing of genres and an example of 'interdiscursive hybridity' (see Chapter 2). The first part of the narrative is in the second paragraph, especially the first sentence which is a highly condensed narrative of quite a complex series of events which can be more explicitly formulated as follows: there was a rapid influx of capital, and this helped to spur high growth rates in Asia, but domestic and foreign markets then lost confidence, then the influx was reversed, and there were then painful recessions which the reversal contributed to. The second sentence of paragraph 2 elaborates on and gives specific examples of 'painful recessions'. The third and fourth paragraphs basically give explanations of the events narrated in paragraph 2, though they also contain narrative elements. The final paragraph extends the narrative to the broadening of the crisis and its spread to other parts of the world.

The crisis is explained as the effect of weaknesses in the countries affected by it. We can make this attribution of responsibility clearer by looking at how agency and responsibility are represented here. In the narrative of paragraph 2, the 'influx' of capital and its 'reversal' are represented as processes without agents. The agents or agencies that brought capital into these countries are not identified. There was simply an 'influx', the action on the part of some agents/agencies of moving capital in (somebody, after all, must have done something) is *nominalized* (Fairclough 2003: 143–4, 220) as 'influx' and thereby transformed from an action into a reified event. The 'influx' was then 'reversed'. This is a strange and mystifying formulation of what would more transparently be represented as two actions with responsible agents – e.g. 'financial institutions a, b . . . moved capital into countries x, y . . . , then they moved it out again'. Grammatically, there is an *intransitive* verb ('reversed') representing a *transitive* action (some agent acting upon the entity at issue here, i.e. capital; on transitivity see Fairclough 2003: 142), which moreover has as its subject 'the rapid influx of capital', the reifying *nominalization* of another transitive action. To put the point simply: who did it and who was responsible for these rapid movements of capital which had such disastrous effects?

If we then look at the first two sentences of paragraph 4, we again find nominalizations of actions ('excessive private short-term borrowing of foreign currencies', 'bad investments') and behaviours ('cronyism', 'corruption', 'lack of financial transparency'). In this case however, unlike paragraph 2, these reified actions and behaviours are negatively *evaluated* (Fairclough 2003: 215, 171–90) either with *evaluative adjectives* ('excessive', 'bad') or through the negative connotations of nouns ('cronyism', 'corruption', 'lack').

Just as we could find more transparent formulations of actions and their agents for paragraph 2 on the basis of social and contextual knowledge, so can we here: we can *infer* (Verschueren 1999: 25–37) that covert agents or agencies in this case are internal to the countries concerned, so that it is the 'locals' who were cronyist, corrupt and so forth, whereas it was external investing agents or agencies that were responsible for the actions inferred, and represented in evaluatively neutral terms, in paragraph 2. So blame is covertly placed on people in the countries affected.

One may think that external investors get off lightly in Eizenstat's representation of events. Investors are explicitly referred to just once ('investors' uncertainty and panic') and this does correct the balance a little, for 'panic' is negatively evaluated and one would think a reprehensible reaction in the circumstances. But it is noticeable that while internal agents/agencies act and behave (badly), investors mainly manifest feelings (as well as 'uncertainty and panic', they 'lost confidence', and we can infer that it was their 'sentiment' that shifted and their 'perceptions' that were changed, see the discussion of *'process types'* in Fairclough 2003, Halliday 1994, van Leeuwen 1995). Overall, then, the actions and reactions of external investors are represented as relatively benign (and perhaps 'understandable').

Let me come finally to the question of how the discourse of globalism is being sustained through adaptation to a situation of perceived failure and loss of confidence. As I suggested earlier, we can see the discourse as a nodal discourse which can be changed through changes in the cluster of other discourses around it while its central elements (including Steger's 'claims') are sustained. Eizenstat actually announces 'a new paradigm' and 'strategy' which the Clinton Administration is 'devising and implementing' – 'namely supporting economic openness and liberalization, which are decades-old principles of U.S. policy, while working to minimize its harshest elements'. Its five 'goals', targeted particularly at 'developing countries', are:

> Restore faith in the global financial system. Ensure that countries have social safety nets in place that help people weather the disruptions caused by globalization. Improve capacity building in both the social and economic realm, among developing nations. Work to improve transparency, good governance and anti-corruption efforts. And, stay the course on economic reform and trade liberalization.

This is an example of *interdiscursive hybridity* (see Chapter 2, and Fairclough and Chouliaraki 1999) in the form of a mix of discourses. One can identify expressions here associated with several discourses which have become increasingly salient in globalist texts as the shifts in the cluster of discourses takes place: 'social safety nets', 'capacity building', and 'good governance'.

These goals are elaborated in the second part of the speech, where the genre is normative argumentation (marked by the predominance of *deontic modality* – what 'must' be done, etc., see Fairclough 2003: 165–71). In the case of the second goal for instance, Eizenstat argues that 'to be willing to continue supporting economic liberalization, citizens must have some confidence that a social safety net is in place that will help them weather the economic disruptions caused by global change'. We can *infer* from this that the 'new paradigm' will do nothing to avert 'economic disruptions', and that 'working to minimize' the 'harshest elements' of economic liberalization amounts only to palliative measures. Eizenstat does argue in elaborating the first goal that 'It is imperative that we look at new ways of reforming the global financial architecture, particularly at this year's G7 summit – in order to prevent recurrence of what President Clinton called the "boom or bust" cycle', but no concrete specifications for such 'reform' are given, and in fact no substantial reform has taken place.

In the case of the third goal ('improve capacity building'), Eizenstat argues that 'developing nations need greater assistance in strengthening their institutional capacity to benefit from the enormous flows of the capital that travel around the globe in search of higher returns and efficient economic systems', including improvements in 'the prudential regulation and supervision of financial institutions', increases in 'transparency and disclosure', and improvements in 'corporate governance'. US assistance 'must be geared toward specific programs that improve the ability of developing nations to cope with the exigencies that these huge capital flows can cause' and 'can go a long way toward building confidence among international investors'. We can see a number of *themes* which have become increasingly prominent within the discourse of capacity building – 'institutional capacity', 'transparency and disclosure', 'corporate governance'. The focus is on development aid to increase the capacity of developing countries to deal with potentially destabilizing 'capital flows', not in any way controlling the flows.

In elaborating the fourth goal ('good governance'), Eizenstat argues that 'we must launch a global campaign for compliance with internationally accepted standards of good governance. Government corruption, wherever it occurs, has a debilitating effect on economic liberalization.' The focus is on corruption in the developing world, and on development aid to improve the environment for 'economic liberalization' in this respect.

We can see in Eizenstat's presentation of the 'new paradigm' elements of the shift in development strategy and discourse noted by Duffield (2001). There is a move towards a more interventionist approach, which targets specific changes in national and corporate governance, in institutions and in social policy (e.g. social safety nets), and increasingly makes the implementation of such changes a condition for receiving development aid. There is also a suggestion of the main shift identified by Duffield, a convergence between development policy and security policy, in the presence of 'political instability' in Eizenstat's argument that 'we must prevent these nations from becoming marginalized in the global economy. This could lead to greater political instability and exacerbated inequality between the haves and have-nots of the world.' Underdeveloped countries are increasingly seen as dangerous countries, and this already existing tendency was to be exacerbated after 11 September 2001 with the declaration of the 'war on terror' (see Chapter 7).

So we can say that there is a change in the strategy and discourse of globalism in the wake of the crises of the late 1990s, but this is not a change in fundamental features of the existing strategy and discourse. On the contrary it is a reassertion and confirmation of them coupled with the attachment of the new discourse of development to the nodal globalist discourse of globalization. The US response to the crises was not to concede that 'economic liberalization' needed to be constrained because of the damage it can do, but to set out to make developing countries fitter to cope with 'economic liberalization'.

Globalism and the KBE

The articulation between globalist strategy and discourse on the one hand and the new strategy and discourse of development on the other is one significant change in the evolution of globalist strategy. Another is its articulation with the strategy and discourse of the 'knowledge-based economy' (KBE, see Jessop 2002: 126–34).

There have been historical shifts in forms of capitalist economy, and there is currently what is widely perceived as a shift from the industrial economy which was predominant from the late nineteenth century until the late twentieth century to a 'knowledge-based economy'. The precise meaning of 'knowledge-based economy' (KBE) is far from clear and highly contentious, but what it broadly suggests is a range of changes in economic production which elevate 'knowledge' to the level of or even above other productive factors. The KBE can be seen as a strategy for economic change and a new 'fix' within the 'global economy', and itself as a 'nodal' discourse which articulates together many other discourses, some of which are indicated by 'buzzwords' such as 'expert systems', 'e-commerce', 'intellectual capital', 'human capital', 'knowledge workers', 'intellectual property' and 'lifelong learning', 'learning society', 'e-government', which are amongst the themes of the KBE. The strategy and discourse of the KBE are not inherently globalist or neo-liberal (Jessop 2004). For instance the European Union has adopted the strategic goal of becoming 'the most successful knowledge-based economy in the world' (Lisbon Council 2000), yet unlike the USA it has defined this goal in conjunction with a commitment to 'social inclusion' and to a 'modernized' (and arguably weakened) version of the European Social Model. Neo-liberal and globalist influence on the EU is increasing, but nevertheless there remain significant differences between the EU and the USA. However, the emergence of the KBE as an international strategy is in large part due to the USA's decision in the late 1980s to base its bid to defend its global economic hegemony from European and East Asian competition on its supremacy in knowledge industries and what came to be called 'intellectual property', and the dominant version of the KBE is the globalist version associated with the convergence of the two nodal discourses of globalism and the KBE.

I want to illustrate this convergence from the Preface to the UK Competitiveness White Paper (Department of Trade and Industry 1998). The UK has since Thatcher's premiership become the leading advocate of globalism and neo-liberalism within the EU, and has closely associated itself with US strategy and policies. The policy content of the White Paper is summed up as follows:

> The Government's White Paper sets out the role it and business need to play in improving the UK's competitiveness. Our aim is to close the performance gap between the UK and other major trading nations. This is a job for business but Government must create the right environment for business success by providing an economic framework which is stable and enterprising. The Government will put in place policies and programmes to help businesses innovate and succeed as we all face the challenge of the knowledge driven economy.

The orientation is to 'the global market', which 'demands innovative and higher quality products and services'. And in the global market, 'knowledge, skills and creativity are needed above all to give the UK a competitive edge. These are the distinctive assets of a knowledge-driven economy. They are essential to creating high-value products and services and to improving business processes.' There is a role for business and a role for government. 'Businesses need to identify, capture and market the knowledge base that drives all products and services. They have to turn into commercial success the scientific and technological knowledge in our universities and research organizations. Companies need to form collaborative partnerships with, amongst others, suppliers, customers, schools and universities to build networks and clusters of excellence to win competitive advantage.' Government's role is to 'invest in capabilities to promote enterprise and stimulate innovation; catalyse collaboration to help business win competitive advantage; promote competition by opening and modernising markets'. With respect to capabilities, Government 'must invest in science, skills, innovative finance and digital technologies'. The Government will for instance 'reward universities for strategies and activities to enhance interaction with business', and 'create a new enterprise culture' by amongst other things 'encouraging the development of entrepreneurship skills, especially amongst school pupils, students and university researchers'. With respect to 'catalysing collaboration', successful businesses are said to 'thrive on a mixture of aggressive competition and intense collaboration as in Silicon Valley in the US. In the knowledge-driven economy, it is more important than ever that they collaborate with other businesses to improve, develop and market products through benchmarking and best practice. However, many businesses do not have the time and resources to collaborate effectively. Government can help' in various ways. The Preface concludes by describing Government and business as 'working together for a successful future. Only business can deliver prosperity and jobs. Government must know when to act, and when to keep out of the way.'

Apart from the focus on 'competitiveness' in 'the global market', one feature of globalist or neo-liberal discourse here is the view of the relationship between business and Government: Government's role is to enable or facilitate, to 'create the right environment', for business, which alone can produce wealth and competitiveness – and Government must know 'when to keep out of the way'. As for the discourse of the KBE, there is the characteristic claim that 'knowledge, skills and creativity' are the decisive assets for competitiveness, that 'capabilities' are something that one 'invests in', and the associated increasingly influential view of universities and research institutes as primarily resources for business: they are 'collaborative partnerships', 'networks' and 'clusters of excellence' with companies, all of which suggest a relationship between equals, whereas the indications are that universities are losing their autonomy and increasingly becoming subservient to business. We can also identify some of the discourses which cluster around the nodal discourse of the KBE – 'partnerships', 'networks', 'benchmarking' and 'best practice', and 'enterprise culture' (a recycled Thatcherite discourse).

Let me turn to the issue of variation, selection and retention of discourses with respect to the KBE, and then with respect to the conjunction of globalism and the KBE. I have already alluded to the significance of US strategy for reasserting economic hegemony in the face of competition for the selection and subsequent retention/institutionalization of the KBE. This was one element in the build-up of one precondition for its selection and retention – the backing of powerful international forces. The strategy for the KBE also received backing from international institutions, notably the Organization for Economic Cooperation and Development (OECD) and the WTO, and, as we have seen, from the European Union, as well as the corporate business sector. Another precondition was that the previously dominant form of capitalism, Fordism, had entered a long-term crisis in the 1970s, and after a long period of uncertainty the KBE proved to be an effective strategy and imaginary for an alternative. This was in part because it captured changes which were underway before the KBE emerged as a strategy and discourse – changes in technologies and especially the development of information and communications technologies, in the labour process (including the steady expansion of service industries), in forms of business organization and so forth (Jessop 2004).

To understand the potency of the conjunction of globalism (and the neo-liberalism it is based upon) and the KBE, it is helpful to bring in another element of (cultural) political economy (Jessop 2002). Many versions of (cultural) political economy incorporate forms of 'regulation theory', which see a specific form of capitalism as constituting a spatio-temporal 'fix' based upon a combination of a particular 'regime of accumulation' and 'mode of social regulation' (Boyer 1990). This is one approach to capturing the view in political economy that economic systems are politically and socially embedded and conditioned. The 'fix', until the crisis which began in the 1970s, was between a Fordist regime of accumulation (industrial capitalism) and a Keynesian welfare state mode of social regulation. Neo-liberalism managed quite successfully to establish the view that the crisis was primarily due to excessive state 'interference' with the market, and so challenged the 'fix' between a regime of accumulation of modes of regulation. One can see the conjunction between globalism (neo-liberalism) and the KBE as constituting a strategy for a new 'fix', combining the pursuit of economic liberalization and 'open markets', which is really about forms of state and modes of regulation and their relationship economies and markets, with the KBE as an accumulation regime. One formulation of the new fix is KBE + competition state (Jessop 2002), reflected in the view we saw in the competitiveness White Paper that the state enables business to succeed in the global KBE by establishing conditions for competitiveness.

Alternatives to 'globalism' among governmental agencies

Eizenstat's speech already represents some concessions to the evidence and perception of the damage that globalism can do, but these concessions do not really address the central issue in debates and controversies around globalization and globalism. Polanyi (1944) wrote a celebrated analysis of the 'great transformation', which established 'laissez-faire' or free market capitalism internationally in the nineteenth century, in which he argued that economic liberalism must be balanced by social protection, that there is a constant tension between the two, and that where they become seriously unbalanced the result is the sort of cataclysm experienced in the world wars of the twentieth century. Circumstances are now very different, but the need for a balance between the free market and social protection still holds true, and the growing evidence that globalism is risking a serious imbalance by conceding too little to social protection is setting off alarm bells all over the world. One expression of this concern is the emergence of new strategies and discourses which more or less directly challenge globalism.

One example is the position taken in the report of the UN Economic Commission for Latin America and the Caribbean 'Globalization and Development' (ECLAC 2002). The report contrasts its 'positive' view of globalization ('the growing influence exerted at the local, national and regional levels by financial, economic, environmental, political, social and cultural processes that are global in scope') which is 'intended to serve the purposes of analysis' with the 'normative' view of globalization as 'the full liberalization and integration of world markets', i.e. the 'globalist' view. The report goes against the central tenet of globalism that globalization is the global spread of a particular neo-liberal version of free market capitalism, claiming that 'there is not just one possible international order', and 'there are many ways to carve out a position in the global economy'. Some of the features which characterize this discourse in contrast with the discourse of 'globalism' are (a) globalization is represented as multidimensional, not just (primarily) an economic process, (b) the 'international order' is seen as emergent and contingent rather than pre-designed, (c) diversity of national economic systems is seen as consistent with a global economy. Moreover, two 'disturbing aspects' of the contemporary globalization process are identified. First, that 'the mobility of capital and the mobility of goods and services exist alongside severe restrictions on the mobility of labour'. This points to a contradiction between the globalist commitment *in discourse* to 'liberalization' and 'deregulation' and 'mobility', and their partial (in both senses of the word) operationalization in practice. Second, a 'lack of global governance', resulting for instance in a lack of 'mechanisms for ensuring the global coherence of the central economies' macroeconomic policies, international standards for the appropriate taxation of capital, or agreements regarding the mobilization of resources to relieve the distributional tensions generated by globalization between and within countries'. What this suggests is a strategy to regulate markets, international regulation of capital tax which would control the 'race to the bottom' (a competition between countries to reduce tax on companies to unprecedentedly low levels) which characterizes current practice, and social policies to offset the damaging inequalities within and between countries which the free market produces. All these are of course anathema to globalists.

A more radical view was taken by Dr Mahathir bin Mohamad, former Prime Minister of Malaysia, at the East Asia Economic Summit 2002 (bin Mohamad 2002, omissions are marked as '(. . .)').

in the 1970s, pressure was applied on countries to go off the Gold Standard and the fixed exchange rate. Henceforth the market, i.e., the currency traders, would determine the rate of exchange of currencies. (. . .) A new business developed to help business deal with the uncertainties of the exchange rate. For a fee, the businesses could hedge. (. . .) Meanwhile the production of goods and services continued. Some failed, and along came the early saviours of failed businesses. They simply bought the businesses, stripped them of their assets and left the minority shareholders gasping. (. . .)

Then came the junk bond peddlers. (. . .) And so began the rampage of the currency traders. Any country was fair game, but most of all the newly emerging economies, rich enough to be fleeced, but not powerful enough to fight back. . . . Perfectly good countries with enormous resources can be truly and really bankrupted.

All the while these countries were condemned for their incompetence, their corruption, their cronyism, etc. The currency traders who sold down the currencies of these countries were never blamed. Indeed they became great philanthropists. . . .

Look at the world today. It is not the prosperous, growing world of the post-war years, especially of the sixties to the eighties. It is a world of economic malaise (. . .) The fact is that we are not doing business anymore, real business that is. We are not producing goods and providing services (. . .) What the world is interested in today is quick money, money that comes from speculation and manipulation; overnight money. The greedy have taken over the economy of the world (. . .)

National governments no anachronism

If the Asian economy is to be revived, Asians must look beyond their continent. They must help bring about a return to sanity. They must do so by ganging up against the greedy who are already shaping the world's economy and finance through the World Trade Organization.

We need to relook very closely at the interpretation of globalization (. . .) We should resuscitate real business, the business of producing things, of providing service. Money should be invested in this and not in buying and selling shares alone or in speculation and manipulation of currencies. (. . .)

We need to go back to the status quo ante, to the good years of the world's growth, to the '60s, '70s and '80s. We must not be afraid to admit that we have gone wrong, and go back to doing real business. Stop the quick profits of asset-stripping, of short selling, of speculation and manipulation of currencies, of monopolizing world business, of the efficacy of size. If we cannot stop them completely, regulate them.

Governments have not become anachronistic. (. . .) They have a good incentive to do the right thing by everyone, including the very poor, simply because, democratic or authoritarian, they know they will be thrown out if they don't care for the people's welfare (. . .)

Malaysia's response to the East Asian crisis was to pull out of the 'global economy' and follow its own economic path, taking its currency off the world market, imposing controls on the export of capital, and imposing tariffs. To the surprise, and perhaps consternation, of many neo-liberally inclined experts, this has proved to be very successful. Bin Mohamad represents the Malaysian strategy as going back to 'the status quo ante', to the good years of the world's growth, to the ''60s, '70s and '80s'. The passage begins with a narrative of globalization in its globalist form which is very different from those of its supporters, and incorporates a different discourse whose *themes* include 'asset-stripping', 'hedging', 'junk bond peddlers', 'speculation', 'manipulation' and so forth. It is worth comparing his account of the East Asia crisis with Eizenstat's (discussed above). According to the latter,

> The rapid influx of capital, which helped to spur high growth rates in Asia, reversed when domestic and foreign markets lost confidence, contributing to painful recessions. (. . .) Excessive private short-term borrowing of foreign currencies increased the economies' vulnerability to shifts in sentiment. Cronyism, corruption, and a lack of financial transparency contributed to a series of bad investments and weakened banks. The crisis exposed weaknesses and changed perceptions of future growth prospects and fed investors' uncertainty and panic, leading to financial instability and eventually recession.

And according to bin Mohamad:

> And so began the rampage of the currency traders. Any country was fair game, but most of all the newly emerging economies, rich enough to be fleeced, but not powerful enough to fight back. (. . .) Perfectly good countries with enormous resources can be truly and really bankrupted. All the while these countries were condemned for their incompetence, their corruption, their cronyism, etc. The currency traders who sold down the currencies of these countries were never blamed. Indeed they became great philanthropists. (. . .)

The representation of international financial dealers and the processes and actions they were involved in is strikingly different. For Eizenstat they are 'investors' and 'foreign markets', whose 'sentiment' and 'perceptions' shift, who 'lose confidence', become 'uncertain' and 'panic', and the 'influx of capital . . . reverses'. For bin Mohamad they are 'currency traders' (he also calls them 'the greedy') who go on the 'rampage', 'fleece' countries, treat them as 'fair game', 'bankrupt' them, and 'sell down' their currencies. Bin Mohamad's narrative is characterized overall by the attribution of the Asian crisis to the activities of a set of external antagonists, sometimes not specifically identified (e.g. the unspecified subjects of the *passive* structures (Fairclough 2003: 145–50): 'pressure was applied', 'these countries were condemned') and sometimes identified ('the currency traders', 'the early saviours of failed businesses', 'the junk bond peddlers', 'the greedy'). As we can see from this vocabulary, bin Mohamad's argument is as much an emotional one as a rational one. Eizenstat does not refer to the actions of 'investors' but their feelings and emotions, as if what was at stake in international finance was the psychological well-being of the players. This is a standard feature of, for instance, reports on financial markets in the press. Bin Mohamad on the other hand represents the 'currency traders' as engaging in acts of vandalism, if not criminal acts. And he responds to the sort of commonplace criticism voiced by Eizenstat ('cronyism', 'corruption' and so forth) by implying that it is hypocritical given that the currency traders 'were never blamed' – adding, ironically, that 'they became great philanthropists'. 'Corruption' is a recurrent theme in criticisms by the major Western governments and international agencies of countries which are unsuccessful in or marginal to the global economy. We can accept that corruption is indeed a real obstacle to development, for instance in the post-communist countries, yet ask why the focus is rarely on corruption in the rich countries of the world, where it is also a major problem (Stiglitz 2002).

The narrative in the bin Mohamad passage is followed by epistemic and normative argumentation. The central claim is that 'we are not doing business anymore, real business that is', and the grounds are that 'we are not producing goods and providing services' and 'what the world is interested in today is quick money, money that comes from speculation and manipulation'. Much of the rest of this part of the extract consists of a list of prescriptions without grounds or arguments. Two other important claims which are at odds with globalism are that 'Governments have not become anachronistic', and that they 'have to do the right thing by everyone, including the very poor'. Bin Mohamad does add that a strong 'incentive' for the latter is the risk of not being re-elected, but nevertheless there is generally a stronger sense of social responsibility for the poor and the victims of change evident in Asian capitalism than in North American or even now parts of European capitalism.

Both Steger (2005) and Saul (2005) suggest that globalism has indeed experienced the 'backlash' which Eizenstat saw as a risk, and this backlash has come from influential quarters in national and international government as well as from elsewhere. Warnings came from such eminent figures as Joseph Stiglitz, the chief economist of the World Bank who later resigned to speak out against the IMF (Stiglitz 2002), and who warned against the sort of misinterpretation of the Asian crisis we saw in Eizenstat's speech, defending the record of the East Asian countries, and later supporting the Malaysian policy. Saul (2005) suggests that the highpoint of globalism was the mid-1990s, and that it has been under increasing pressure (indeed faced with 'collapse') since then. My view is that globalism is weakened, but far from dead.

Non-governmental agencies

There are thousands of non-governmental agencies whose activities impinge in some way on globalization. The category of 'NGOs' has expanded enormously in recent years, and it covers an increasing range of organizations of different types. The first example I shall discuss is from the 'Manifesto' of the 'Make Poverty History' campaign organized by Christian Aid, which describes itself as a 'development agency' and is supported by churches in Britain and Ireland. It is taken from the 'Make Poverty History' website (which is actually entitled 'Pressureworks', with the homepage 'Act Now'), and the Manifesto is the most expository item on the site, in the sense that the aims of the campaign are most fully formulated and argued in it. This is a campaigning organization whose primary objective is to get people to act, on their own behalf and on behalf of others. The Manifesto, in setting out the primary objectives of the campaign, formulates a strategy for changing how globalization works in its dominant globalist form.

1 Trade justice

- Fight for rules that ensure governments, particularly in poor countries, can choose the best solutions to end poverty and protect the environment. These will not always be free trade policies.
- End export subsidies that damage the livelihoods of poor rural communities around the world.
- Make laws that stop big business profiting at the expense of people and the environment.

The rules of international trade are stacked in favour of the most powerful countries and their businesses. On the one hand these rules allow rich countries to pay their farmers and companies subsidies to export food – destroying the livelihoods of poor farmers. On the other, poverty eradication, human rights and environmental protection come a poor second to the goal of 'eliminating trade barriers'.

We need trade justice **not** free trade. This means the EU single-handedly putting an end to its damaging agricultural export subsidies **now**; it means ensuring poor countries can feed their people by protecting their own farmers and staple crops; it means ensuring governments can effectively regulate water companies by keeping water out of world trade rules; and it means ensuring trade rules do not undermine core labour standards.

We need to stop the World Bank and International Monetary Fund (IMF) forcing poor countries to open their markets to trade with rich countries, which has proved so disastrous over the past 20 years; the EU must drop its demand that former European colonies open their markets and give more rights to big companies; we need to regulate companies – making them accountable for their social and environmental impact both here and abroad; and we must ensure that countries are able to regulate foreign investment in a way that best suits their own needs.

This is a very different text from the ones I have discussed so far. It is produced by an organization committed to action, and it is designed not just to persuade people of a point of view, but to stir them into action. So I shall begin with some comments on the genre. The three main sections of the Manifesto are 'Trade justice', 'Drop the debt', and 'More and better aid', and I have taken just the first. They all begin with a set of bullet points which are formulated as *imperative* sentences (Fairclough 2003: 115–18) and can be taken as the 'demands' of the campaign. This is the first of a mix of different genres, which also includes epistemic argumentation in the first of the paragraphs, and normative argumentation in the second and third.

The first paragraph consists of a factual claim with *epistemic modality* (sentence 1, see Fairclough 2003: 165–71) followed by two factual assertions which provide grounds supporting this claim (sentences 2 and 3). The second and third paragraphs consist of hortatory prescriptions ('we need trade justice . . .', 'we need to stop the World Bank . . .', 'the EU must drop . . .', 'we need to regulate . . .', 'we must ensure'), the first of which is followed by an extended multipart explanation ('This means . . .'). 'We' is used in its *inclusive* sense meaning 'all of us', people in general, rather than in its *exclusive* sense (where there is a contrast between 'we' and 'you' or 'them', see Fairclough 2000a: 35–7, 151–4). The whole extract is rhetorically interesting, but let us just note some features of the second paragraph: the binary contrast (a textual *classification*, Fairclough 2003: 88–9) between 'trade justice' and 'free trade', and implicitly between 'justice' and 'freedom' in its neo-liberal sense, which is tersely formulated ('We need trade justice **not** free trade') and works well as a slogan; the highlighting of *not* and *now* in bold typeface; and the repetition and *syntactic parallelism* within the explanation – 'This means' – 'it means ensuring' – 'it means ensuring' – 'it means ensuring').

This is a dialogical and polemical text. It enters into dialogue with antagonistic positions and contests the discourse of globalism. The core theme and value of the discourse of globalism, 'free trade', is rejected in favour of 'trade justice', and the universal invocation of free trade as a solution to economic ills is implicitly contested in the first bullet point: 'These will not always be free trade policies.' 'Export subsidies' are interpreted not as helping farmers in the rich countries but 'damaging the livelihoods of poor rural communities'. 'Eliminating trade barriers' is placed in what we can reasonably interpret as 'scare quotes' – a way of marking it as 'their' language not 'ours'. The sentence in which it occurs might also be read as a somewhat oblique criticism of the discourse of globalism on the grounds that there is a difference between words and actions: although 'poverty eradication', 'human rights' and 'environmental protection' are all, along with 'eliminating trade barriers', part of its vocabulary and significant themes within the discourse, what happens in practice is that 'eliminating trade barriers' is given priority. The globalist tenet of deregulation, excluding states from economic regulation in favour of the free play of market forces, is also contested: 'poor countries' should be able to 'protect their own farmers and staple crops', and 'governments' should be able to 'effectively regulate water companies'.

There are many significant *assumptions* or presuppositions, propositions that are assumed or taken for granted, in the second and third paragraphs (Fairclough 2003: 55–61). In the second paragraph, that free trade is not just; that countries can only feed their people by being able to protect their farmers and staple crops; that governments can only effectively regulate water companies if water is excluded from world trade rules; that world trade rules can undermine labour standards. In the third paragraph, that the World Bank and International Monetary Fund (IMF) do force poor countries to open their markets to trade with rich countries; that the EU does demand that former European colonies open their markets and give more rights to big companies; that companies are not made accountable for their social and environmental impact; and that countries are not able to regulate foreign investment in a way that best suits their own needs. These presuppositions are also dialogical and polemical in that they are implicit counter-claims to the claims and arguments of globalism. They also contribute to the mobilizing power of the text in assuming a great deal of common ground between authors and readers and addressing readers as a group of like-minded and motivated people.

As a strategy, this is largely negative rather than positive. It does not advance a fundamentally new and different way of regulating international trade. It is a strategy for modifying the existing regulatory system. Notice the number of verbs which share the general sense of 'stopping': 'end', 'stop', 'put an end to', 'stop' (again), 'drop', and one might add 'keep out'. This is not the whole picture: some of the demands are formulated positively (e.g. 'we need to regulate companies . . .'), and one might argue that the constraints called for on the existing regulatory system amount to creating a significantly different system. But as in many alternative strategies, existing globalist practices and regulatory systems are taken as the point of reference, and we should question whether radical hegemonic change can be achieved in this way. Let us move to more radical alternatives.

Limits to growth

The section title is the taken from a report which was published over thirty years ago, in 1972, by the Club of Rome, called *Limits to Growth* (Meadows *et al.* 1972). The conclusions of the report were:

1   If the present growth trends in world population, industrialization, pollution, food production, and resource depletion continue unchanged, the limits to growth on this planet will be reached sometime within the next one hundred years. The most probable result will be a rather sudden and uncontrollable decline in both population and industrial capacity.

2   It is possible to alter these growth trends and to establish a condition of eco-logical and economic stability that is sustainable far into the future. The state of global equilibrium could be designed so that the basic material needs of each person on earth are satisfied and each person has an equal opportunity to realize his individual human potential.

This report can be regarded as the precursor of many alternative strategies which, in one way or another, challenge globalism on what is perhaps its most fundamen-tal value and raison d'être: 'economic growth'. 'Economic growth' is an *assumed good* (see Fairclough 2003: 55–8 on 'value assumptions') in countless texts many of which one could not call globalist, and questioning 'economic growth' as a value is still a scandalous thing to do in most contexts in most countries. On the other hand, the idea of 'limits to growth' has been widely integrated in a superficial way into official policy, which is why many influential economists and politicians now set their objectives as 'sustainable growth'. But critics would argue that the policies which have been developed on national and inter-national levels to achieve 'sustainability' do not even begin to approach what would be needed for the 'state of global equilibrium' envisaged in the report.

I shall discuss extracts from the Manifesto of the Green Party for England and Wales (Green Party of England and Wales 2005) to illustrate more radical eco-nomic strategies. Here first of all are the opening paragraphs of the section on the 'Global Economy':

> EC900 National economic systems operating in isolation cannot resolve the problems of trans-boundary pollution, exploitation of global resources and inequitable relationships between rich and poor countries. Resolution of the global economic and ecological crises requires a new order of cooperation between nations with the development of new international institutions and agreements, in which a green European Confederation could play an impor-tant role. (See 'International' policy)

> EC901 Economic globalization is integrating national economies and labour markets more tightly together as the flow of goods, services, and investment across borders expands. This is locking producers, both North and South, into an increasingly competitive system, while lower social and environ-mental standards are increasingly being used to facilitate trade expansion. But competitiveness is a zero-sum game: one country can become more

competitive only at the expense of another. For poor countries, and for poorer people in the industrialised countries, globalization has meant marginalization; and for the environment, it has meant increasing destruction.

EC902 Formidably powerful and publicly unaccountable trans-national companies are becoming ever more footloose, their strength and mobility facilitated both by technological advances, and by the progressive withdrawal of investment controls by governments and by multilateral institutions such as WTO. TNCs are now increasingly able to exploit differences in social and environmental standards between countries in order to maximise profits.

EC903 The rush towards globalization is neither inevitable nor desirable. It is leading to the sharp reduction in powers of local and indigenous communities, states, and even nations, to control their futures, as economic power is transferred to global institutions. A worldwide homogenisation of diverse, local, and indigenous cultures, social and economic forms, as well as values and living patterns increasingly reflect the new global monoculture.

EC904 New global agreements are urgently needed to regulate international trade and investment in the interests of equity and sustainable development. Green policies are based on the principle that we need to reduce to a minimum the overall volume of international trade, and to revitalise local communities by promoting maximum self-reliance, economic, social, and political control, and environmental sustainability. These policies will also greatly increase employment opportunities.

This simultaneously argues for 'new international institutions and agreements' on the grounds that 'global economic and ecological crises' (which are assumed rather than asserted) cannot be resolved nationally, and argues against what is first called 'economic globalization' but then simply 'globalization', on the grounds of its negative effects ('lower social and environmental standards', 'marginalization', 'destruction' etc.). The latter appears superficially to be an argument against globalization as such, but the claim that 'global' problems need to be dealt with by 'international institutions' might be interpreted rather as a strategy for a radically different form of globalization. This is not made clear. There is what we could call an 'argumentative chain' which links the argument against economic globalization to an argument for 'maximum self-reliance' for 'local communities', which means reducing international trade.

The argument against economic globalization includes as grounds the claims that it 'locks producers' into an 'increasingly competitive system'. 'Competitiveness' is claimed to be a 'zero-sum' game, 'one country can become more competitive only at the expense of another' – a claim which is precisely the opposite

of the globalist claim made by Eizenstat: 'In an increasingly globalized and interdependent economy, the quest for prosperity is the opposite of a zero sum game.'
One contradiction in globalist discourse is that it urges everyone to be competitive, yet assumes everyone will benefit, as if competition did not imply winners
and losers. Another globalist claim that is directly refuted is 'inevitability': 'The
rush towards globalization is neither inevitable nor desirable.' In these respects,
this text like the 'Make Poverty History' text above is *dialogical* and polemical
(Fairclough 2003: 41–5, 128). The argument for 'self-reliance' can be seen as
grounded by the claims of 'sharp reduction in powers of local and indigenous
communities, states, and even nations, to control their futures' and a 'new
global monoculture' (the *warrant* for this argument – that loss of ability to control
one's own future and 'worldwide homogenization' are bad things – is left implicit
and taken for granted), as well as 'equity and sustainable development' and
'employment opportunities'.

The 'objectives' of economic policy are as follows:

Ecological sustainability

EC200 To conserve natural planetary resources and to maintain the integrity
of natural life-sustaining cycles; to regenerate areas made waste and take steps
to avoid further ecological disaster; to reduce demand for energy and raw
materials; to favour low energy non-polluting processes based on renewable
resources.

EC201 To this end, the Citizens' Income will allow the current dependence
on economic growth to cease, and allow zero or negative growth to be
feasible without individual hardship should this be necessary on the grounds
of sustainability.

Equity and social justice

EC202 To achieve an equitable distribution of resources, wealth, opportunity
and power which ensures access for all to the means of sustenance and of
personal and social development.

Decentralization and devolution

EC203 To devolve economic power to the lowest appropriate level, thereby
rendering participants in the economy at all levels less vulnerable to the
damaging effects of economic decisions made elsewhere and over which
they have no control; to support the 'informal' sector (notably by provision
of a Citizens' Income for all) thus reducing the impact of the formal economy.

Self-reliance with interdependence

EC204 To liberate and empower all sections of society to meet their needs as far as possible from their own resources through activities which are socially enhancing; to encourage all to contribute to society according to their abilities, recognising as they do so, responsibility for themselves, for others, for future generations and for the planet.

The particular cluster of discourses (*interdiscursive hybridity*, see Chapter 2) indicated by the headings ('ecological sustainability', 'equity and social justice', 'decentralization and devolution', 'self-reliance') differentiates this economic discourse from mainstream economic discourses, even though some discourses in the cluster are appropriated within the latter. The discourse of 'ecological sustainability' has now been integrated within most economic discourses, though not usually with the salience it is given here (it is often a footnote or afterthought to the main economic strategies). Most of the main *themes* of this discourse have also been widely appropriated, though again often marginally, in mainstream economic discourses ('conservation', 'regeneration', 'renewable resources'), but actually reducing demand for energy and raw materials is not a common proposal, and maintaining 'the integrity of natural life-sustaining cycles' points to a specifically Green ontology.

The policy envisages the cessation of the 'current dependence on economic growth' without individual hardship through a 'citizen's income', which will be sufficient to meet basic living costs, will be universal rather than means-tested, and will not be conditional on employment. Whether growth is positive, 'zero' or 'negative' depends upon ecological 'sustainability'. As I pointed out above, questioning 'economic growth' as a value is widely regarded as a scandalous thing to do, an indication of how deeply entrenched and thoroughly naturalized what we might call the ideology of growth is – the assumption that human development means economic growth.

This assumption has recently been strongly challenged by radical economists including Amartya Sen, winner of the Nobel Prize for Economics (Sen 1999), who has developed what has become known as the 'capabilities' approach to development. He views 'free and sustainable agency' as 'a major engine of development', and sees development therefore as 'a process of expanding the real freedoms that people enjoy', that is, their 'capabilities' to act, to be agents. Development requires 'the removal of major sources of unfreedom: poverty as well as tyranny, poor economic opportunities as well as systematic social deprivation, neglect of public facilities as well as intolerance and overactivity of repressive states'. Economic growth, standardly measured by increase in the Gross National Product (GNP) per head of the population, is one means to 'development as freedom', but there are other means (e.g. increasing public expenditure on health care or education) that do not always require economic growth, and do not always happen when there is economic growth. The conventional view of development as measured only by economic growth is hopelessly reductive and inadequate from this perspective.

The redistributionist discourse of EC202 has been excluded from mainstream economic discourse with the rise of neo-liberalism, and it is formulated in a 'capabilities' way as including 'the means of . . . personal and social development' as well as 'sustenance'. Although 'devolution' is now a common theme in mainstream discourse, 'devolving economic power to the lowest appropriate level' is a radical interpretation of it, as is supporting the 'informal' sector and 'reducing the impact of the formal economy'. EC204 is the most distinctively Green section. 'Self-reliance' and meeting one's needs from one's 'own resources', requiring economic activities to be 'socially enhancing', and seeing everyone as responsible 'for future generations and for the planet', are way beyond mainstream economic discourses.

Here finally, also in the spirit of 'limits to growth', is a statement by Václav Havel, former President of the Czech Republic, and one of the foremost anti-communist dissidents:

> I believe that, for the rest of the world contemporary America is an almost symbolic concentration of all the good and the bad of our civilization – ranging from the fantastic development of science and technology generating more welfare and the profundity of civil liberty and strength of democratic institutions, to the blind cult of perpetual economic growth and never-ending consumption . . . Who thinks today about future generations? Who is concerned about what people will eat, drink, breathe in one hundred years, where they will get energy when there are twice as many people living on this planet as today?
>
> (Václav Havel 1997)

Conclusion

I have argued that the neo-liberal globalist 'nodal' discourse of globalization, despite coming under considerable pressure because of the widely perceived flaws and failures of globalist strategy, has proved to be resilient, and that its advocates have been largely able to meet challenges and maintain the continuity of the strategy and the discourse by integrating new discourses into the cluster which is attached to the node. Furthermore, a powerful convergence has developed between globalism and the strategy and discourse of the KBE, projecting a new 'fix' between the KBE as regime of accumulation and a neo-liberal mode of social regulation.

But the hegemony of this nexus of strategies and discourses is never fully secure. It constantly has to be actively sustained and re-made as new events occur, and new circumstances and challenges emerge. One part of the challenging environment within which hegemony has to be secured is the existence of alternative discourses of globalization associated with alternative strategies, some of which are backed by powerful and influential agencies. I have given necessarily selective examples of some of these discourses.

I have analysed a number of texts, and it may be useful to sum up the range of textual features which I have commented on: genres drawn on in texts, and interdiscursive hybridity of genres; discourses and interdiscursive hybridity of discourses, and themes associated with particular discourses; argumentation, particular argumentative genres (epistemic and normative argumentation) and fallacious arguments; narratives; differences between discourses in the representation of social agents and their actions (process types); assumptions; modality; nominalization; inference; inclusive/exclusive 'we'; classification in texts, and relations of equivalence; dialogicality and polemic; evaluation in texts; rhetorical and persuasive features of texts.

My discussion of discourses and the strategies associated with them has been very general in that I have not been concerned with how such strategies and discourses figure within processes of globalization in particular places (countries, regions, cities, etc.). This is precisely my concern in the next chapter.

4 Re-scaling the nation-state

In this chapter I shall take up the view of globalization as changes in 'scales' and relations between scales which I discussed in Chapters 1 and 2 (Jessop 2002, Harvey 1996, Collinge 1999, Boyer and Hollingsworth 1997). From this perspective, globalization is not just a matter of the construction of a global scale, it is also a matter of new relations between the global scale and other scales (e.g. 'glocalization' as a relation between global and local scales, Robertson 1992), and wider changes in the set of scales and relations between them caused by the construction of a global scale. Contemporary globalization is also associated with the construction of other scales than the global scale, including the 'macro-regional' scale (e.g. the European Union or the North American Free Trade Area), the scale of cross-border economic regions such as the Pearl River Delta (China, Hong Kong, Macau), and the scale of 'global cities'.

The chapter will focus on a case study of re-scaling at the level of the nation-state: Romania, one of the 'post-communist' countries of Eastern Europe. I shall begin with some points about the categories 'scale' and 're-scaling', and this will be followed by a general discussion of 'transition' in Romania. The third section will look from a discourse-analytical perspective at the recontextualization of what I shall call 'small practices' such as 'mentoring', 'branding', and 'self-evaluation', which I shall suggest have a deeper impact on practices but also values, attitudes and identities than they might initially seem to. In the following two sections I shall discuss two specific areas of re-scaling in Romania, which can be seen as aspects of both globalization and Europeanization. These are: reform of higher education in the wake of the 'Bologna Declaration' (1999) on European higher education, and the developing 'Bologna process' which has arisen out of it; and reform of social policy, specifically of policies for dealing with poverty and social deprivation, and the recontextualization in Romania of EU strategy for combating 'social exclusion' and achieving 'social inclusion'. I shall refer comparatively at certain points to other countries.

Scale and re-scaling

The significance of scale and relations between scales is indicated in this quotation from Smith (1992):

> The theory of geographical scale – more correctly the theory of the production of geographical scale – is grossly underdeveloped. . . . And yet [scale] plays a crucial part in our whole geographical construction of social life. Was the brutal repression of Tianamen square a local event, a regional or national event, or was it an international event? We might reasonably assume that it was all four, which immediately reinforces the conclusion that social life operates in and constructs some sort of nested hierarchical space rather than a mosaic.

Scales, as the quotation indicates, are not naturally given, but socially constructed. Moreover, the social construction of scale is closely associated with relations of and struggles over power. Scale is:

> The arena and moment, both discursively and materially, where socio-spatial power relations are contested and compromises are negotiated and regulated. Scale, therefore, is both the result and the outcome of social struggle for power and control . . . [By implication] theoretical and political priority never resides in a particular geographical scale, but rather in the process through which particular scales become (re)constituted.
>
> (Swyngedouw 1997)

A scale is a space where diverse economic, political, social and cultural relations and processes are articulated together as 'some kind of structured coherence':

> There are processes at work . . . that define *regional spaces* within which production and consumption, supply and demand (for commodities and labour power), production and realization, class struggle and accumulation, culture and lifestyle, hang together as some kind of structured coherence within a totality of productive forces and social relations.
>
> (Harvey 2001)

If we focus on processes of globalization in any particular spatial 'entity' (and this might be for instance a small local community such as a village, a large urban centre, a cross-border region, an international regional bloc such as the European Union, or a nation-state), we can see these processes as 're-scaling' (Jessop 2002) the 'entity' concerned, namely positioning it within new relations between scales. One aspect of contemporary globalization is that 'the national scale has lost its taken-for-granted primacy' (Jessop 2002). The sort of spatial 'entity' I shall focus on in this chapter is the nation-state, taking the particular case of one of the post-communist countries of Eastern Europe, Romania, as my main example, though also referring to other countries including Britain. But since processes of re-scaling affecting Romania centrally involve relations between the national scale and the European scale (of the EU), there will also be extensive discussion of the latter.

The category of scale can be integrated into the cultural political economy approach to globalization which I am taking in the book (Chapter 2). Strategies to achieve a new 'fix' between a regime of accumulation and a mode of social regulation, which I discussed in Chapter 3 in relation to the convergence between (or nexus of) globalist strategy and the strategy for the KBE, include strategies to construct new scales, organize the relations between scales in particular ways, and re-scale spatial entities including nation-states (re-locate them in new relations between scales). So there are both structural and strategic dimensions (Jessop 2002) to scale and re-scaling: on the one hand changes in scales and relations between scales, on the other hand strategies to push such changes in particular directions, to gain economic or political advantage from relations between scales, or to defend the existing positions or carve out new positions for particular social agents or agencies. The strategists involved may be national governments, political parties, international agencies, members of local communities, etc. A final point is that changes in 'vertical' relations between scales impact upon and interact with changes in 'horizontal' relations between social fields or institutions within particular spatial entities – for instance, to anticipate an example I discuss below, changes between the national scale and the macro-regional scale of the EU in the case of Romania impact upon relations between education, government and the market in Romania through EU-initiated processes of educational reform.

Romania and 'transition'

Romania, like other 'post-communist' countries of Central and Eastern Europe, is represented in neo-liberal economic discourse as in 'transition' (Chiribucă 2004, Dăianu 2000, 2004, Holmes 1997, Outhwaite and Ray 2005, Pickles and Smith 1998, Simai 2001, Stark and Bruszt 1998, Zamfir 2004). The basic narrative of transition, which began as a predictive narrative (i.e. a story about what will happen in the future) is that the centralized economies and single-party states of the past (the socialist period) will be transformed into market economies and Western-style multi-party democracies through making a number of policy changes now. Studies of aspects of transition which have been carried out from a discourse analytical perspective include Fairclough (forthcoming), Ieţcu (formerly Preoteasa, 2004) and Preoteasa (2002).

The (Western) architects of transition adopted the globalist strategy for and discourse of globalization, envisaging transition as a part of the global spread of capitalist economies based open neo-liberal principles of liberalization, open markets and free trade. Countries in transition were subject to various pressures and inducements to adopt (recontextualize) and implement the World Bank–IMF 'structural adjustment programme' which is widely known as the 'Washington Consensus' (Dăianu 2000, Lavigne 1999). The narrative associated with the Washington Consensus links a past (continuing into the present) of economic failure due to state interference in the economy which wastefully subsidizes inefficient and loss-making state industries, excessive state spending, state regulation of economic activity (finance, retail prices, trade), barriers to foreign investment and so forth; a future of economic success associated with 'open markets' in which private companies operate free from state regulation and interference; and a present in which policies are implemented to achieve this – 'liberalization' of finance and trade, 'deregulation' of economic activity, 'fiscal discipline, 'privatization' of state-owned enterprises and so forth.

The terms in quotation marks are elements of the vocabulary of neo-liberal economic discourse. More than that, they are major *themes* of the new discourse around which established and recurrent narratives and arguments cluster. They have been recontextualized in countries like Romania and, with varying degrees of hesitation and delay, operationalized through legislation and practical policy initiatives, though often in ways which were very different from what was anticipated.

For instance neo-liberal narratives depicted 'privatization' as a means of restructuring and relaunching economies, through massive injection of new investments, introduction of efficient managerial models, and eliminating chronically inefficient sectors of economies. In practice, 'privatization' often took place through corrupt deals which transferred public assets to private individuals, often members of the old 'nomenklatura', at virtually no cost. Privatized companies exploited companies which remained in the state sector. Potentially profitable privatized companies were closed down for the short-term profit of the new entrepreneurs, and former public monopolies became private monopolies which derived huge profits from overcharging captive markets (Dăianu 2000, Pickles and Smith 1998, Stark and Bruszt 1998, Zamfir 2004).

We could say that recontextualization changed the meaning of 'privatization', that it was not understood as in neo-liberal discourse as a route to economic efficiency and sound entrepreneurial values and practices, but as a route to the extravagant self-enrichment of a small minority simultaneously with the impoverishment of the great majority, without the dramatic economic take-off which was promised. It is an illustration that real change is 'path-dependent'. It depends upon history, upon changes in the past and their impact on current circumstances, the institutional frameworks, the capacities and values and attitudes of people, and these factors are likely to shape the transformations which strategies and discourses undergo as they are recontextualized. What strategies for 'transition' failed to take into account were the actual circumstances in the post-communist countries, as well as the massive differences between them (Dăianu 2000, Pickles and Smith 1998, Stark and Bruszt 1998, Zamfir 2004).

'Transition', then, is a part of globalization in the globalist sense, aimed at drawing the post-communism countries into the process and the project of the global dissemination of neo-liberal free market capitalism, into the 'global market'. Although different forms of capitalism (e.g. East Asian forms) exist and have proved their viability, transition to a market economy in Romania and other 'post-communist' countries has been generally assumed, with little questioning or challenge, to be transition to neo-liberal capitalism, though with an increasing European (EU) inflection which I come to below. The post-communist countries of central and Eastern Europe have tended to adopt particularly extreme versions of economic liberalism, perhaps as a way of clearly distancing themselves from their socialist past. The political left in a Western European social democratic form tends to be weak, and there is often (certainly in Romania) an intolerance of even moderate social democratic or even politically liberal ideas (Miroiu 1999, Szacki 1994).

But 'transition' is a very dubious way of representing economic and social change, because it implies not only a given starting point (socialist economies and states) but also a known destination. There is a certain irony here. Socialist economists were criticized by liberals for assuming that economic change could be centrally planned, whereas in fact no central planner can have knowledge of all the contingencies which determine how economies will actually evolve. This supposedly shows the superiority of market economies over centrally planned economies. Yet theorists of 'transition' often themselves seem to assume that the process can be planned, controlled and managed with precision. We can see the error of the architects of transition as partly a misunderstanding (or perhaps a feigned misunderstanding) of the constructive effects of discourse: the discourse of 'transition' could contribute and has contributed to the (re)construction of social life, but in ways which are contingent upon the causal effects of other factors which vary from country to country, so that its actual effects could not be predicted, and are proving to be in many ways different from what was predicted.

If the re-scaling of Romania and other post-communist countries has partly been shaped by the globalist strategy and discourse of the architects of 'transition', it has also had an increasingly important 'macro-regional' dimension: 'Europeanization', associated with the planned accession of the countries to the European Union. Ten countries from the region joined the EU in 2005, and Romania and Bulgaria are due to join in 2007. International regional blocs such as the EU have an ambiguous status with respect to the dominant globalist strategy for globalization. On the one hand, they are a mechanism for giving countries greater impact on the 'global market' which globalism has had most influence in shaping. On the other hand they can potentially impede the unification of the 'global market' by supporting divergent economic, political and cultural forms, practices, values and so forth.

An illustration of this ambiguity is current debate and anxiety over 'the European social model' (Delanty and Rumford 2005). There is a continuing commitment to a European 'social agenda' which has hitherto distinguished the EU from its main competitor, the USA. This is shown for instance in the formulation and development of the strategic goal of the Lisbon Declaration (2000), which is a knowledge-based economy but in combination with policies to achieve greater social cohesion and 'social inclusion'. But economic problems and concerns about 'competitiveness' in the European Union are leading to increasing pressures to scale back (or 'modernize') social welfare, and to arguments for the EU to move in a more globalist and neo-liberal direction (Muntigl *et al.* 2000). It is also generally the case that there is more active support for the 'social agenda', social policies and social welfare in parts of Western Europe (especially the Scandinavian countries) than in Eastern Europe. So although Romania has inevitably been drawn into the EU social agenda (it has for instance committed itself to the strategic goal of the Lisbon Declaration, and therefore policies for greater social inclusion as well as the strategy for the KBE), globalist and neo-liberal positions continue to have a great deal of influence.

Economically, politically, socially and culturally, Romania is a complex, contradictory, disorganized or partially and unevenly organized, and rather chaotic country (Chiribucă 2004, Gallagher 2004). For instance the most dynamic and the dominant sector of the economy is the emerging Western-style market sector, but there is still a substantial state sector though that is now shrinking rapidly, and a huge 'black' or 'unofficial' economy where the regulation which the official economy is subject to (e.g. payment of taxes and social insurance contributions) does not apply (Chelcea and Mateescu 2004, Chiribucă 2004, Dăianu 2000). Many strategies and discourses have been recontextualized from 'the West', but the extent to which and the scale on which they have been institutionalized, and the extent to which and the forms in which they have been implemented, vary a great deal.

Processes of re-scaling are clearly under way. For instance European standards, practices, modes of regulation and governance, values and identities are evident in the economy, in politics, in education and so forth, but sporadically and unevenly, and coexisting with standards, practices, modes of regulation and governance, values and identities inherited from the communist period and even before, in highly complex and contradictory forms of combination (Heintz 2005). For example, clientelist and nepotistic social relations and 'status groups' of a form that has existed for many decades in Romania are still extremely powerful in all social fields (Matei 2004, Mungiu-Pippidi 2002). Recontextualization and re-scaling do not therefore result in any simple process of harmonization and integration of Romania at the European or global scales, but complex, contradictory and unpredictable mixtures of old and new.

Projects and practices: the case of 'mentoring'

Let us move towards matters of discourse. I want first to mention the significance for re-scaling of a wide variety of what we might call 'small' or 'micro' practices which appear to be just details within much bigger processes of change and which affect the activities and behaviour of particular categories of social agents in particular contexts. Examples of such practices include 'branding', 'benchmarking', 'self-evaluation', 'team working' and the practice I shall focus on here, 'mentoring'. There are experts in these practices, and they are disseminated through what Giddens (1991: 18) calls 'expert systems' which deploy 'modes of technical knowledge which have validity independent of the practitioners and clients who make use of them', and independent of particularities of time or space. Such practices are in Giddens' terms 'disembedded', 'lifted out' of the particular social contexts and social relations in which they originate and 'rearticulated' (or in my terminology, recontextualized) 'across indefinite tracts of time and space'. There is more to such practices than meets the eye. Their dissemination is of particular importance for re-scaling because they impact not only on public action and behaviour but also on private values, attitudes and senses of self-identity, and can quietly introduce and disseminate 'Western' values (including characteristically Western forms of individualism) and potentially have a profound cultural impact (see also Ong and Collier 2005, Strathern 2000).

New strategies and discourses do not just 'flow' into particular spaces. They are so to speak 'carried' there by particular agencies. The agencies that are strategically operative in a country like Romania are not just internal (Romanian); there are also external agencies who have internal power, because they provide finance, because they can influence the international position of Romania (e.g. its 'credit-worthiness'), and so forth. Both Romanian and internally operating external agencies have put their weight behind strategies, discourses and their operationalized forms in practices through a huge number of 'projects' which have been initiated, usually with finance from external agencies (such as the EU, World Bank, foreign governments) and involving 'partnerships' with Romanian public and private agencies. These projects cover a highly diverse set of areas, but they often combine practical objectives with aims of projecting discourses, values, attitudes and 'good practices', relying upon 'multipliers' (government agencies, private corporations, NGOs and individuals) to disseminate them beyond the limits of the 'project' into the wider society.

Educational projects, for instance, introduce new ways of working (e.g. 'project-focused'), learning (e.g. 'e-learning') and evaluation ('self- and peer-evaluation' based upon ideas of 'quality'), and cultural effects in the form of new values (e.g. collaborative orientations to 'teamwork') and attitudes (e.g. understanding and acceptance of cultural differences). All these expressions in quotation marks are themes in recontextualized discourses. One example is the World Bank's Rural Education Project (2003–9), whose objective is to 'have rural school students benefit from improved access to quality education'. Although the project addresses the acute lack of material resources in rural schools, its main objective is 'change in behaviours'. This includes 'professional development of teachers', introducing them to new ideas such as 'needs-based learning' through school-based training involving 'mentors', and increasing 'community-participation' in schools and 'democratic school governance'. Such projects cumulatively invest considerable resources and finance into disseminating essentially Western ideas, practices, values, attitudes and, from a discourse-analytical perspective, discourses, genres and styles.

Take 'mentoring', for instance. According to Clutterbuck and Megginson (1999), mentoring is 'off-line help by one person to another in making significant transitions in knowledge, work or thinking'. The Coaching and Mentoring Website (2005) gives a list of what 'mentors' do which includes:

- Facilitate the exploration of needs, motivations, desires, skills and thought processes to assist the individual in making real, lasting change.
- Use questioning techniques to facilitate client's own thought processes in order to identify solutions and actions rather than take a wholly directive approach.
- Support the client in setting appropriate goals and methods of assessing progress in relation to these goals.
- Observe, listen and ask questions to understand the client's situation.
- Encourage a commitment to action and the development of lasting personal growth and change.
- Maintain unconditional positive regard for the client, which means that the coach is at all times supportive and non-judgemental of the client, their views.

The idea of 'mentoring' was until recently virtually unheard-of in Romania. As this extract indicates, there is a totally new discourse to learn (themes and terminology include 'mentoring', 'facilitating', 'exploring needs', 'setting goals', 'personal growth' and so forth). There is a whole new way of behaving for both 'mentors' and 'mentees' to learn, and that includes new forms of interaction, i.e. new genres, including the genre of mentor/mentee interaction which is alluded to in the extract. This cannot be done properly (though it might be mimicked) without new attitudes to work, new relationships with colleagues (relationships based on professionalism and trust are assumed) and indeed oneself, or without changes in workplace ethics and values. And these in turn include, in terms of discourse, new styles, new semiotic resources of expressing and enacting changed identities. In other words, a large-scale multidimensional change in people and organizations is entailed by this apparently minor idea, and 'small' practice, of mentoring.

In Romania, it has been introduced in educational contexts, and is now spreading to business contexts for instance. Mentoring, after all, can be enacted wherever beginners inhabit the same space as people with experience. Mentoring and other such practices tend to initially be established in particular areas of and sometimes small 'islands' within educational and other systems rather then right across systems. One example is language centres such as the PROSPER-ASE language centre in Bucharest which was set up (as an NGO) in 1994 with the support of the British Council and under the aegis of the Academy of Economic Studies to offer high quality language training to adults for professional purposes or for study abroad (Mureşan 2004). PROSPER-ASE contributed to setting a national quality assurance network for language centres with support from the British Council and the Goethe Institute. Mentoring and other practices such as self-evaluation and 'learning partnerships' are a part of quality assurance and professional development in this network of language centres.

In principle, and to some extent in practice, such 'islands' within the educational system can operate as a vanguard for change within the system more generally. However, the language, behaviour, attitudes and values of mentoring and other 'small practices' are radically different from the language, behaviour, attitudes and values which still predominate in work, education, public administration and so forth in Romania (Heintz 2005). This means that the introduction of such practices can cause a great deal of difficulty, tension and unease, in some cases be resisted, and perhaps lead to forms of hybridization between new practices and established practices. The case of mentoring and similar small practices illustrates the general picture in contemporary Romania: an uneven, patchy, contradictory, sometimes chaotic, sometimes tense state of co-existence between new and old, including new and old discourses, genres and styles. One effect of this situation is the social divisions it introduces, for instance between those who can derive economic value from their knowledge of and command over new practices, ideas, values, discourses, genres and styles, and those who cannot.

Reform of higher education

The reform of higher education in the EU and candidate states is a good example of the social construction of space and time (and 'space-times') as described by Harvey (1996 – see Chapter 1), and the 'carving out' of new scales within a specific 'sub-system' or field (that of education in this case) discussed by Jessop (2002, see also Robertson 2002). Until recently, education policy was seen within the EU as the prerogative of member states, and the establishment of a

European scale subject to governance at EU level has been a sensitive and contentious process in which the education ministries of member states have shown caution and some reluctance (Dale 2005).

The new scale is explicitly referred to as the 'European Area of Higher Education', one of many 'European areas' or 'spaces' which have been discursively and in part materially constituted (through operationalization and implementation of discourses) in recent years as part of the broader process of constructing a European scale. Its emergence is closely associated in turn with EU strategy for constructing the KBE adopted at the Lisbon Council (The Council of the European Union 2000). The Lisbon Declaration itself calls for changes in education (including higher education) which are necessary to achieve the KBE. These include a 'European Area of Research and Innovation', the development of 'lifelong learning', and changes in education and training:

> Europe's education and training systems need to adapt both to the demands of the knowledge society and to the need for an improved level and quality of employment. They will have to offer learning and training opportunities tailored to target groups at different stages of their lives: young people, unemployed adults and those in employment who are at risk of seeing their skills overtaken by rapid change.

It also sets a 'target' for member states of defining 'means for fostering the mobility of students, teachers and training and research staff' including 'through greater transparency in the recognition of qualifications and periods of study and training'.

The mutual recognition of qualifications has been a central issue. A legal basis for cross-national recognition of qualifications has been supplied by the UNESCO Lisbon Convention (1997), which most countries involved in the Bologna process have signed up to, and there are moves by UNESCO and the OECD to extend the regulatory apparatus for international recognition of qualifications. International recognition of qualifications is recognized as one of the obstacles to the completion of the WTO General Agreement on Trade in Services, which would disallow restrictions by national governments on the provision within their territories of services (including education) by foreign agencies and individuals. These points suggest that higher education reform is linked to the discursive and material construction of the 'global economy' as 'knowledge-based', and to a view of the 'liberalization' of trade in services as an important part of the KBE, and to the competitiveness of the EU in education and other sectors.

The Bologna Declaration by European Ministers of Education (1999) set a number of specific objectives: 'a system of easily readable and comparable degrees' through the implementation of a 'Diploma Supplement' (containing a detailed record of studies undertaken); a system based on two main 'cycles', undergraduate and graduate (normal lengths for undergraduate, Master's and Doctoral degrees were later agreed as 3–4, 1–2 and 3 years respectively); a unitary system of 'credits' for courses of study; promotion of 'mobility' of students and academic and administrative staff; cooperation in 'quality assurance', aiming to develop comparable criteria; promotion of 'necessary European dimensions' in higher education (i.e. a European 'content' in courses of study). A further recommendation was that undergraduate degrees should be 'relevant to the European labour market'.

These objectives are legitimized in terms of increasing the 'international competitiveness' of European higher education and the 'employability' of citizens, as well as 'an awareness of shared values and belonging to a common social and cultural space'. Further meetings of Ministers of Education took place in 2001 (Prague), 2003 (Berlin) and 2005 (Bergen), at which the objectives were elaborated and added to, within an evolving 'Bologna process'. Although as in this case the legitimization of reform in documents within the Bologna process generally draws upon both an economic discourse and a discourse of European cultural values and identity, the former has become progressively more prominent, with an increasing emphasis on 'international competitiveness'. This reflects a convergence or 'nexus' between EU strategy for university reform and EU competiveness strategy as developed by the Competitiveness Advisory Group (Wodak 2000, Fairclough and Wodak forthcoming). At the same time an apparatus has been developed for the regulation and 'governance' of university reform at an EU scale. We can see the Bologna process as contributing to the discursive and material re-scaling of European universities as a sector operating within a knowledge-based 'global market'.

The Bologna process in Romania

At governmental level in Romania, there is a commitment to the Bologna strategy and discourse ('cycles', 'mobility', 'quality', 'competitiveness', 'employability' and so forth) and to implementing the Bologna reforms. The official selection of this discourse is virtually an automatic effect of Romania's imminent accession to the EU. Its retention, institutionalization and operationalization have in part been secured through legislation. Law 288 (2004) on the organization of university studies introduced a system of three 'cycles' (undergraduate or 'licentiate' 3–4 years, Master's 2–3 years, PhD 3 years), stipulated that undergraduate degrees should cover general subject areas leaving specialization for Master's degrees, and introduced the Bologna system of 'credits' and the 'Diploma Supplement'. Degrees in each cycle require a range of general and specific 'competences' as well as subject knowledge. The new system was put into operation from 2005. There is a law on 'quality assurance' in preparation, but it has not yet (autumn 2005) been adopted.

The way in which the change to the three cycles has been recontextualized in Romania reflects repeated complaints on the part of the government and others that there is a serious mismatch between higher education and the needs of the labour market (this was for instance one of the main problems foreseen in the Romania National Report to the Bergen meeting of Education Ministers in 2005). This is evident in the detailed specification within Law 288 of a range of general and specific 'competences' as well as subject knowledge for each cycle, the requirement that undergraduate degrees include a 'practical' component, and a controversial government decree which specified which subject areas would be recognized in undergraduate studies, excluding many existing specialisms.

The justification for the new law provided by the government in the parliamentary debate is also revealing in this regard: the reorganization would 'eliminate excessive specialization', contribute to the 'development of professions which are short of specialized and economically and culturally necessary personnel', contribute to 'the development of new qualifications related to current needs and . . . the labour market', and be in line with 'the dynamics of the labour market at national, European and international level' (all the extracts which I quote in this section and the next are my translations of Romanian originals). So the government's interest was more or less entirely economic, and there were no references to other legitimations which have been prominent in the Bologna documentation such as student mobility or European culture and identity. The new system was put into operation from autumn 2005.

There is a general recognition that progress towards implementing the Bologna reforms has been slow in Romania. This has perhaps been partly because of the generally poor state of the system of higher education. The general view is that standards have declined during the 'transition' period, and this is linked to a massive reduction in public spending on education, an unregulated move from an elite to a mass system of higher education leading to a sharp decline in quality, salary levels and conditions of work which have impoverished and demoralized academics, and so forth. The implementation of the Bologna process in Romania would imply truly radical reform of universities. Undergraduate degrees in Romania have taken four years or more (and will now mostly be reduced to three), been highly specialized, with a large number of specializations many of which would seem to be anything but relevant to the labour market. And although there are areas of distinction, there has been no system of 'quality assurance'. The following extract from a press statement on the doctoral degree issued by the Ministry of Education on the occasion of the publication of a new law (2005) is indicative of the scale of the problems: 'In recent years, the doctorate has undergone a continuous decline leading to the erosion of confidence in the quality of doctoral degree granted by qualified institutions in Romania.'

The operationalization of the Bologna strategy has been very much 'top-down' in Romania, starting from the government. Yet the EU documentation envisages a process of 'partnership' and participation' throughout the university system (e.g. the Berlin Declaration of 2003: 'it is ultimately the active participation of all partners in the Process that will ensure its long-term success. . . . Students are full partners in higher education governance'), but in Romania student consultation has been virtually non-existent. Many staff knew nothing about the reforms until they began to be imposed from the top, and the discourse of governance which represents all relevant groups as 'partners' actively 'participating' in 'partnerships' is at odds with the extremely hierarchical and clientelist nature of social relations in universities, where students are often subject to favouritism and whims of staff, and junior staff to those of senior staff (Miroiu 1999).

The combative and polemical tone of its supporters in government and universities is an indication of the opposition and resistance which the reform faces in universities. For instance, referring to changes in undergraduate degrees, the Minister of Education said (March 2005): 'If we organize admission and undergraduate degrees in terms of (general) subject areas, then we create a mechanism . . . through which university provision meets the needs of students. The student knows that he or she will obtain a diploma for a broad subject area', whereas with the existing system 'we create a mechanism for choosing specialisms which are often out of date, inefficient, and only continue to exist through pressure from the "academic tribes" within the universities' and do not correspond with 'the needs of the students or the demands of the labour market'. The 'demands of the labour market' may be clear, but 'the needs of the students' is an ambiguous expression which should be treated with caution: is it what the students see themselves as needing, or what others see the students as needing? This is perhaps a small fragment of globalization in itself: advocates of higher education more effectively serving the market in Britain, Romania and many other countries have rhetorically appealed to 'the needs of the students'.

The Minister's reference to 'academic tribes' (also often called 'clans') can be interpreted as a derogatory allusion to established relations of power in the academic field as in many other fields of Romanian public life (see my earlier comment on clientelism), the dominance of 'status groups', in Max Weber's sense (Matei 2004, Mungiu-Pippidi 2002). Romanian public life is highly personalized – everything depends upon who you know, who you can legitimately call on for help or support on the basis of favours owed, common friends or contacts, or loyalty. In Weber's conception, members of a status group are not necessarily members of the same social class. They share a common interest in defending and increasing the prestige of their group and its values and practices, and raising the position of their group in status hierarchies. Status groups in Romanian universities are internally hierarchical and are typically dominated by a powerful senior academic on whom other members are dependent (for jobs, promotion, and various perks and favours) and to whom they owe allegiance and loyalty. These groups have pursued their own strategies to obtain and hold on to positions of power in higher education and elsewhere, and the reforms can be seen as a threat to their position, for instance in introducing a transparency (in quality assurance, for example) which could undercut their privileged access to information and decision-making, and removing their power to control which specialisms are taught. These groups can be seen as having adopted mainly defensive 'foot-dragging' strategies towards reform rather than positive alternative strategies, and these notoriously include 'simulation' – adopting the rhetoric of reform while resisting real change – as well as forms of self-legitimation in terms of for instance 'preserving standards' or 'resisting subservience to the market'. But the strategic options of such groups seem now to be narrowing as the political pressure for reform increases.

University of Bucharest: Manual of Quality Control

I shall discuss as an example of the top-down, combative and polemical character of public documentation the opening section of the University of Bucharest's 'Manual of Quality Control', which was published on the university's website in 2004 (University of Bucharest 2004). It clearly presupposes opposition, resistance and 'foot-dragging', and gives insight into the strategy of authorities in this particular university to achieve implementation of the Bologna reforms. It also shows that the process of re-scaling is in part a textual process: the document represents the university as located within a new set of scalar relations, and we might say that it 'textures' the re-scaling of the university in the sense of producing the re-scaling in discourse as one necessary moment of making the re-scaling actual.

The *texturing of new scalar relations* is summed up in the section title, 'The University of Bucharest in the National and International Context', and the first sentence ('The University of Bucharest, like all the great universities of the world, is currently faced with major challenges') locates the university within an elite group of universities on a global scale. The rest of the section sets out seven 'challenges'. The discussion of the first ('Rapid innovation in the area of information and communication technologies') concludes: 'If the University of Bucharest were to ignore the challenge of information and communication technology, it would mean condemning itself to exclusion from the elite educational market.' Again it locates the university within a global elite, but significantly represents this as a 'market', a concrete illustration of my point above that re-scaling has consequences for the 'horizontal' dimension of an emerging 'fix', in this case shifting the boundary between higher education and business and including the former within the latter (manifested in *interdiscursive hybridity* between educational and economic discourses). The idea of higher education being a market has long been familiar in countries like Britain, but is relatively new in Romania.

A striking feature of this document which is also illustrated here is that change is *legitimized* in a negative way in terms of the need to avoid risks and dangers. This is a *hypothetical conditional sentence* with the *pragmatic force* of a warning, and characteristically legitimizes present action in terms of predictions about the future (the future consequences of failure to act in the present). Legitimization through such warnings of risk is also indirectly linked to the polemical character of the document: given the assumption of resistance and foot-dragging in the university, emphasizing the dangers of inaction is an understandable strategy.

The second 'challenge' ('Processes of globalization with their multiple forms and consequences') again represents the university as an actor on the global scale, claiming that processes of globalization are 'objective', warning that they 'cannot be avoided or ignored', and asserting that the university must be an 'active agent within globalization', working for the possibilities it opens up for students, but also as an agent in defence of national cultural identity in the context of the dangers of cultural globalization.

The third 'challenge' ('The development of mass higher education') represents the university as part of a system at the national scale which has failed to respond to the challenge of mass higher education, claiming that in other countries it is seen as 'progress, offering all young people the opportunity' of higher education, and so suggesting that Romania is failing on international comparisons. The final sentence ('If this issue is ignored or treated with hypocrisy, the quality of higher educational qualifications will be badly affected, and universities will lose prestige') again legitimizes present action in terms of the need to avoid predicted future dangers (again it is a conditional sentence, though not in this case hypothetical, with the pragmatic force of a warning). 'Hypocrisy' is interesting: there is an *assumption* or presupposition that these challenges might be 'ignored or treated with hypocrisy', and 'hypocrisy' introduces a covert polemic with those who resist reform by implying that they are hypocrites – perhaps that they pay lip-service to reform without actually implementing it.

The fourth 'challenge' ('Internal and international competition') thematizes 'competition', and again hybridizes the discourse of the market with educational discourse. It represents the university as subject to 'intense competition' within the changing 'Romanian market', which now includes private universities, new state universities and fees for state higher education. The university is also subject to 'severe international competition', both because Romanians can choose to study abroad and will do so 'increasingly often if the educational offers of foreign countries seem more attractive', and because foreign universities are establishing themselves in Romania. The polemic against the internal resistance becomes more explicit and targeted, recounting the experience of 'certain faculties' as a cautionary tale ('The University of Bucharest cannot avoid this process of competition, constantly invoking its prestigious past and considering this a sufficient argument to attract students. Certain faculties of the University of Bucharest which have

used this way of thinking have experienced for several years the negative consequences of a fall in applications and have had to correct their attitude'). What is
asserted in the second sentence is *assumed* in the first – that some parts of the university have tried to 'avoid this process of competition' by invoking the 'prestigious past'.

The fifth challenge ('Loss of monopoly over higher education') locates the university within a Romanian 'educational market' in which universities have lost
their 'monopoly' because non-university institutions now award higher educational qualifications. Again change is legitimized in terms of risk: 'If universities
wish to keep a competitive position in the educational market, they must become
flexible and capable of adapting rapidly to the needs of the labour market.'

In the seventh challenge, the university is located within universities on a
national scale in relation to policies for the 'compatibility' of national systems
of higher education on a European (EU) scale. It is claimed that the process of
reform, which according to the Bologna Declaration countries voluntarily sub-
scribe to, will be 'imperative' for candidate countries (for 'universities cannot
be responsible for creating difficulties for the Government in accession nego-
tiations'). Again there seems to be an element of polemic with internal antagonists (principles for change agreed by the University Senate 'were only partially
implemented') and legitimation of change through risk which is predicted as potentially cataclysmic ('we risk being overwhelmed by reality') and which requires
immediate preventive action.

Let me summarize. The text contributes to the discursive re-scaling of the university ('textures' the university in a relationship to national and international
scales) as an organization which must operate at a global as well as a national
scale, and operate on both scales as a competitor in increasingly competitive
markets. The text argues for radical reform which is *legitimized* in terms of the
risks and dangers arising from these changes in its location at both national and
global scales. The *representation of time* is also an interesting feature of the text:
a predicted future of risks and dangers requires urgent present action in the
context of changes, errors and failures in the past. The strategy of legitimation
in terms of risks and dangers is perhaps motivated by an awareness of resistance
and foot-dragging within the university, and there is also an element of *polemical*
engagement with those who resist or oppose reforms.

Let me note finally a stark contrast between this text and the positive, upbeat
representation of the university's involvement in reform in the Rector's Preface:

> The University of Bucharest is in the forefront of higher education reform,
> working for the integration of our country into Europe, for the creation of
> a European Higher Educational Area and a European Research Area.
>
> The institution is deeply involved in improving the quality of processes of
> teaching and learning through continuous reflection on didactic activities,

through a sustained research effort, through the solidarity of staff and students
in seeking creative solutions for education in the present and in the future.

There seems to be a slippage here between fact and imaginary – between the way
the university currently is (which other parts of this document suggest is far from
what is suggested here), and an imaginary projection of how the university could
and should be. Perhaps the strategy of the university leadership is to stimulate
change by alternating between visionary futures and prophecies of doom.

Higher education reform in Romania and other countries

Higher education reform in Romania is at a very early stage, compared with a
country like Britain, whose recent report to the Bergen meeting of Ministers of
Education (2005) claimed, with some reason, that the Bologna reforms had for
the most part already happened in the UK. For instance, systems of quality assurance have been established for some years in the UK. This is not so in some other
established members of the EU. In Austria, for instance, the Bologna reforms
were initially used by the right-wing government to justify a reactionary university
reform that reversed processes of democratization which had been going on for a
number of years and re-established authoritarian and clientelist university leadership, which was neither required nor justified by the Bologna process (Fairclough
and Wodak forthcoming).

Comparison between the Austrian, Romanian and other cases indicates that
recontextualization and re-scaling in the area of higher education as in others
do not follow a single pattern but vary according to the specific characteristics
and circumstances of the recontextualizing context. Outcomes of the Bologna
reforms are likely to be different in different countries. They are difficult to predict, and cannot be fully controlled and managed. In the Romanian case, specific
circumstances include an acute lack of resources (of teaching space, libraries,
ICT facilities, secretarial support – indeed most of what is taken for granted in
Western Europe); a system of social relations and power structures based upon
'status groups' which is deeply hierarchical and undemocratic; an atmosphere
of disinterest, foot-dragging and resistance to reform especially amongst a demoralized and badly paid academic staff. The strategy and the discourses are in circu-
lation, but they have not yet been operationalized on anything like a general scale
in changes in institutions, procedures, social practices, orders of discourse (discourses, genres, styles), values, attitudes. The authorities are faced with a dilemma:
it seems that the reforms will not be implemented unless they are imposed from
above, yet they cannot ultimately work as intended without the active participation of and 'partnership' between all parties which is not only at odds with top-
down imposition but also at odds with entrenched relations of power. It seems
reasonable to expect a development and outcome which is significantly different

from other countries, perhaps some sort of hybrid combination of aspects of the existing order and aspects of the reformed order. Yet to some degree the reforms will take place, because it is difficult to see how universities can survive otherwise in a higher education 'market' which they are thrown into willy-nilly.

When reform took place in Britain in the 1980s, there was a sense of having to choose between the devil and the deep blue sea. As in Romania, the old order was too discredited to be defended except by a few die-hards, but the alternative was higher education as a market, which was and remains deeply distasteful to many academics. What did not happen in Britain, and has not happened in Romania, is the emergence of a credible alternative strategy for reform.

Quality assurance

In this section I shall focus on one aspect of the Bologna reforms, quality assurance, because it is an example of broader changes in governance which are themselves an important part of Europeanization and globalization. It also connects with my earlier discussion of 'small practices' – 'mentoring' and other practices are seen as contributing to 'quality' in education. And it is the aspect of the Bologna reforms whose operationalization and implementation are most problematic in Romania for the sort of reasons I referred to in discussing 'mentoring': it has profound cultural and personal as well as institutional implications, entailing social relations, attitudes, values and identities which are very different from those which predominate in Romanian higher education.

The promotion of European cooperation in 'quality assurance' was one objective in the Bologna Declaration, and quality assurance has become a more prominent issue at subsequent meetings of Ministers of Education. Quality assurance has come to be seen as the key to other objectives, especially mutual 'recognition of qualifications' and 'mobility'. At the Berlin meeting (2003) Ministers stressed the need to develop 'mutually shared criteria and methodologies on quality assurance', and called upon the European Association for Quality Assurance in Higher Education (ENQA) to 'develop an agreed set of standards, procedures and guidelines on quality assurance, to explore ways of ensuring an adequate peer review system for quality assurance and/or accreditation agencies or bodies', and to report back to the Ministers' meeting in Bergen 2005. This was done, and the ENQA proposals (ENQA 2005) were approved.

The main proposals were that there will be 'European standards for internal and external quality assurance, and for external quality assurance agencies', the European quality assurance agencies will be regularly reviewed and a European register of quality assurance agencies will be produced. The setting and regulation of standards on a European scale accords with similar processes of regulating quality assurance and agencies for quality assurance internationally (including in the USA). In this sense, developments on quality assurance within the Bologna process are not specifically European. They are part of the global process I referred to earlier in which reform of higher education is seen as linked to the development of a 'global economy' conceived as a 'knowledge-based economy'.

The methodology for quality assurance is centred upon 'self-examination' and 'self-evaluation' ('small practices' which involve new discourses, genres and styles), and the principle that 'providers of higher education have the primary responsibility for the quality of their provision and its assurance' (ENQA 2005). They should establish an inclusive 'culture of quality' (ENQA 2005) (inclusive in the sense that students, academic staff, administrative staff and other 'stakeholders' are a part of it) which recognizes the importance of quality and seeks its continuous enhancement. The role of external quality assurance is to ensure that this process of internal quality assurance is adequate.

In internal quality assurance, 'institutions should have formal mechanisms for the approval, periodic review and monitoring of their programmes and awards'; 'students should be assessed using published criteria, regulations and procedures which are applied consistently'; 'institutions should have ways of satisfying themselves that staff involved with the teaching of students are qualified and competent to do so'; that 'the resources available for the support of student learning are adequate and appropriate' and that they 'collect, analyse and use relevant information for the effective management of their programmes of study and other activities'. Quality assessment should be made public: 'institutions should regularly publish up to date, impartial and objective information, both quantitative and qualitative, about the programmes and awards they are offering' (ENQA 2005). The idea of a 'culture' of quality is sometimes extended to a view of individuals as having an ongoing responsibility to monitor and improve the quality of their own work.

'Quality' is a problematic and contentious concept. If one asks a specialist in quality assurance what quality is in for instance teaching, one is likely to be referred to a set of 'performance indicators' (e.g. how clear the aims of the course are to the students, how adequate the bibliographical information provided to students is, how useful lecture handouts are and so forth). Behind such 'indicators' there are ideas of 'good practice' or 'best practice' and 'benchmarks'. Given a particular understanding of what 'best practice' is, one can devise a set of indicators which measure to what extent a particular course or programme measures up to 'best practice'. What is more problematic is providing secure and uncontentious grounds for deciding what 'best practice' is, and justifying the assumption that quality (in a more general ordinary language sense) depends upon or is guaranteed by adherence to some unitary model of 'best practice' or more broadly of 'excellence', or is something which can be measured in terms of a set of 'indicators'. Clearly, there are diverse views of what makes good teaching (or good research), and the danger is that quality assurance systems will produce uniformity and standardization, encourage conformity, and discourage diversity and creativity.

Quality assurance is an example of more general changes in governance which are also an aspect of globalization. It is just one application of a new model or technology of governance which is based upon a principle of 'self-management', 'monitoring' and 'assessment' combined with external 'audit', 'rituals of verification'. 'Where audit is applied to public institutions – medical, legal, educational – the state's overt concern may be less to impose day-to-day direction than to ensure that internal controls, in the form of monitoring techniques, are in place' (Strathern 2000). This new technology of governance is closely associated with the idea of the 'accountability' of public institutions. These developments in governance fall under the general rubric of 'new public management', which is consistent with neo-liberal principles of converting public services into competitive markets (Rose 1999). On the face of it, institutions are 'empowered' to make their own way in the market free of bureaucratic control, but their autonomy is largely illusory, because they are subject to 'audits' which monitor how effective their mechanisms and procedures are for 'assuring' standards of 'quality' which are imposed upon them.

From a discourse analytical perspective, what is of interest here is not only the new discourses which are associated with this new technology of governance, but also the genres. We can see quality assurance as enacted through procedures which are discursively constituted as *genre chains* (Fairclough 2003: 31–2, 66, 216), groups of genres which are linked together in systematic and predictable ways, which entail regular and predictable linguistic changes as material is moved from genre to genre. Let me refer to my own experience of one part of the system for quality assurance in Britain, 'staff appraisal', drawing upon material from an appraisal training session (Fairclough 2003). In essence, it is a process which takes place at regular intervals in which the performance of an employee is evaluated against targets decided upon at the previous appraisal, and which results in new targets being decided upon. In discourse analytical terms, it is a discourse, but also a chain of genres which constitute the procedure, as well as styles, in which participants enact the procedure. Let us focus on the genre chain.

The main stages of the procedure are: preparation, discussion, recording, dissemination. Preparation involves the production of documentation by the appraisee, including an up-to-date CV, plus other relevant material such as feedback from colleagues or students, and 'a reflective document' on one's work. The 'appraisal discussion' is a meeting between the appraisee and appraiser (an experienced colleague with knowledge of the appraisee's work, chosen by the appraisee) in three stages: reviewing the appraisee's current situation and the issues arising from it, developing 'preferred-scenario' possibilities and how these might be translated into viable goals, and developing a plan of action. Recording involves the appraiser producing a report which is agreed with the appraisee, including conclusions, agreements and goals. The report is disseminated only amongst the appraiser, appraisee and head of department. This is a genre chain, in the sense of a fairly well-defined set of diverse genres which are linked together to constitute the procedure as a larger whole, with relatively predictable relationships between the genres. So, the documentation supplied by the appraisee combines diverse genres (CV, feedback and a 'reflective document' – generic diversity is possible for any of these, but the tendency is for a fairly limited range of standard forms to develop), the appraisal discussion has a specified generic form as I have indicated, which is further elaborated in guidance to appraisers (which I shall not go into, see Fairclough 2003: 250–2), and the appraisee's documentation is likely to be brought into the discussion in fairly predictable ways, and finally the appraisal report is a genre which is also procedurally specified in terms of what it should cover, and is likely to relate to the appraisal discussion and the appraisee's documentation in fairly predictable ways.

There is a good deal of flexibility in this particular genre chain (indeed the flexibility of the procedure in emphasized by managers as a virtue), but it nevertheless constitutes an institutionalized discursive entity. Staff appraisal is a social practice (a 'small practice'), constituted as a procedure, which like mentoring can be recontextualized 'horizontally' in different social fields (education, business, health care and so forth), and 'vertically' at different scales, and which has potentially quite significant implications for the way people behave, relate to each other, see themselves, and for their attitudes to work and to colleagues and their values as workers. It is an exemplification of the new technology of governance I discussed above in that it is centred upon a process of self-assessment and self-management which is broadly framed by the 'mission' of the institution and the 'plans' of the department, and 'peer-reviewed' in what is generally a non-threatening way – though in some institutional contexts, staff appraisal is much more threatening than in the British university I have been referring to.

One innovation of the EU Lisbon Council was in governance: a new 'open method of coordination', which is of interest from a discourse analytical perspective. Here is the relevant passage from the Presidency Conclusions (The Council of the European Union 2000):

> Implementation of the strategic goal will be facilitated by applying a new open method of coordination as the means of spreading best practice and achieving greater convergence towards the main EU goals. This method, which is designed to help Member States to progressively develop their own policies, involves:
>
> - fixing guidelines for the Union combined with specific timetables for achieving the goals which they set in the short, medium and long terms;
> - establishing, where appropriate, quantitative and qualitative indicators and benchmarks against the best in the world and tailored to the needs

of different Member States and sectors as a means of comparing best
practice;

- translating these European guidelines into national and regional policies
  by setting specific targets and adopting measures, taking into account
  national and regional differences;
- periodic monitoring, evaluation and peer review organised as mutual
  learning processes.

One can see this as the implementation at a different level of the technology of
governance I have just been discussing. Just as in the case of quality assurance,
common EU standards ('guidelines') constitute the framework for self-regulation
by member states, with periodic external monitoring and evaluation. The discourse of the fourth element of the method is interesting in that it extends educational discourse ('peer review' is primarily understood as the process applied to
papers submitted by academics for publication in journals) into the field of intergovernmental relations, and we actually see the discourse of quality assurance in
the second element ('indicators', 'benchmarks', 'best practice'). This *interdiscursive hybridity* itself indicates a technology of governance which transcends
particular fields or institutions.

And again there is a *genre chain*. In practice, the 'open method of coordination'
is an interconnected set of documents and meetings/discussions, cyclically
repeated, in which both forms of written language and forms of spoken interaction
are predefined and regulated. To take one example, periodic progress reports
from countries which are a part of the Bologna process conform to a particular
genre of report, i.e. they are organized in accordance with specific generic
conventions. Indeed the reports prepared for the Bergen meeting of Education
Ministers (2005) had to be presented according to a standardized 'template' consisting of sections (e.g. on quality assurance and mobility) containing specific questions or requests for information.

Quality assurance illustrates how different dimensions of globalization cluster
together within specific globalization processes. I have indicated economic dimensions of the reform of higher education, how it is linked to the deregulation of
trade in services, to the emergence of a global market in higher education as
well as to the increasing importance of higher education in other sectors of the
economy, and to the knowledge-based economy. I have also indicated how it
connects with a new technology of governance which is being established internationally in various sectors apart from education. But the reform of higher education also involves forms of cultural globalization, and again this is particularly
clear in quality assurance. The idea of a 'culture' of quality and an ongoing
concern to improve quality through self-monitoring and self-assessment implies
changes in 'the way people perceive themselves in relation to their work, to

one another and to themselves', changes in 'professional, collegial and personal identity' (Shore and Wright 2000).

It will perhaps be clear to readers from what I have said about Romania and about quality assurance why the latter poses the most acute problems in operationalizing and implementing the Bologna reforms. The practices, social relations and professional and collegial identities of Romanian education are, as I have indicated, very different from those entailed by systems of quality assurance, as also are the forms of regulation and governance. Quality assurance entails social relationships which are open and relatively egalitarian, practices which are transparent and subject to effective institutional regulation, and people who are professionally committed to the institution and well disposed to continuous learning. The general situation in Romanian universities is that institutional regulation of practices is poor and opaque. Social relations are highly hierarchical and predominantly clientelist and the distribution of goods is controlled in often arbitrary and personalized ways by a professorial elite, and people in some cases cynically seek to maximize their own interests, and in most cases are demoralized and alienated by abysmal salaries and conditions and what they perceive as an under-resourced and unjust system. However an effective quality assurance does exist in 'pockets' or 'islands' of the educational system such as the network of language centres I referred to earlier.

There is a general public cynicism in Romania about government discourse and legislation which is constantly expressed in public discourse, including the mass media, in terms of a gap between words and realities. And there is considerable scepticism about whether Romanian universities have, or can come to have in the near future, the institutional and cultural characteristics which are prerequisites for the Bologna reforms to be actually operationalized and implemented in a full and adequate form. A common response in the mass media and elsewhere to such perceived gaps between discourse and reality is that Romanian 'mentalities' are the problem, and that real change requires change in 'mentalities' which, it is often added, will take 'decades'. I prefer as I have indicated to see the problem as one of institutions and social and power relations within them, which of course affect 'mentalities' (attitudes, values, behaviours). The successful operationalization and implementation of changes in the 'pockets' or 'islands' I have referred to demonstrate (if any demonstration was needed) that the obstacles are not deep-seated features of the Romanians as such.

Systems of quality assurance are already being developed and universities will be legally required to implement them. The optimistic view is that systems and procedures will contribute to the profound transformations I have indicated. The pessimistic and perhaps more realistic view is that existing social relations and interests are so entrenched that in many areas of higher education lip-service will be paid to forms of quality assurance without much in the way of substance, and certainly nothing resembling a 'culture of quality'.

Poverty and 'social exclusion'

'Poverty' has been a long-standing concern within social policy in Britain as in many other countries, but one early initiative of the 'New Labour' government elected initially in 1997 was to change the discourse, and shift the focus to 'social exclusion'. 'Social exclusion' is generally seen as 'more than just poverty', and it entails (a) a multidimensional view of disadvantage including education, health, housing and social networks and participation as well as income; (b) a dynamic analysis of how social exclusion comes about over time, often through a clustering of diverse factors, (c) a relational view of disadvantage, as a relationship between an included majority and an excluded minority; (d) policies to 'include' the 'excluded', getting them off welfare and back to work (Room 1995, Levitas 1998, Fairclough 2000b, Silver and Miller 2002).

Cameron and Palan (2004) make the interesting suggestion (referred to in Chapter 1) that the construction of poverty and social deprivation as 'social exclusion' is actually a part of globalization as it is discursively/materially constructed in a 'globalist' way. Their view is that globalization is the interconnection between three different 'imagined' (and in part realized, institutionalized) economies: the 'offshore', 'private' and 'anti-'economies, the 'anti-economy' being a space of 'social exclusion' which, in contrast to the other two, lies outside the emergent global order. The three 'economies' are interrelated as follows: the necessity for the state to 'go private', curtail its public responsibilities for its citizens, and become the 'competition state' follows from the 'inevitability' of globalization in a neo-liberal form, and therefore of a competitive struggle for survival between national economies; the 'inability' of the state to address poverty except in the limited and inadequate guise of 'social exclusion' and policies for 'inclusion' follow from the priorities of the competition state (which include producing a competitive labour force but exclude all but limited care for the victims of globalization).

The pressure for Romania like other post-communist countries to adopt the strategy and discourse of combating 'social exclusion' and achieving 'social inclusion' for dealing with its daunting social problems has come from the EU. The fight against social exclusion was included in the objectives of the EU by the Amsterdam Treaty (1999), and the 'strategic goal' enunciated in the Lisbon Declaration (2000) included 'more and better jobs and greater social cohesion'. In an EU Commission Communication on the Social Agenda (Commission of the European Communities 2005), economic growth and 'social cohesion' are represented as 'mutually reinforcing. It is a precondition for better economic performance that we create a society with greater social cohesion and less exclusion.' Member States should co-ordinate their policies for combating poverty and social exclusion on the basis of the 'Open Method of Co-ordination' we met earlier, given the 'common objectives':

- to facilitate participation in employment and access by all to resources, rights, goods and services;
- to prevent the risks of exclusion;
- to help the most vulnerable;
- to mobilize all relevant bodies.

Employment is said to be 'the best safeguard against social exclusion', and promoting 'quality employment' requires developing the 'employability' of the unemployed through policies to promote 'the acquisition of skills and life-long learning'. Social protection systems are to be organized to 'guarantee that every-one has the resources necessary to live in accordance with human dignity' includ-ing access to decent housing and healthcare, but also to ensure that employment results in increased income, and to promote 'employability'. Policies are to be put in place to 'prevent life crises' which can lead to social exclusion (e.g. indebted-ness) and to 'preserve family solidarity', and particular help is to be given to the disabled, children, immigrants and areas of high social exclusion. The 'mobiliza-tion of all relevant bodies' includes 'mainstreaming' the fight against social exclu-sion in all relevant policy areas at national, regional and local level (given the 'multidimensional' character of social exclusion – 'housing, education, health, information and communications, mobility, security and justice, leisure and culture'), 'promoting dialogue and participation' between all relevant bodies including 'the social partners, NGOs and social service providers', fostering the 'social responsibility' of citizens and business, and promoting 'the participation and self-expression of people suffering exclusion, in particular in regard to their situation and the policies and measures affecting them'.

The emphasis on employment accords with a 'social integrationist' discourse of 'social exclusion' which Levitas (1998) identifies as the main discourse in the EU strategy. She suggests that there are significant differences of interpretation which amount to different discourses of 'social exclusion', which imply different under-standings of what 'inclusion' might mean: a redistributionist discourse in which poverty is the main factor in exclusion, a 'moral underclass' discourse in which differences of culture (negatively valued in moral terms) are the main factor, and a 'social integrationist' discourse in which lack of paid employment is the main factor. According to Levitas, public discourse 'slides between' them. While the EU itself predominantly adopts the social integrationist discourse, other discourses may be more or less salient in the national (regional and local) recontextualization of EU strategy.

The EU strategy represents the societies of the EU in a way which fore-grounds certain aspects of them and backgrounds others. For instance, the socially destabilizing and disruptive effects of economic and social change associated with 'globalization' are sometimes referred to as a rationale for an active strategy to combat social exclusion, but what many would see as the inherently exclusionary dynamics of the new form of capitalism that is emerging (suggested by the Cameron and Palan analysis) are less represented or analysed. The discourse pre-supposes societies in which the majority are 'included', and draws attention away from growing inequalities of wealth and power within the 'included', while con-struing 'exclusion' as residual, peripheral and pathological rather than endemic (Levitas 1998). The implication is that the societies which the 'excluded' are excluded from have legitimacy and work harmoniously and well for the 'included'. The strategy for social inclusion can appear as a utopian project for creating a cohesive and benign society. But from the perspective of different discourses which represent contemporary capitalism as a class-divided society in which poverty, injustice and exclusion are endemic, it can appear as ideology. That is, it minimizes the deprivation, suffering and need of the victims of change, and legitimizes the withdrawal of the state from the responsibility of ensuring the well-being of all its citizens by redistributing wealth.

The recontextualization of EU strategy in Romania

In what follows I shall refer to the Romanian National Action Plan against Poverty and for the Promotion of Social Inclusion (Comisia Anti-Sărăcie 2001, henceforth NAP), and the Romanian National Development Plan for 2004–6 (Ministerul Integrării Europene 2002, henceforth NDP) whose third strategic priority is 'Development of human resources, increase in levels of occupation and combating social exclusion'. The extracts from these documents which I discuss are my trans-lations from the Romanian originals.

The complexities and difficulties of recontextualizing EU strategy in Romania are indicated in the following quotation from Chapter 15 of NAP:

> Poverty and social exclusion in Romania are not a marginal product of a system which functions reasonably efficiently, but the result of the failure of the system: first the profound crisis of the socialist project then strategic errors of transition responsible for a disastrous economic collapse and the absence of a compensating social policy.

The result was 'an explosion of poverty' and 'a serious polarization' of the popu-lation: the rapid enrichment of a small section of the population 'which benefited spectacularly from new opportunities', the impoverishment of the majority of the population, and the 'severe poverty' of a small section combined with 'human and social degradation', the 'lack of basic resources for a civilised life'. In 2001, income from salaries plus social benefits was 42 per cent of its 1990 level. What this amounts to is a radical difference between problems of poverty, social deprivation and marginalization in Romania on the one hand, and in the countries which the EU strategy was originally designed for on the other. It is simply not true that societies like Romania work relatively well for an 'included' majority. As in the case of higher education reform, the selection of the strategy and discourse were effectively automatic consequences of Romania being a candidate for EU membership. The difficulties of trying to square the circle and make the strategy and discourse of social exclusion/inclusion fit the realities of social deprivation in Romania can be shown through an analysis of the documents.

'Social exclusion' is defined (NAP, Chapter 1) as the 'positioning of a person outside normal forms of social life, as a result of multiple deprivations, with reduced possibilities of reinsertion in normal social life. The result of discrimination, lack of opportunity, accumulation of deprivation, degradation/non-development of capacities for normal social functioning, or of a style of individual or collective life which marginalizes.' 'Extreme poverty generates, through its permanent character and its reproduction across generations, social exclusion which is difficult to reverse.' And other processes than poverty can lead to exclusion: 'criminality . . . , street children, young people coming out of children's homes, families which have lost their homes . . . , broken families, families with chronic unemployed, cases of alcoholism and drug dependence, and finally a significant part of the Roma population which accumulates many social handicaps'. What is emphasized is 'the paralysis of capacities for redress, 'the degradation of capacities for social inclusion': 'many unemployed have become chronically unemployed, incapable of readjusting their professional capacities, progressively losing contact with the labour market . . . Perhaps most seriously, the new generation has appeared with a severe deficit of capacity for efficient insertion into the labour market . . . Poverty has become aggravated through conversion into persistent social exclusion, the consumption deficit becoming linked to a deficit of capacities, which in turn makes poverty more chronic.' Chapter 15 of NAP concludes: 'Romania is not confronted with a state of poverty/exclusion produced from developments within the parameters of a normal social dynamic, but with an explosion of poverty and social exclusion produced by a major cumulative crisis of socialism and transition, over more than a quarter of a century.'

The third priority in the NDP, 'Development of human resources, increase in the employment level, and combating social exclusion' links social exclusion specifically with un/employment and 'employment capacity', and through the latter with education. Priority 3 is explained and justified as follows:

> The general objective . . . is to increase the employment capacity of the workforce as well as to combat social exclusion. This priority is justified by the need to deal with problems appearing in the labour market, including the increasingly poor quality of services to promote employment possibilities, especially the limited capacity of the education and professional development system to match the changing needs of the labour market, as well as structural problems in the labour market: an unemployment rate among young people

above the EU average, a significant level of long-term unemployment. These problems appear because of the social exclusion of traditional target groups such as handicapped people or the Roma population . . . but also, more importantly, the growing social marginalization in the rural areas.

Four main strategies are identified: increased 'investment' in, as well as reform of, education and professional development; 'investment in the development of human resources through continuous education' using the internet (which entails policies for widening access to and use of the internet); special training schemes to help unemployed and socially excluded people find permanent jobs; and strengthening the social service system especially for vulnerable people in the poorest areas of the country.

The documents represent poverty and social disadvantage in terms of a number of categories, and the contradictions appear in the way these different categories are related. For instance, 'social marginalization' is said to be 'a term used mainly with the same content as "social exclusion", referring to the position of a person/group outside ("at the margin" of) the "normal" social life of a community. In recent years it tends to be replaced by the latter' (NAP, Chapter 1). Yet the extended quotation from NDP above ends with a sentence that attributes labour market problems to 'the social exclusion of traditional target groups' and 'more importantly, the growing social marginalization in rural areas'. A very large proportion of the population live in the rural areas in Romania even in comparison with other post-communist countries – 35.7 per cent of jobs were still in agriculture in 2003 (42.3 per cent in 2001). Many of the rural population suffer from the 'multiple deprivations' which NAP associates with 'social exclusion' – poverty or extreme poverty, poor education (provision is worse than in urban areas, drop-out rates are high, and only 2 per cent of students in higher education are the children of agricultural workers), worse health service and social services than people in urban areas, and so forth. So we might ask why this sentence differentiates 'social exclusion' and 'social marginalization', given the claim that the terms are used 'mainly with the same content'. We can see this as one of a number of textual symptoms of the difficulty of representing poverty and social disadvantage in Romania in terms of the discursive categories of the EU strategy: if we add up 'social exclusion in traditional target groups' and 'social marginalization in rural areas' as a measure of 'social exclusion', it would begin to appear that there are more 'excluded' people in Romania than 'included' people, which is nonsensical in terms of the strategy and discourse of 'social exclusion'.

'Social exclusion' is defined in NAP as exclusion from 'normal forms of social life', implying that it is an abnormal condition. The conclusion I quoted above from Chapter 15 of NAP is clearest in problematizing this: Romania faces not 'a state of poverty/exclusion produced from developments within the parameters of a normal social dynamic', but an 'explosion of poverty and social exclusion' produced by an extended period of crisis. If Romania has been in crisis for a quarter of a century, the distinction between 'normal' and 'abnormal' becomes difficult to draw. We can connect this to what is said about another category, 'relative poverty': it is defined (in NAP) as 'a standard of life within decent limits but which, in relation to collective life aspirations, creates discomfort and frustration'. Yet it cannot 'be measured in relation to average earnings' in Romania because median net income does not itself guarantee a 'decent' standard of life. Collective definitions of a 'decent minimum' have two points of reference according to the document: in relation to the standard of living of fellow Romanians, and to Western standards of living. This makes the category of 'relative poverty' 'very difficult to define', and it 'maybe includes as many as a third' of the population.

Furthermore, another category, 'relatively low income' is defined as 'people with income significantly lower than the average for the community', 'lack of conditions of life collectively regarded as decent'. In Romania however it is an indicator which 'estimates economic polarization more than poverty as such'. The standard EU measurement of 'relatively low income' as less than 60 per cent of average income would include only 16.8 per cent of Romanians, a figure which is actually lower than the average in the EU, and clearly quite meaningless in a country where the majority have very low incomes.

This is very confusing, but it gets more so. In the NAP, 'poverty' as such is defined as 'lack of the necessary financial resources for a normal life in terms of the standards of the collectivity in question'. '*Extreme* poverty' is defined as 'such a serious lack of financial resources that the conditions of life of the people concerned are absolutely unacceptable in a civilized society; serious deterioration of the dignity of human life, producing rapid deterioration which is difficult to reverse of capacities for normal social functioning. Extreme poverty tends to become chronically established in marginalization and social exclusion, so that possibilities for escaping from a situation of poverty become insignificant.' '*Severe* poverty' is defined as 'a level of resources which offers extremely modest conditions of life . . . which impede normal social functioning but without excluding efforts to escape from poverty and establish oneself in a situation in which resources return to normal.' 'Extreme poverty' in Romania is estimated at around 1 per cent at one point in the document and 'several per cent' at another, 'severe poverty' at 12 per cent, and 'poverty' at a further 17 per cent. Given that 'poverty' is defined as lack of resources for a 'normal' life, on these figures some 30 per cent of Romanians are 'excluded' from 'a normal life'.

All this indicates the difficulty of construing Romanian problems in terms of EU categories, given that it is not the case that there is a majority who live a 'normal' life at a 'decent' standard, in relation to which certain groups can be identified as 'socially excluded'. As we have seen, on the figures and definitions given in these documents some 30 per cent of Romanians are excluded from a 'normal' life. Let us bring into the picture the 'Barometer' of public opinion (produced by the Soros Foundation) for October 2004: 39 per cent of respondents agreed that 'We don't have enough for the essentials of life', 40 per cent that 'We only have enough for the essentials of life', 14 per cent that 'We have enough for a decent life but we cannot afford to buy expensive goods', 4 per cent that 'We can afford to buy expensive goods by only by cutting short on others', 1 per cent that 'We can afford to buy everything we need.' This suggests that some 80 per cent of Romanians see themselves as having less than enough for a 'decent life'. The EU discourse seems increasingly beside the point.

From a discourse analytical perspective, there is hybridity or mixing of different discourses: the discourse which was developed by researchers within Romania in the 1990s for representing poverty, and the EU discourse. And it is this hybridity, motivated it seems by pressure to 'fit' Romania into the EU model, which is the source of the confusion and contradictions I have noted. Let us take as an example a sentence quoted above: 'Extreme poverty generates, through its permanent character and its reproduction across generations, social exclusion which is difficult to reverse.' The category of 'extreme poverty' ('sărăcia extrema') has (like the category of 'severe poverty') been developed by Romanian researchers (Stănculescu and Berevoescu 2004) who specifically reject 'social exclusion' as 'inadequate for the specific reality of our country', where 'a large part of the population experience a situation of poverty' (2004: 25). It is very unclear what 'extreme poverty generates . . . social exclusion' can mean – in fact I would say that it is meaningless. I suggest that this is because whoever wrote the sentence has treated what are actually categories from different theoretical discourses ('extreme poverty' and 'social exclusion') as if they were different, co-existing real conditions, one of which 'generates' the other. This is compounded by a *semantic incongruity* (Cruse 2000): 'social exclusion' is attributed a property (being 'difficult to reverse') which is implied by the property of 'extreme poverty' which causes it to 'generate' 'social exclusion' – 'its permanent character and its reproduction across generations'.

Turning to the positive side of the strategy, achieving 'social inclusion' is defined as 'the process of reinsertion in normal life, normal social functioning, of people in situations of social exclusion/marginalization or at high risk of marginalization, through the development of capacities and construction of opportunities' (NAP, Chapter 1). The objective is an 'inclusive society', the creation of 'a prosperous society, economically, politically and socially active, with a high level of collective and individual responsibility, socially cohesive, with a high level of opportunity for all'. A number of 'principles' for constructing such a society are formulated (NAP, Chapter 2). These indicate that the discourse of 'social inclusion' can be seen as a 'nodal discourse' which articulates together three main additional discourses: the discourse of personal and economic responsibility (making people 'active', 'independent' and 'responsible'), the discourse of partnership governance (including the 'excluded' as 'participants' in 'partnerships'), and the discourse of human capital (social policy as 'investment' in people'):

- 'Principle of activation': 'poverty and social exclusion become self-reproductive not only because of the lack of minimum conditions but also because of a state of passivity . . . adapting through acceptance the situation of marginalization and poverty, degradation of capacities to constructively face up to difficulties and avoid risks'. Activation involves 'revival of capacities to function socially, reinsertion in the system of economic activity, stimulation of participation in public life, development of capacities for and involvement in construction of one's life and those of one's family'.
- Principle of 'responsibilization': 'people who are responsible, for themselves, their families, friends, colleagues, neighbours, their communities', within 'a new public morality'. Even 'people on social assistance are not exempted' – they should contribute according to their resources.
- Principle of 'social support as an instrument of social inclusion': social support 'should at the same time be seen as an instrument of activation and responsibilization . . . and stimulant for social inclusion. The person assisted should not be treated as a child to whom something is given, but an adult who is helped to become independent, to support him/herself, but at the same time assume responsibilities'.
- Principle of 'moving from cure to prevention': 'cure is expensive and runs the risk of perpetuating the problem. Prevention means a development from the start of capacity for self-sufficient life and constructively facing up to risks.'
- Principle of 'avoiding discrimination against the less poor in favour of the more poor': it is 'important that giving various social benefits to the very poor . . . does not lead to bias against those who face up to their position with difficulty but have a somewhat better economic position through their own effort. A social policy too centred on only helping 'the poorest of the poor' risks accentuating their social exclusion and going against the morality of work and contribution to collective welfare'.
- Principle of 'investing in social and human development': which 'represents the most effective instrument in the fight against poverty and exclusion', or 'prevention and recovery through re-insertion'.
- Principle of 'partnership and participation': 'representative groups and organizations should be involved in the process of planning social policies; local communities, NGOs and, not least, beneficiaries will be involved in a wide participative process'.

There is more than an undertone of what Levitas called the 'moral underclass' discourse in the construal of 'social inclusion': policies for 'social inclusion' include combating what are explicitly or implicitly registered as flaws in those who are 'excluded' – 'passivity', a failure to take 'responsibility', a lack of 'independence', forms of criminality, exclusion from the 'morality of work and contribution to collective welfare'. Of course it is always possible, and easy, to argue that people could do more to help themselves. But the poor in Romania generally have few opportunities to better themselves. There are major structural problems which need to be addressed, not least a massive rural population dependent on agricultural labour which is totally unsustainable within the EU, and a steady decline in the number of jobs in the economy. These demand radical policies for structural change which will further damage the well-being of millions of people unless equally radical policies for social support and welfare are introduced. The strategy and discourse of 'social exclusion' and 'social inclusion' are inappropriate and largely irrelevant to the scale of the problems. The danger of 'moral underclass' discourse is that it can legitimize lack of social support by blaming the victims for their own plight.

Initiatives to operationalize the discourse of social exclusion/inclusion are elements in many of the 'projects' I referred to earlier, including the example I mentioned, the World Bank's Rural Education Project (2003–9). Its main objective of helping rural school students 'benefit from improved access to quality education' is itself a significant attempt to correct the social exclusion of people in rural areas, and its focus on 'change in behaviours' can be interpreted as aiming at social inclusion – for instance increasing 'participation' of local communities in the governance of schools, which also entails enlarging people's repertoires of genres and styles. This in itself strikes me as laudable. The point is not to suggest that a social exclusion/inclusion strategy and discourse is of no benefit, but rather that it is not up to the scale of the problem, and can furthermore damagingly misrepresent it.

Conclusion

This chapter has shown that the re-scaling of spatial entities such as nation-states can be a complex process with uneven, contradictory and unpredictable outcomes. This is because re-scaling involves the recontextualization of strategies and discourses, and recontextualization is an active process of appropriation in which the extent and nature of the selection, retention (institutionalization), operationalization and implementation of strategies and discourses depends upon economic, political, social and/or cultural characteristics of the recontextualizing context – including its history, its structural properties, features of its institutions, social relations and relations of power and struggles between different social and political groups, the values, attitudes and identities of its population.

I have focused on two cases which involve change in the relations between the Romanian national scale and the European (EU) scale, the Bologna strategy for higher education reform, and EU strategy for combating social exclusion and achieving greater social inclusion. In both cases, Romania's status as future EU member means that these EU strategies and associated discourses virtually selected themselves rather than being selected at the national scale. In the case of the social exclusion/inclusion strategy, I have argued that this was an unfortunate 'selection' in that it is based upon assumptions about social reality which are wrong in the case of Romania. This has led to contradictions and confusions in policies for operationalization and implementation which are evident in the official documentation, as I have shown.

In the case of the Bologna strategy and discourse, although the reforms have been legally institutionalized and some measures have been or are being implemented, there are major tensions between the sort of institutions, practices, social relations, professional and collegial relations which the Bologna strategy and discourse presupposes and those that actually exist in Romania, so that it is difficult to predict or manage with any precision the actual outcomes of reform. So the re-scaling of Romania, and specifically here its re-positioning in relations between the national and European scales, is taking place, but in a rather chaotic way, with the sort of obstacles, complexities and contradictions I have indicated. Change in structures, institutions, practices, people and (orders of) discourse is uneven and unstable. I should add that Romania is by no means exceptional in this regard, though it has specific characteristics which make its particular trajectory distinctive in some ways.

The main features of texts which I have discussed in textual analysis in this chapter include: nodal discourses and other discourses which cluster around them, interdiscursive hybridity in the form of the mixing of discourses, contradictions, legitimization, genre chains, the representation of spatial relations (relations between scales) and of temporal relations.

I have referred only in passing to the mass media, yet they clearly have an important place in processes of re-scaling, in disseminating, legitimizing or de-legitimizing strategies, discourses, and changes in institutions, practices, values, attitudes and so forth. The mass media and mediation will be my concern in the next chapter.

5 The media, mediation and globalization

The mass media play an important part in the constitution of new scales, the transformation of relations between scales, the re-scaling of spatial entities, and the construction and consolidation of a new 'fix' between a regime of accumulation and a mode of social regulation (which I discussed in Chapter 3). All of these processes depend upon the social dissemination of discourses, narratives, ideas, practices, values and so forth, upon their legitimization, upon the positioning and mobilization of publics in relation to them, and upon the generation of consent to or at least acquiescence with change. And in contemporary societies the mass media are the primary social field and agency for these processes, and mediation is the primary mechanism (Silverstone 1999, Thompson 1995, Tomlinson 1999, Virilio 1997). Politics and government are now substantially mediated, and most public reflection, debate and contestation over globalization, Europeanization and other processes of change take place within the mass media, which have become the primary space in contemporary public spheres (Barnett 2003, Blumler and Gurevitch 1995, Franklin 1994). Moreover, the construction of what cultural political economy identifies as the cultural conditions for economic and political systems and changes largely depends upon the influence of the mass media on beliefs, practices, values, attitudes and identities, with the proviso that people's social experience is now a complex combination of unmediated experience (through direct interaction and exchange with other people) and mediated experience, in which each shapes and inflects their response to the other (Tomlinson 1999).

My objectives in this chapter are first to extend the theme of Chapter 4, the re-scaling of the nation-state, to include media and mediation, and second to discuss what we might see as a particular contribution of mass media to the construction of a global scale, the partial constitution of a 'global public'. I shall discuss three examples. The first concerns the 'mediatization' of politics (Fairclough 1995) in Romania, and specifically the emergence of political 'branding' (part of a more general current preoccupation with 'branding' in Romania). The second example illustrates the construal of women's gender identity in the Romanian version of

Cosmopolitan. I shall discuss both examples in terms of the effects of mass media on the re-scaling of Romania. The third example concerns the representation of the suffering of 'distant others' in media coverage addressed to a global public, referring specifically to coverage of the attacks on the World Trade Center and the Pentagon on 11 September 2001 (Boltanski 1999, Chouliaraki 2004, 2005, 2006). But before I get to the examples, I want to discuss the concept of mediation, and aspects of the political economy of contemporary mass media.

Mediation

The concept of 'mediation' is tied to overcoming distance in communication, communicating with 'distant others'. Mediation is associated with 'space-time distanciation', the 'detachment of a symbolic form from its context of production' and its 're-embedding in new contexts which may be located at different times and places' (Thompson 1995: 21, see also Giddens 1981, Ricoeur 1981). Modern forms of telecommunication (the telegraph and telephone, then radio, television, and then the internet) have resulted in the 'uncoupling of space and time' (Thompson 1995: 32), in the sense that communication with 'distant others' is no longer subject to the delays resulting from the need to physically transport symbolic forms (e.g. letters or printed material). Changes in information and communication technologies and the emergence of new media have vastly expanded the possibilities for overcoming distance in communication, making possible instantaneous communication over unlimited distances at little cost, and they are generally regarded as a crucial element of contemporary processes of globalization.

But the concept of 'mediation' also includes the notion of communication through a *medium* which has specific properties which affect the nature of the communication, which intervenes in the process of communication. Specific media have both particular technical properties which constitute possibilities and constraints for communication – an obvious example is that television is a visual as well as auditory medium whereas radio isn't, so television allows communication which is multi-modal. But that is not all. Specific media also develop sets of 'semiotic codes, conventions, formats and production values' which use the technical possibilities in conventionalized ways, and which affect, for instance in the case of television, strategies of camera work, narrative strategies, genres, modes of address and so forth (Tomlinson 1999: 155). If we further see mediation as 'the movement of meaning from one text to another, from one discourse to another, from one event to another' then this involves 'a constant transformation of meanings' which is shaped by the specific properties of the medium or media employed (Silverstone 1999). For instance, when events are reported in news narratives, their form and meaning are transformed according to the genre conventions of news narratives (van Ginneken 1998). We can see this is a case of what I have been calling 'recontextualization' (see Chapter 4).

Political economy of the global communications industry

An important part of contemporary globalization is the globalization of modern information and communication technologies and new media, and the impact this has had on globalization generally (Hamelink 1994). There has been a rapid international dissemination of new technologies and media including television, video, internet and mobile telephones, although there are still significant inequalities of access between different regions of the world and for instance between urban and rural areas and between the rich and the poor. It is reasonable to say that we have entered an era of global communication, but we cannot appreciate its character without considering questions of political economy (McChesney *et al.* 1998, Wilkin 2001).

The emergence of a global communications industry, dominated by powerful trans-national corporations (e.g. AOL-Time Warner, Vivendi, News Corporation, General Electric, IBM, Microsoft) is itself a significant element of the emergent 'global economy'. The role of these corporations in global political economy is twofold: first, they have provided the infrastructure (hardware and software) that has enabled changes in the pattern of production; second, they are 'the major purveyors of news, information, entertainment and knowledge about the world in general' (Wilkin 2001: 126). They are the main source of views and ideas, of a sense of what is right and what is possible, and the main providers of credibility and legitimacy for the powers that be. They have contributed to the dissemination of globalist discourse, claims and assumptions, and of the values, attitudes and identities which are cultural conditions for the successful implementation of globalism, on the basis of an intimate relationship between these corporations and other sectors of business, the public relations industry, governments in the most powerful states and other agencies. This is not to say that the media as a whole are a mere echo-chamber for globalism. Influential independent newspapers and broadcasting still exist in many countries, and they have in many cases played a crucial role in challenging aspects of globalism as well as orchestrating opposition to war (especially in the case of Iraq). But the independent role of the media as a 'fourth estate' fulfilling a public service role, providing accurate and dispassionate information, and, where necessary, exposure and criticism of social ills, is being progressively undermined as the transnational corporations become dominant in the media field internationally (Blumler and Gurevitch 1995; on changes in the media during 'transition' in post-communist countries see Sparks 1998).

The global communications industry has a general influence on what we can roughly distinguish as both the contents and the forms of media which contribute to globalization of media and bear upon its impact on globalization in the wider sense. With respect to contents, taking the particular case of news media, one can see the partial emergence of a global news agenda whose coverage depends upon a common resource of news agency reports and film, addressed to an increasingly global audience, and producing globalized representations and meanings around particular events (Thompson 1995, van Ginneken 1998). The agenda shows the influence of the most powerful news agencies which are largely situated in the USA and Europe and of the most influential news outlets (especially newspapers and television channels). In the case of television coverage of news and current affairs, patterns of 'visibility' (and 'invisibility'), in the sense of the sort of issues and the sort of people that are made visible, to varying degrees, partly reflect these international influences. The influence on content is also partly due to the international market in programmes, where the USA is the leading exporter in television programming – Hollywood films are, for example, part of the staple fare in television networks all over the world. The emergence of a global dimension to media content is particular clear in the case of news items which top the global agenda such as the attacks on the World Trade Center in New York and on the Pentagon in 2001, or the 'tsunami' of December 2004, wars (most recently the Iraq war), the death of prominent individuals (such as Pope John Paul II), or major international political events such as meetings of G8 or the WTO.

With respect to the forms of media, Microsoft software has a – controversial – international dominance which means that forms of electronic communication are virtually the same in many parts of the world, and a casual inspection of programming on television stations in many different countries shows the global diffusion of a similar range of programme types (news and current affairs programmes, soap operas, 'reality TV' shows). On a more specific level, the formats of, for example, news programmes may vary internationally, but there is a tendency for the formats of the most widely disseminated global channels (such as CNN) to constitute points of reference, if not benchmarks, for television news in many countries (Hamelink 1994).

These developments are well known. What is more controversial is how to evaluate them with respect to globalization. One interpretation ties the globalization of media to the 'cultural imperialism thesis' (Schiller 1969, Thompson 1995) according to which the dominance of especially American corporations over world media is leading to a spread of Western values and the weakening of local cultures. In my view, there is something in this. For people living in poverty or under oppressive political regimes, visions of affluence, democracy and consumer lifestyles on television have certainly fed dissatisfaction with local practices, traditions, values, misery and poverty, and aspirations for Western lifestyles, practices, identities and so forth. In terms of economic and political ideas, it has also fed commitments to liberalism and to Western capitalism, including latterly globalism.

But the 'cultural imperialism thesis' has to be treated with some caution. First, because the content and forms of media, despite the convergences I have indicated, are considerably more varied than this thesis suggests – even American television is very far from projecting a unitary set of values and lifestyles. And, as I have argued, recontextualization is a complex phenomenon, involving not a simple colonization, but also an active process of appropriation whose character and outcomes depend upon diverse circumstances in diverse contexts. I argued above that people's experience is now a complex mixture of unmediated and mediated experience and that what they do on the basis of this experience is affected by its hybrid character. One effect is in Thompson's words (1999: 174) the 'hermeneutical character of appropriation', that 'the significance that media messages have for individuals and the uses to which mediated symbolic materials are put by recipients depend crucially on the contexts of reception'.

Mediatization of politics: political 'branding'

The tendency for political discourse to become 'mediatized' is now well established and thoroughly familiar (Blumler and Gurevitch 1995, Fairclough 1995, Negrine 1996, Newman 1999, Wernick 1991). An institutionalized relationship between politics and media can be traced back to the emergence of the national press in Europe and North America in the eighteenth and nineteenth centuries, but the character of that relationship has changed dramatically, especially since the emergence of television and since watching television became a virtually universal practice in most countries in the world. The boundary between the social fields of media and politics has been redrawn, producing a substantial if partial intersection between the two: political debate and persuasion, the making and implementation of policy, and the whole business of government have so to speak migrated to a significant degree from specialized institutions in the political field to the media. It is because of this restructuring of relations between fields that I used the term 'mediatized' rather than just 'mediated'. This development is most pronounced in countries such as the USA, the older-established EU countries, Japan and Australia, but the tendency for politics to become mediatized is a global tendency – which does not mean, as we have seen, identical outcomes. It is associated with a 'professionalization' of 'communications' within government and political parties and the management of the mediation of political 'messages', and the emergence of 'spin doctoring', seeking to put a positive 'spin' on political messages, for which for instance the New Labour government in Britain after 1997 became notorious (Fairclough 2000b).

Part of these developments is the extension to politics of the commercial strategy of 'branding'. 'Branding' has become a global industry in its own right, with its own galaxy of highly paid experts, branding consultants, who are spreading the branding 'message' across the globe. The idea of the 'brand' was originally applied to commercial goods in the traditional sense (e.g. soap powders), but has been extended to less tangible goods (such as the 'Cosmo brand' of the women's magazine *Cosmopolitan* which I discuss later, see Machin and Thornborrow 2003) and to universities, political parties, political leaders, cities (Flowerdew 2004) and even countries (Pride 2001). The technique of branding is based upon certain simple principles: your brand should reflect your strengths, commitments and values – your 'brand values'; your brand is your promise to your customer; you should consistently communicate your brand values in what you do and how you behave.

An example of brand thinking in politics is Gould's (1998: 211) account of a paper he produced in 1994, when Tony Blair became leader of the Labour Party in Britain, called 'Consolidating the Blair identity'. He summarizes his position as follows:

> Tony Blair should not be what he is not. This will not work and will be counterproductive. He should not try to avoid the problem of youth by behaving with excessive gravitas. Nor try to avoid looking soft by behaving with excessive aggression. What he must do is build on his strengths, and build an identity as a politician that is of a piece with the political positions he adopts. He must be a complete, coherent politician who always rings true.

We can recognize here the first of the principles of branding I listed above: 'reflect your strengths, commitments and values – your brand values'. The technique of branding was applied to New Labour and to Tony Blair as the embodiment of New Labour. This entailed not only using Blair's strengths but 'building on' them. One of Blair's weaknesses was for instance identified by Gould as not seeming to be tough enough, and this was addressed at various levels in the branding of Blair: through the early and highly successful sound-bite 'tough on crime, tough on the causes of crime', through developing Blair's capacity to 'talk tough' and sound tough in his speeches, and look tough. All this was in line with New Labour's 'brand values' (i.e. 'of a piece with the political positions he adopts'), and added to Blair's 'coherence' as a politician in the sense of developing a style and image consistent with 'brand values' (policies). At the same time, New Labour made extensive use of 'focus groups' to ensure that their 'promise' to their 'customers' was what they wanted, and of 'spin doctoring' to ensure consistency in the communication of 'brand values' (Driver and Martell 1998, Fairclough 2000b).

Political branding, like the application of branding strategies in other areas, is becoming global. Parliamentary and presidential elections were held simultaneously in Romania in November–December 2004. The victorious presidential candidate, Traian Băsescu, had previously twice been elected as major of Bucharest, and had been advised for all three elections by GMP Advertising. GMP director Felix Tataru claimed in an interview shortly after Băsescu was elected president that he was the first Romanian politician to be treated as a 'brand'. He spelt out what that means: 'You should not create a false image, a mask, for politicians, invent things which are not their own. You should give a politician a coat which suits him, in which he feels good, which he likes wearing. We did not try to do things which were not him.' This is strikingly similar to Gould's comments on Blair.

The Băsescu brand was built upon features of his personality which made him an unconventional figure in Romanian politics, with the suggestion that he would bring a new, more direct, 'hands-on' approach in a context where conventional politics and politicians were widely discredited. The branding of Băsescu as the unconventional, controversial and often disruptive figure who would 'break the mould' of post-1989 Romanian politics involved cutting across boundaries which had conventionally separated the field of politics from the fields of popular entertainment and commercial advertising and from everyday life, through a hybridity (including *interdiscursive hybridity*) which articulated together a wider range of communicative resources (genres, discourses, styles, tones or 'keys') than are normally found in Romanian politics. This was evident in the campaign for the re-election of Băsescu as Mayor of Bucharest earlier in 2004. The campaign literature had the character of a rather cleverly executed and humorous commercial advertising campaign in which Băsescu was symbolized as a red chilli pepper (*ardei* in Romanian), a symbol which evokes his tendency to flare up at unpredictable moments, suggests that he adds spice to Romanian politics, and so forth.

A central issue in the Băsescu campaign was to achieve a majority for the 'Justice and Truth' Alliance (National Liberal Party and Democratic Party) in the city council. After four years he had to work with a council dominated by his political opponents (the Social Democratic Party, which was also at that time the party of government). Let me describe one advertisement related to this as an example. The dominant colour is orange, used by the Justice and Truth Alliance in all their publicity. On the left is a large red chilli pepper, on the right a bottle of peppers with the label (D.A. PNL-PD – a Romanian abbreviation for 'Justice and Truth. National Liberal Party-Democratic Party'). The headline is 'Vote for him/it. But don't leave him/it on its own . . .' (the pronoun in the Romanian text can mean either 'him' or 'it' – we are clearly to take the pepper ('it') as symbolizing Băsescu). The text in the body of the advertisement begins: 'Băsescu is a great guy! He does what he says and he says what he does. He has big plans for Bucharest but no-one to taste them with because of an abstinent Council.' And with the same prominence as the headline at the bottom of the page: 'He does a lot on his own. With a Council he will do everything.'

This is amusing and irreverent, and new in Romanian politics. It brings commercial advertising into politics in a more technologically and semiotically sophisticated way than people had previously experienced. It combines entertainment with politics, and it recontextualizes colloquial spoken language within politics (especially the expression I have translated as 'a great guy'). The printed publicity for the presidential campaign was somewhat similar. It depicted Băsescu, a former captain in the merchant navy, saluting, and the slogan ('Sa traiţi bine!', 'May you live well!') was a *wordplay* on the expression which accompanies a salute in the armed forces, 'Sa traiţi!' (literally 'May you live'). Băsescu's behaviour on television is consistent with this tone: he has the look of a funny man, with an impish grin, a tendency to joke and laugh a lot, and to act in what struck me at times as a somewhat clownish way. He can also be serious and engage in serious and effective political argument, as well as act in authoritarian ways. The irreverence, unconventionality and clowning were also evident on his website during the election, which included for instance computer games with Băsescu and other politicians as characters.

Băsescu's unconventional range of communicative resources was illustrated in the final TV debate between the candidates (Năstase and Băsescu) just before the second round of the presidential election, on 8 December 2004. I shall refer to one part of the debate which was widely commented on, in which Băsescu raised the issue that both of them had been communists before 1989. Băsescu begins by announcing that the two of them have a 'big problem', and very effectively *holds the 'floor'* for several minutes before stating what the 'big problem' is — not as it turns out that they were both communists (though the fact that people only have a choice between two ex-communists is referred to in the course of this section as a 'curse' on 'this people'), nor is it in fact a problem for both of them, but for Năstase — his inability to understand that institutions have to function by themselves without interference or manipulation. Băsescu is alluding to the main theme of his campaign, the 'corruption' of the previous administration.

What is interesting is the range of communicative resources he uses. They include the genre of *conversational narrative*, including accounts of a conversation with colleagues and, most strikingly, of a conversation he claims to have had with himself in the mirror ('Then I kept looking at myself, sometimes I was looking at myself in the mirror, and I say "Hey, Băsescu old son, do you have respect for the Romanian people?" I was asking myself. I say: "I do." "Have you made a mockery of the Romanian people?" I don't have the feeling that I ever did that.') In the context of the section as a whole, he is doing what people often do in everyday conversation — using narratives in *argumentation*, to make an argumentative point. What I have translated as 'Hey, Băsescu old son, do you have respect for the Romanian people?' was in Romanian 'Mă, tu ai respect pentru poporul român, Băsescule?', and included two markedly *colloquial features*: the interjection 'mă', which is stigmatized in Romanian education as impolite, and the colloquial vocative 'Băsescule', with the vocative suffix 'le'. This is one of many points in the debate where Băsescu, unlike his opponent, draws upon the communicative resources of colloquial conversation.

Another example, concerning *pronouns* and forms of the *verb*, is that Băsescu initiates a shift from the *formal* and polite second personal plural (which would be expected in this sort of exchange) to the *informal* second person singular (from 'voi' to 'tu', equivalent to 'vous' and 'tu' in French). Delivery, *'paralinguistic' features* and *'body language'* also contribute to the colloquial style. For example, he often gives the impression through a combination of pausing and 'body language' of searching for words, of speaking spontaneously, whereas comments on Năstase represented him as merely reproducing prepared material in a somewhat 'wooden' way. Băsescu drew extensively upon the expressive resources of colloquial speech, Năstase did not. Such colloquial language, which is not expected in Romanian political debate, contributes to constructing Băsescu as an authentic personality, an ordinary person like the rest of us – as well as a man who is honest enough to have doubts about himself, and to 'confess' them in a public context such as this. This is a part of the Băsescu brand.

A controversial programme (on the Realitatea TV channel) after the debate seems to give some confirmation to aspects of this analysis. The two candidates were awarded points out of 10 for their performance in the debate by a panel consisting of a theatre director, a psychologist, a political analyst and a 'specialist in images'. Băsescu was awarded 8.5, Năstase 6. Marks were awarded for: 'scenic presence, attitude, discourse, and charisma and style'. Comments included: Năstase's 'gestures' showed 'insecurity', his 'discourse' was 'very complicated' and 'monotonous', whereas Băsescu's 'tone' was 'very direct'. Năstase was 'reserved' and 'had a presence centred upon himself', whereas Băsescu was 'cooperative'. Băsescu was more 'dynamic', 'flexible', 'emphatic' and 'simple', and less 'distant'. One panellist said about Băsescu: 'It seems to me that the fact that he said "I don't know" made him, personalized him as, everybody's friend.' This is attractive for some people, but not for others. For some Romanians, Băsescu behaves in a way which is quite inappropriate in politics and certainly for the President of the country.

The result of the election was extremely close. Although Băsescu won by a narrow margin, his party actually lost the parliamentary elections to the Social Democratic Party. And analysis and commentary in the press have suggested that only a rather small number of younger urban voters voted for Băsescu because they positively liked the brand (rather than, for instance, to keep Năstase out). However, a year after the election Băsescu was by far the most popular political leader in the country, considerably more popular than the Prime Minister or other members of the government, or the leaders of the opposition. Many people like Băsescu, though whether it is simply the man or also at least partly the brand that they like is a somewhat imponderable question.

The remarkable extension of branding from commercial goods to virtually any institution, to persons such as politicians and to spatial entities like cities, can be seen as part of the operationalization of neo-liberal discourse, specifically of its representation of virtually all areas of social life as markets or potential markets. The remarkable dissemination of branding across the globe – its globalization – can be largely attributed to globalism, which is as we have seen a strategy for spreading capitalism based on such neo-liberal principles to all countries. Branding is an example of the 'small practices' I discussed in Chapter 4, which have more profound implications than they may appear to have because they entail changes not only in practices and behaviour but also in cultural values, attitudes and identities. In Romania, branding is at the time of writing (2005–6) a significant preoccupation in public discourse, with many books appearing on the subject as well as articles in newspapers and journals. There seems to be very little public questioning of the neo-liberal assumptions that branding is based upon – that anyone or anything can be treated like a commodity – though there is plenty of private cynicism. The issue which has attracted most public debate is the 're-branding' of Romania itself, but most of the soul-searching seems to be about whether the country has a sufficiently coherent identity and set of values to be branded rather than whether (re-)branding a country is a reasonable or decent thing to do.

In the case of politics, the impact of branding on political culture includes what Ramonet (1999: 134–5) calls the 'personalization' of politics:

> Political life becomes a clash of men (or women), corporeal, filmable, rather than a clash of ideas. . . . [The political leader is judged not] on his analysis of the situation or on his action [but on whether] he is 'found convincing'. It is in effect the person himself who is being judged, his character, his facility, and not his politics.

The emergence of political branding and personalization can be linked to the relative demise of national political systems based upon struggles between different political ideologies, primarily between the left and the right. This in itself can be seen as part of a shift in the role of national states associated with the dominance of neo-liberalism and globalist strategy for globalization. Neo-liberalism redefines the role of the national state as facilitating markets without regulating them (or 'interfering with' them), and drastically reducing commitments to social welfare. In so far as states have moved in this direction, ideological differences between mainstream political parties on fundamental economic and social issues have tended to be minimized, and a broad consensus between them has developed on key economic and social issues. (This does not mean that political differences and struggles have ended (Mouffe 2005), it means they are less effectively reflected in parliamentary politics.) In this scenario, the choice between political parties in elections is becoming largely a matter of image, the personalities of leaders, and brands (Franklin 1994). This obviously presupposes the mediatization of politics in that communicating image, political personality or 'brand values' requires high visibility in mass media.

These international tendencies in the politics of democratic countries are appearing in the post-communist countries including Romania, and are a part of processes of re-scaling. Although Romania has had a multi-party political system with democratic elections since 1990, the political system has been unstable, and clear and consistent differences in political ideologies between parties have not developed (Mungiu-Pippidi 2002, Roper 2000). Major political objectives and policies (joining the EU and NATO, carrying out the economic, political, legal, administrative and other reforms necessary for EU accession) have been shared across the political spectrum, though a major focus of controversy has been the failure of governments to implement them. The dominant party has been the Social Democratic Party which has been in government for eleven of the sixteen years of 'transition'. Its policies are not social democratic in any clear or consistent sense, and it has moved increasingly towards neo-liberalism. The opposition has been fragmented and has depended upon unstable alliances between parties to fight elections. The 'Justice and Truth' alliance of the National Liberal Party and the Democratic Party (a breakaway from the Social Democratic Party) fought the 2004 elections mainly on the negative issue of government corruption, without putting forward a substantively different political programme, and has proved (like its predecessor in 1996–2000) to be an unstable government because of differences and conflicts between the governing parties. Proposals since the election to merge the two parties are not based on compatability between their policies but on electoral calculations that a single large 'centre-right' party is needed to keep out the Social Democratic Party. In this scenario, a move towards Western mediatized, personalized and branded politics is not surprising. Băsescu perhaps gained a slight but crucial advantage in the closely fought 2004 elections by having made this move before others did.

Many of those active in the overthrow of the Ceauşescu regime in 1989 were inspired by the vision of a democratic society with a vigorous civil society and public sphere, but the blossoming of public debate and activism after 1989 was short-lived (Gallagher 2004, Zamfir 2004). As made-over managers and technocrats under the former regime, as well as some people who had held senior political or Securitate (secret police) positions, secured the reins of power, including control over major sections of the mass media, people grew disillusioned and cynical. On the face of it, the mediatization of politics makes it more transparent, subjects politicians to examination and interrogation by journalists before the tribunal of the public and places the public in a better and more democratic position to evaluate policies and politicians. In practice, there are indeed cases where the media in Romania as elsewhere successfully expose weaknesses in policies, flaws in politicians, abuses of power and cases of corruption. But there is also a widespread sense that this is a façade, and that most of the major decisions, activities and abuses go on behind the scenes. Mediatization from this perspective tends to turn citizens into passive consumers and/or cynics, and allows both government and corporate business interests to manipulate the public more effectively. Certainly there is little evidence in contemporary Romania of active citizenship or a vigorous public sphere. The branding of parties and politicians may produce leaders like Băsescu or Blair who enjoy for a time considerable public popularity and trust, but it also extends the scope for public relations experts to manage public opinion. This is not particularly a problem for Romania or other postcommunist countries, but it is a general problem of democratic deficit in mediatized democracies. The irony is that post-communist countries are importing it in their 'transition' from a democratic deficit of a very different sort.

Cosmopolitan Romania

I now want to move from the role of media and mediation in re-scaling within the field of politics to an example of their contribution to cultural globalization, specifically the recontextualization of broadly 'Western' gender identities. My example will be from the Romanian version of the women's magazine *Cosmopolitan*. This magazine is published in thirty-two languages and sold in more than 100 countries, and can seen as part of the global media. Machin and Thornborrow (2003) discuss the global marketing of the 'Cosmo brand', which they sum up as 'independence, power and fun' (the descriptor 'Fun Fearless Female' appears in many international editions). They suggest that typical Cosmo images of women at work and in sexual interaction have the following functions: 'They use abstraction and stylistic harmony to index a fantasy world; they depict a smooth, idealized and beautiful world in which women's beauty and sexuality empowers them; they signify agency by depicting energy and motion.' Although there are national differences in editions of the magazine, images of this sort regularly appear, as well as distinctive ways of discursively representing Cosmo women. One feature which they identify is the strongly educative character of many articles: readers are often assumed to be naïve, inexperienced and lacking in knowledge, while at the same time their capacity for independence, agency and 'taking-charge' in accentuated, and this apparent contradiction is 'seamlessly' achieved in article after article. Another key feature is 'fun', playfulness and a 'tongue-in-cheek' character, the sense that it is only a game, a fantasy which women can act out through certain forms of consumption (the clothes and make-up they buy, their leisure activities and so forth).

I shall discuss an article from the edition of Romanian *Cosmopolitan* of April 2005 entitled 'The Cosmo guide to big decisions' (*Cosmopolitan* 2005), with the sub-heading 'Do you often use the expression "missed opportunities"? Read the article below and learn how to take decisions in a "professional" way. All you need is the courage to chose, instead of just allowing yourself to be chosen.' The article begins as follows:

The life of a woman who is active (as well as up-to-date, attractive, etc.) is sometimes like a fast train, events and emotions succeed each other so quickly. But also dozens of decisions which have to made each day: coffee with vanilla or moccacino? A layered skirt or slashed blue jeans? Going to the *Alexandru* or to the *In Vino Veritas*?

Yes, it's true that these are not life-or-death problems, but they can cumulatively have a negative effect on your capacity to make major decisions in the long term. If this sounds familiar, then it means that at least once you also have fallen into 'decision breakdown', i.e. under pressure of time, you've been paralysed in a situation when prompt action is needed. Of course having lots of choices is good in theory, but the secret is not to lose time weighing up every situation too much. Because hesitation affects your confidence in yourself: generally you end up regretting the choices you make, or not making them at all.

To escape from this awful 'embarras du choix', and to stop always asking yourself 'What if . . .?' here is our guide in five stages:

1   Talk to your heart.
2   Act like a man!
3   Take advice – but be selective . . .
4   Throw away your list of 'pros' and 'cons'!
5   When you've made a choice, get used to the idea and enjoy it!

The first 'stage' ('Talk to your heart') recommends relying on 'instinct' but also ensuring that one is well informed. The second urges the woman to 'act like a man!' (a humorous allusion to the Romanian dramatist Caragiale, 'Fii bărbată!') in the sense of not allowing concerns about others to get in the way of a choice which is good for her. The third recommends seeking advice, but ensuring that the friends or experts one turns to have the relevant experience or knowledge. The fourth discusses the value but also the dangers of making lists. The fifth urges the woman not to agonize about choices she has made but get the most out of them. The decisions referred to are diverse – relationships, jobs, investments, purchases – and there are a number of stories about particular individuals' choices. There is also a questionnaire framed within the article which differentiates between two types of 'choice-makers', a 'judge' who 'resolves problems quickly and easily', and a 'researcher', 'curious and open, who likes to consider all possibilities'. There are two photographs of the same woman, one leaning rather alluringly on a wall in front of stylish white house dressed in a cocktail dress (with the caption 'Instinct only "works" in combination with concrete – and correct – information'), the other standing against a window with arms crossed in a business-like posture dressed in jeans and a sweater.

The women addressed here are by implication the 'active, up-to-date and attractive' women referred to, and, as suggested by the photographs, successful and affluent. They are *directly addressed* (the second person *pronoun* 'you' is used; they are asked questions, and given advice in the imperative sentence of the list of five 'stages'), and there is an interesting alternation in the Romanian original between the pronouns of *formal* and *informal* address (analogous to 'tu' and 'vous' in French) which indicates at the same time a partial transfer of and a certain discomfort with the informal way in which readers are addressed within the Cosmo style. The contradiction identified by Machin and Thornborrow is also evident in this example: the article is directed at the Cosmo woman who is able to take decisions and take charge, yet the assumption is that readers can have (or perhaps generally have) difficulty in achieving these assumed aspirations, and the 'guidance' offered assumes women are naïve and inexperienced in the basic practicalities of life (and need telling, for instance, about the elementary technique of listing 'pros' and 'cons' in making decisions). There is also the element of playfulness which Machin and Thornborrow identify and the sense that this is just 'fun', for instance in the formulation of the answers one needs to chose between in the questionnaire, e.g. 'When you order in a restaurant, do you (a) Choose the first thing you notice and that makes your mouth water? (b) Read every description on the menu – for two hours – before choosing?'

So we can say that the discourse of 'Cosmo woman' has been recontextualized in Romania, and that the repertoire of possible identities for women has thus been extended to include the 'professional', independent, 'active', 'up-to-date' career woman who succeeds on the basis of her elegance and sexual attractiveness, along with the consumerist and individualist values which are a part of Cosmo woman. But as the discussion of recontextualization in Chapter 4 indicated, this in itself tells us nothing about the impact of the discourse on women's practices, values, attitudes and identities. One major constraint on the impact of this discourse is economic, and is connected to the class structure of Romanian society, and the huge difference in wealth between a small elite (around 5 per cent–10 per cent of the population) and the great majority (Zamfir 2004). The only women who have the resources and opportunities to be Cosmo women are the few who have senior positions in private business (which is heavily dominated by men), and the wives and daughters of men who have such positions. The option of being a Cosmo woman is thus much more socially restricted in Romania than in Western European countries – most professional women have very small incomes and have to take on several jobs to survive. No doubt there are others (e.g. employees in successful private businesses and banks) indirectly connected to the elite who might aspire to this 'lifestyle', though even the cost of the magazine (6.40 new lei, or around 2 euros) is prohibitive for most women.

Romania is a conservative society and in many ways a deeply patriarchal society (Miroiu 1999, 2004, Pasti 2003), and, within the business elite where the Cosmo lifestyle could in principle be an option, gender relations and identities are particularly male-dominated. Perhaps the 'post-feminism' of Cosmo woman is attractive in this milieu because only this pale shadow of feminism could be accepted. There is on the other hand a tradition which has been inherited from the socialist period of 'strong women' who have senior posts especially in the public sphere (e.g. in education), as well as having almost exclusive responsibility for management and decision-making in domestic contexts. But the 'activeness' and 'independence' of the Cosmo woman, with its emphasis on sexual attractiveness and 'fun', is of a totally different character from the more serious and austere activeness and independence of these women, who are likely to regard this aspect of 'Western' culture with contempt.

Summing up, people are exposed to all sorts of cultural identities, attitudes and values in the mass media, some of which like Cosmo woman are heavily promoted. But whether discourses or styles come to be selected and retained and have a major cultural impact depends upon conditions of various sorts in the recontextualizing context, as I argued in Chapter 4.

Distant suffering: 11 September 2001

I now want to shift the focus from the contribution of media and mediation to re-scaling the nation-state, to their role in the construction of a global scale, and specifically a 'global public'. The issue I shall discuss is the mediation of the suffering of distant others in natural disasters, major accidents, wars and so forth, and the particular example I shall take is coverage of the attacks on New York and Washington on 11 September 2001.

Mediation has been seen on the one hand as making a positive contribution to globalization through its capacity to give 'immediacy' to the lives, practices, problems and suffering of distant others and thus make possible a better understanding of others and a greater empathy with them, and on the other hand as having the negative effect of turning people into mere spectators of the lives of others, into voyeurs (Tomlinson 1999). But neither extreme optimism nor extreme pessimism would seem to be justified: the lives of distant others are mediated in a variety of ways, with a variety of effects. I shall focus on 'distant suffering' (Boltanski 1999) for a number of reasons: because 'disaster news' (Chouliaraki 2006) is one of the main forms in which distant others are represented, because some 'disaster news' stories virtually become global stories which address global audiences (e.g. news of major terrorist attacks or natural disasters such as the 'Tsunami' of December 2004), and because 'disaster news' can have a mobilizing effect in many countries and localities (be it mobilizing to provide emergency aid or to build up political pressure for action) which raises the issue of how mediated experience interacts with unmediated experience, and of the effects of mediation on public spheres.

Chouliaraki (2004, 2005, 2006) has developed an approach to distant suffering in terms of the 'analytics of mediation',

> a framework for the study of television as a space of appearance that presents . . . human suffering within particular regimes of pity, that is within specific semantic fields where emotions and dispositions to action vis-à-vis the suffering of 'others' are made possible for the spectator.
>
> (2005: 146)

This framework helps us connect ways in which suffering is represented on television with ways in which audiences are positioned to respond and react to it (and, ultimately, with ways in which they do actually respond and react), and how the mediation of distant suffering is framed by relations of power.

Television as a medium provides a repertoire of resources for representation which includes both visual representation and verbal representation and the relationship between the two (recall my discussion of the semiotic codes and conventions of different media in the section on mediation above), and depends upon the 'allowances' of the technologies of television (i.e. what they make possible, what they 'allow'). One part of Chouliaraki's framework is the identification and differentiation of different ways which are recurrently used in the representation of distant suffering on a range of global and national television channels. A range of options or choices is available to news-makers in both visual and verbal aspects of representation, and these tend to combine in particular ways. The options include: whether the news is primarily (or only) presented in the studio, or on location; whether the focus is on facts or on evoking compassion, indignation or other feelings; what kinds of visual representations are used (graphics, photographs, archive film, live transmission); in the case of video and film, what choices are made in angle, distance (e.g. close-ups versus long shots) and so forth; whether the news narrative is primarily description, or story-telling proper, or analytical exposition; whether the verbal and visual elements are strongly or weakly connected, whether the visual is interpreted verbally or allowed to 'speak for itself'. A particular news story may well mix options (e.g. be partly description, partly story-telling proper, partly analytical exposition). The framework also gives prominence to the representation of space and time, and to agency – for instance whether suffering is represented as proximate to or distant from the audience, in the present or in the past (and with or without implications for the future), whether sufferers are represented as agents (for instance whether they speak, whether they interact with others or directly with the spectator), which other agents (notably the benefactors who alleviate suffering, or the perpetrators of suffering) are represented. Different categories of news about distant suffering can be distinguished on the basis of which options are chosen, and how they are combined.

This framework provides the resources for a more analytical approach to certain inequities in mediation which are well established in social science, the effect of global relations of power on how places and people are positioned within the implicit hierarchies which inform 'newsworthiness'. As is well known, the lives of certain 'distant others' are generally represented as counting for more than the lives of others in the media, receiving more media attention and a different quality of media attention. Put crudely, the life of an American or a European tends to count considerably more than the life of a Bangladeshi or a Nigerian. Chouliaraki's framework allows us to investigate such differences in terms of the representational resources that are devoted to reporting distant suffering in different places and affecting different people. What is of interest from the perspective of globalization is the extent to which the repertoire of ways of representing distant suffering is being globalized (in the sense that television channels across the world are tending to use the same repertoire, though this tendency is conditional upon their technological resources), and the extent to which the news values which govern selection amongst the options available within this repertoire according to notions of 'newsworthiness' are also being globalized.

These are complex questions which I don't presume to answer here. But the example I shall discuss, the mediation of the events of 11 September 2001 (see Edwards and Martin 2004), is of interest with respect to globalization in several ways. First, it was a global story which dominated the news in countries across the world for a considerable period of time. Second it was a story addressed to a global audience; the suffering was located in the USA (though the victims were of many nationalities), but it was presented as relevant to people all over the world. The global channels such as CNN and BBC World took a leading role in broadcasting this global story to a global audience, but their treatment of the story also greatly influenced that of many national channels. Third, global power relations heavily influenced the way in which the story was interpreted and the direction taken by responses and reactions to the events of 11 September. The mediation of the events themselves and the distant suffering which they caused shaded into the mediation of a narrative and an interpretation of the events initiated by the US government which was presented as demanding retaliatory action on an international basis: a 'war on terror' (see Chapter 7). Thus the global story became a vehicle for global mobilization against 'terrorism', which was in part legitimized by the claim that the events of 11 September amounted to an attack on the global economy, symbolized in an attack on one of the pillars of the global economy, the World Trade Center in New York (Honderich 2003, Jackson 2005). Of course, there were some countries and television channels which distanced themselves from this unfolding of the story, and there were millions of people in other countries who were distressed both by the human suffering and by the political interpretations and implications placed upon it by American officials and their supporters elsewhere.

Chouliaraki's analysis of the mediation of these events (2004) emphasizes its complex character (the diverse sets of representational resources which were drawn upon, and the diverse ways in which audiences were positioned in relation to the suffering of 11 September) by analysing different parts of the coverage of the story on Danish national television. The first is an interview between the anchorperson in the studio and the Danish Consul in New York over a telephone link, interspersed with street shots from Manhattan characterized by erratic camera movement, imperfect focus and framing, camera lenses covered in white dust. The consul describes the situation as a first-hand witness, expresses his own feelings, and evaluates the longer term consequences. The focus is upon 'sentiment', the emotional and empathic engagement of the audience, both through the 'instantaneous proximity' which the camera gives the audience, positioning people as witnesses of the events as they unfold, the destruction, the dust, people running or walking away, relief workers with helmets on, and through the consul's vivid description of the suffering and his expression of his own feelings (e.g. 'dramatic, shocking, indescribable'), and then a shift towards contemplation as the consul tries to evaluate the consequences ('we are entering a new phase', 'worry, deep anxiety, a terrible, terrible, terrible event with deep political consequences for all of us'). The theme that 'things will never be the same again' was pervasive in the mediation of the events, from many quarters, and I return to this below. The consul's formulation conveys the extraordinary character of the attack and of its consequences through indicating his own apprehension ('worry', 'anxiety'), repetition of 'terrible', emphasizing import by twice using the adjective 'deep', and being specific about the general or even universal nature of the consequences ('for all of us').

Chouliaraki's second sequence is a two-minute chronology of events, primarily a visual text, beginning with shots of the burning tower, then the second plane crash, Bush's first public statement, the collapse of the two towers and the burning Pentagon. The verbal text is exclusively details of time, place, flight routes and numbers, and numbers of victims. The Bush statement is shown, not reported, and it gives the sequence a focus on 'denunciation', referring to 'an apparently terrorist attack against our country', and promising 'to hunt down those folks who committed this act' (see below).

The third sequence is a long shot from a distance (an exceptional eight minutes in duration) of Manhattan burning. The verbal voice-over comes from a panel of experts discussing causes and consequences. These visual and verbal elements distance the audience from the concrete specificities of the events. In contrast to the positioning of the audience in a relationship of 'sentiment' and 'denunciation' with the events in the first two sequences, the audience here is positioned in a relationship of 'contemplation'. The visual image here is a sort of 'tableau vivant' which Chouliaraki (after Boltanski 1999) associates with the 'sublime', and which can evoke an aesthetic appreciation which excludes empathy with the human suffering, but which can also open up a different moral dimension, for instance reflection on the false sense of security which people in general have as inhabitants of the metropolis ('if it can happen there, where next?').

What Chouliaraki is arguing is that the mediation of the events of 11 September articulated together a set of representational resources which made available to audiences a particular range of moral horizons and orientations to the suffering of these 'distant others'. There are two points to be made here. The first is that as complex and diverse as the mediation of these events was, it also excluded certain possible orientations to suffering, including reflections on the relationship between this suffering and suffering at other times and in other places which might allow people to address the questions, 'why here, why now?', and including also the possibility of bringing the perpetrators of this suffering to justice without embarking upon retaliation and eventually war.

The second point is to reiterate that although the way these events were mediated offered, so to speak, to audiences globally a particular range of orientations towards the suffering, nothing dictated that these offers should always be accepted. Particular ways of mediating events may significantly affect people's perception of them and reaction to them, as I would suggest they did in this case, but in no sense do they determine them. There was all over the world a wave of horror at the attacks and sympathy for the victims of the attacks, a global reaction which was similar to those in response to the death of Princess Diana or the tsunami of December 2004, which we can say was caused not just by the nature of the events themselves but by the way they were mediated. After all, equally terrible events have happened, which have caused suffering to many more people, but in the absence of media coverage on this scale they have not impressed themselves on 'global public opinion' in anything like the same way. But we should not overstate the common human reaction to the events of 11 September: for millions of people, sympathy with the victims was inflected with a sense that the Americans 'had it coming'.

One feature of the mediation of these events which many viewers were aware of and which has since been extensively discussed is that the reporters were initially lost for words, a most unusual situation which is comprehensible given the unusual character of the story. Most news reports are produced after the events which they report, even if shortly after. But this was 'breaking news', events which were instantaneously caught on camera and transmitted across the world as they unfolded, itself an indicator of great advances in media technology. The nature of the events was clear enough, but what was not immediately clear was how to interpret them, what meanings to attach to them. There was a 'void of meaning', and all viewers heard from journalists as they watched the aircraft crash into the twin towers and the buildings collapse were repeated anguished cries of 'Oh my God!' (Jackson 2005). Jackson (2005) notes that many initial eyewitness accounts gave a sense of hyper-reality, that what we were watching was like a film: 'I looked over my shoulder and saw the United Airlines plane coming. It came over the statue of Liberty. It was just like a movie. It just directly was guided into the second tower' (Laksman Achuthan, Managing Director of the Economic Cycles Research Institute). The 'void of meaning' was filled by an emerging narrative of the events which was built up mainly by American government officials.

Jackson (2005) has identified four features of this narrative. First, it represents the events as a 'national tragedy' for the USA, and the USA as the primary victim of 'terrorism'. Second, it represents the attacks as an 'act of war', rather than for example a crime against humanity. Third, the attacks are represented in a way which establishes intertextual relations with other events in US history, and with a set of myths which have a powerful resonance for Americans: the Second World War and especially the Japanese attack on Pearl Harbor, the Cold War, America's historical role in the struggle for civilization and against barbarism, and the narrative of America as spreading freedom and democracy across the globe, 'freedom' understood as economic and not just political freedom ('free trade') and linked to 'globalization' in the globalist sense. Fourth, the narrative suppresses alternative accounts of the events, especially those which see them as a rebuff to the iniquities of American foreign policy.

Basic elements of this narrative were already in place in government statements made on the day of the attack, including the second and longer of two statements by President Bush (Bush 2001) which is reproduced below (the symbol '(. . .)' indicates an omission):

> Good evening. Today, our fellow citizens, our way of life, our very freedom came under attack in a series of deliberate and deadly terrorist acts. The victims were in airplanes, or in their offices; secretaries, businessmen and women, military and federal workers; moms and dads, friends and neighbors. Thousands of lives were suddenly ended by evil, despicable acts of terror.
>
> The pictures of airplanes flying into buildings, fires burning, huge structures collapsing, have filled us with disbelief, terrible sadness, and a quiet, unyielding anger. These acts of mass murder were intended to frighten our nation into chaos and retreat. But they have failed; our country is strong.
>
> A great people has been moved to defend a great nation. Terrorist attacks can shake the foundations of our biggest buildings, but they cannot touch the

foundation of America. These acts shattered steel, but they cannot dent the steel of American resolve.

America was targeted for attack because we're the brightest beacon for freedom and opportunity in the world. And no one will keep that light from shining.

Today, our nation saw evil, the very worst of human nature. And we responded with the best of America – with the daring of our rescue workers, with the caring for strangers and neighbors who came to give blood and help in any way they could.

Immediately following the first attack, I implemented our government's emergency response plans. Our military is powerful, and it's prepared. Our emergency teams are working in New York City and Washington, D.C. to help with local rescue efforts.

Our first priority is to get help to those who have been injured, and to take every precaution to protect our citizens at home and around the world from further attacks. (. . .)

The search is underway for those who are behind these evil acts. I've directed the full resources of our intelligence and law enforcement communities to find those responsible and to bring them to justice. We will make no distinction between the terrorists who committed these acts and those who harbor them.

I appreciate so very much the members of Congress who have joined me in strongly condemning these attacks. And on behalf of the American people, I thank the many world leaders who have called to offer their condolences and assistance.

America and our friends and allies join with all those who want peace and security in the world, and we stand together to win the war against terrorism. Tonight, I ask for your prayers for all those who grieve, for the children whose worlds have been shattered, for all whose sense of safety and security has been threatened. And I pray they will be comforted by a power greater than any of us, spoken through the ages in Psalm 23: 'Even though I walk through the valley of the shadow of death, I fear no evil, for You are with me.'

This is a day when all Americans from every walk of life unite in our resolve for justice and peace. America has stood down enemies before, and we will do so this time. None of us will ever forget this day. Yet, we go forward to defend freedom and all that is good and just in our world.

Thank you. Good night, and God bless America.

I shall take Jackson's second point first. There is already a clear indication that the attacks are seen and will be responded to as acts of war. Bush asserts that America and its 'friends' and 'allies' stand together to 'win the war on terrorism', which makes the *assumption* that this a war, and the claim that 'Our military is powerful, and it's prepared' *implies* that they will be used. He also refers to those responsible for the attacks as 'enemies' ('America has stood down enemies before, and we will do so this time'), and offers an explanation for the attacks ('These acts of mass murder were intended to frighten our nation into chaos and retreat. But they have failed; our country is strong . . . America was targeted for attack because we're the brightest beacon for freedom and opportunity in the world. And no one will keep that light from shining') which suggests a strategizing opponent, and ties in with the otherwise superfluous description of the attacks as 'deliberate' (such attacks could hardly be accidental). In a formulation which was to become familiar in the 'war on terror', he states that 'We will make no distinction between the terrorists who committed these acts and those who harbor them.' If the intention were legal redress, there would of course be a distinction. Within a few days, Bush's interpretation of the attacks as acts of war demanding military reprisals was more explicit: 'War has been waged against us by stealth and deceit' (14 September).

The attacks are clearly interpreted as attacks on America ('Today, our fellow citizens, our way of life, our very freedom came under attack in a series of deliberate and deadly terrorist acts . . . America was targeted for attack. . . .'), and one can see implicit *intertextual* allusions to the American myths I referred to above, an allusion to the Cold War which implicitly equates terrorism with communism as threatening 'our way of life, our very freedom', and a more general allusion to America's heroic past in confronting and defeating enemies ('America has stood down enemies before, and we will do so this time'), as well as an explicit claim that America was targeted because it is 'the brightest beacon for freedom and opportunity in the world'. In the following days and months, intertextual allusions to these myths became more explicit: 'Americans have known wars – but for the past 136 years, they have been wars on foreign soil, except for one Sunday in 1941' (Bush, 20 September), 'By sacrificing life to serve their radical visions – by abandoning every value except the will to power – they follow in the path of fascism and Nazism and totalitarianism. And they will follow that path all the way . . . to history's unmarked grave of discarded lies' (Bush, 20 September), 'our struggle is similar to the Cold War. Now, as then, our enemies are totalitarians, holding a creed of power with no place for human dignity' (Bush, 1 June 2002), 'This is not, however, just America's fight. This is the world's fight. It is civilization's fight. This is the fight of all who believe in progress and pluralism, tolerance and freedom' (Bush, 20 September).

Part of the suppression of alternative narratives of the events of September 9 is a denigration of the enemy which rules out any account of their actions as those of rational political actors pursuing just solutions against overwhelming odds. Yet there is evidence that this is what people like Osama bin Laden are doing, whether one agrees with them or not (Bergen 2001). In this speech as in many others, terrorist acts are represented as 'evil' and 'despicable', the product of 'evil, the very worst of human nature'. One issue which I leave for Chapter 6 is the meaning of 'terror' and 'terrorism' and the rhetorical deployment of these terms. But let me note here that representing terrorism and terrorist acts in religious terms as 'evil' excludes questions of political difference, political grievances and conflicts, questions about American politics in especially the Middle East and possible political solutions. If these people and their acts are 'evil', then normal political relations and processes cannot apply. As Jackson (2005) notes, the essential rhetorical move is to represent the reasons for attacks such as these as rooted in the identity and nature of the attackers, not in politics.

The extended and extensive global mediation of the events of 11 September can be seen, perhaps somewhat cynically, as simultaneously contributing to bringing the world together in response to human suffering on a large (if by no means the largest) scale, and providing a platform for a political narrative of these events, and for building international support at popular as well as governmental levels for a 'war on terror'. This was as I have said a global story which was addressed to a global audience. Like other stories such as the coverage of the tsunami in December 2004, it can be said to have contributed to the formation of something akin to a global public. In cases like the tsunami where emergency aid is at issue, global mediation can bring people together across the world both in making their own donations to appeal funds and building up public pressure for a substantial relief effort from governments. In this sense it can contribute to increasing 'cosmopolitanism' (Tomlinson 1999) or 'civic cosmopolitanism' (Delanty 2000), a sense of universal humanity and an 'ethics of global responsibility' (Thompson 1995), and the slow emergence of a 'cosmopolitan public sphere' (Delanty 2000).

But the effective hijacking of the humanitarian response to the events of 11 September for national political purposes is a reminder that global mediation is dependent upon a global communications industry which is strongly interwoven with the interests of those who are globally powerful. The mediation of 11 September is also a particularly good example for making the point that what is at issue with global news is not simply whether or not it contributes to constituting a humanitarian, ethical, global public. Relations of power are also always at issue, and the globally hegemonic power may seek to transform international politics into a fight between right and wrong, good and evil, in order to sideline the political struggle between right and left, between neo-liberalism and political positions which are centred upon principles of social justice (Mouffe 2005).

Conclusion

My concern in this chapter has been with the influence of mass media and mediation on processes of globalization. There are five main points that emerge. The first is that the mass media are a crucial element in the global dissemination of information, news, reactions to and interpretations of information and news, new strategies, discourses, ideas and practices, new norms and values in economic activities, political systems and processes, social institutions, organizations, and the conduct of ordinary life, changes in attitudes, sentiments and identities and so forth. Virtually all aspects of social life are now affected by the media and mediation, including even the conduct of private and domestic life and of personal and intimate life, and media 'messages' about all aspects of life are circulated globally.

The second point is that these 'messages' are not in any sense neutral. They are mediated, and that means that whatever aspects of social life are represented in the mass media pass through the particular semiotic codes, conventions, norms and practices of the specific media, and that their forms and meanings are transformed in this particular form of recontextualization. There is, third, another sense in which these 'messages' are not neutral. The global dominance of trans-national media corporations within the mass media, and their intricate interconnection with centres of power in politics, government and business, mean that the latter can to an extent use the mass media as relatively compliant vehicles for disseminating their own 'messages' in the furtherance of their own strategies. The fourth point is that the impact of mass media and mediation cannot however be taken for granted because it depends upon the recontextualization of media 'messages' in many diverse recontextualizing contexts whose specific structural, historical, institutional, social and cultural characteristics and circumstances shape the ways in which media 'messages' are received, interpreted, and reacted to, and the impact they ultimately have.

The fifth and final point is that the globalization of the mass media has contributed to a limited extent to the construction of a global public, global public opinion, and even a global 'cosmopolitan public sphere' in which debate, action and mobilization on a global basis are generated. Although there is a discernible tendency in this direction, it is still a limited and emergent phenomenon in several respects. First, because a global public has so far been constructed around a limited range of issues and coverage, within which 'disaster news' has a prominent place. Second, because its content is managed largely by the trans-national media corporations and the centres of power they are interconnected with. And third, because the national scale remains the most important one – for most countries, a national press and national broadcasting system (even if they are in part under foreign ownership) covering national issues, and covering international and global issues largely from a national perspective, is still the centre of gravity.

Let me conclude by noting the main features I have referred to in analysis of textual extracts: interdiscursive hybridity including the incorporation of commodity advertising and colloquial conversation in political discourse, wordplay, control of the floor in interaction, conversational narrative, argumentation, assumptions and implication, formal and informal second-person pronouns, paralinguistic features, body language, direct address to audiences and intertextuality.

6   Globalization from below

In this chapter I focus on what Falk (1999) and Burawoy *et al.* (2000) refer to as 'globalization from below', or 'grounded globalizations' (see also Wapner 1996). As in previous chapters I shall be concerned with strategies, but now with strategies of individuals or groups in specific places, in many cases defending themselves against negative effects of processes of globalization or taking advantage of new possibilities offered by these processes. These include strategies against globalism and for alternatives to it (see for instance Callinicos 2003). The character of these strategies is affected by what Harvey calls the 'dialectics of space and place', how the changing spatial relations which I have represented as changing relations between scales affect the constitution of 'places', and the resources available to people for local and particularistic activities and interactions and the development of strategies in particular places. Globalization makes available new resources for local action which include new discourses and practices and identities (including genres and styles) in which these discourses are internalized and operationalized. By 'places' I mean the localities (cities, towns, villages, regions) in which most people still largely live out their lives. People's strategies also depend upon their particular positioning (in terms of social class relations, gender relations and so forth) within these places. The focus, then, is on the 'local', or 'place', as productive of its own forms of globalization.

But I shall also address the dialectic between 'militant particularism' (Williams 1989) and generalism or universalism in people's struggles and campaigns for a better world, and how contemporary globalization affects the particular forms this dialectic takes (Harvey 1996). The issue is not a new one: Williams (1989: 249) refers to attempts in working-class self-organization to connect particular struggles to a general struggle, and notes the 'extraordinary claim that the defence and advancement of certain particular interests, properly brought together, are in fact the general interest'. There is a dialectic between 'particular' interests, concerns, objectives, strategies and discourses and 'general' interests, concerns, objectives, strategies and discourses: local struggles can be more effectively developed by internalizing these general resources, and can also contribute to them, for instance by providing models for action. There can also be contradictions and tensions between particular and general interests, strategies, discourses and so forth. Contemporary globalization affects the forms which this dialectic takes not only by enhancing local access to general or universal resources, but also by facilitating coalitions and alliances between places, and between groups or organizations acting on a local scale and those acting on a national, macro-regional or global scale. This brings local struggles into contact with new forms of 'transnational activism' (Tarrow 2005) and 'global' organizations such as Greenpeace.

I shall begin with a short discussion of some of the academic literature and perspectives and concepts within it which bear upon the concerns of this chapter, in part reviewing material I referred to in Chapter 1, and then discuss three examples. The first relates to the strategies of unemployed workers for coping with unemployment in Britain during the Thatcher era, and shows an unemployed worker appropriating neo-liberal economic discourse to legitimize a strategy which involves breaking the law. The second and third examples relate to local struggles over issues with regional or global ecological implications, though it is clear in both cases that struggles over environmental issues are also struggles over social issues such as the power of corporations, democratic control of government and corporate policies, and so forth. The second is from Hungary and shows how people involved in a local political dispute over a hazardous waste incinerator draw upon discursive and other resources made available by globalization in developing opposing strategies. The third is from Thailand and concerns resistance to the construction of a large coal-burning power station in the industrial city of Map Ta Phut. Both cases illustrate the effects of globalization on the dialectic of particularism and universalism, but this is particularly true of the third, with the involvement of South-East Asian environmentalist organizations and the global campaigning group Greenpeace.

Some relevant perspectives and concepts in the academic literature

A trap which some academic analysis of globalization falls into is treating globalization only in terms of structural changes and the strategies of 'global' agencies, agents and 'players' ('globalization from above', Falk 1999), and simply making assumptions about the impact of global processes and tendencies on local contexts and on people living their local lives in these contexts, and their actions and strategies in response to these processes and tendencies, rather than recognizing the need for locality-based analysis to establish these (Burawoy *et al*. 2000, see also Bauman 1998 on the distinction and relationship between 'globals' and 'locals'). There is also a significant theoretical issue here: the trajectory of globalization can be seen as depending upon how tensions, contradictions and struggles within and over globalization are played out, including those between the strategies of powerful agencies seeking to drive 'globalization from above' and the strategies of situated and localized social agents which contribute to 'globalization from below' (Falk 1999).

I have already begun to address this issue to a degree, arguing in the discussion of the re-scaling of Romania (Chapter 4) that the 'internal' effects of external strategies and discourses depend upon the strategies of 'internal' agencies and agents, how they react to these external elements, to what extent they appropriate them within their own strategies, and so forth. But I have not so far discussed situated action in 'places'. The general point is that people are social agents with capacities for acting and strategizing, not merely the passive objects of larger social processes and changes, and they can develop their own ways of acting in response to them and within them. But these capacities are dependent on circumstances and conditions: people's capacity for action may sometimes be very limited and they can sometimes suffer the effects of change but be unable to do much about them, and be victims of change.

In Chapter 1 I discussed Tomlinson's work on globalization and culture (Tomlinson 1999). Tomlinson discusses cultural globalization in terms of the concept of 'deterritorialization', the weakening of the ties between culture and place, a process of 'globalizing culture' which does not however entail the emergence of a homogeneous 'global culture'. Global events 'may add to the extension of the individuals' "phenomenal world": people probably come to include distant events and processes more routinely in their perceptions of what is significant for their own personal lives' with an 'ever-broadening horizon of relevance in people's routine experience'. This interpenetration of global and local has been referred to as 'glocalization' (Robertson 1992, Thompson 1995). Deterritorialization has 'ambivalent effects' on self-identity, on the one hand freeing self-identity from the limiting constraints of particular places, but on the other hand undermining the security and certainties of being tied to a particular place. Deterritorialization is often associated with cultural 'hybridity', the 'mingling of cultures from different territorial locations'. There are two provisos: first, that deterritorialization is dialectically linked to 'reterritorialization': cultural mixtures can stabilize; second, that power relations can structure such mixtures in ways which give certain cultural elements salience over others.

Tomlinson's arguments are focused on culture, but in the dialectical-relation approach I am adopting (see the Introduction and Chapter 2), culture is not isolated from other elements or 'moments' of the social. It is dialectically interconnected with them. The concept of 'deterritorialization' can be extended to economic, political and social as well as cultural aspects of people's lives, and the complex dialectical interconnections between them. Most people continue to lead local lives, in the sense that they live largely within bounded localities, but the social activities and interactions they engage in are less and less tied to these localities and increasingly transcend them, connecting with activities in other localities and involving new relations between scales. The media are the major source of new resources for people to act and develop strategies locally with respect to aspects of their increasingly deterritorialized lives. And as Tomlinson also argues, people's experience is now a complex mixture of un-mediated and mediated experience which enhances their resources for agency in changed circumstances (see Chapter 5).

Tomlinson discusses 'deterritorialization' and its consequences without any real attention to discourse, but as I noted in Chapter 1 it is clear that for instance the 'hybridity' associated with deterritorialization includes 'interdiscursive hybridity' (Chapter 2), the mixing of different discourses, different genres and different styles. And there is also a growing ethnographic literature on globalization ('global ethnographies', see Burawoy *et al.* 2000, Burawoy and Verdery 1999, Anăstăsoaie *et al.* 2003) which, like the literature on globalization more generally, quite often refers in general terms to discourse but rarely includes any real analysis of discourse. My third (Hungarian) example is based upon an ethnographic study by Gille (2000), and one aim is to show through a re-analysis of extracts from the data which she includes in the paper how a more systematic and detailed treatment of discourse might contribute to 'global ethnographies'.

Unemployment and survival strategies

My first example relates to the strategies of survival which people develop to deal with the effects of globalization, such as unemployment. In the following extract (from the data discussed in MacDonald 1994) we have three unemployed people in a town in the North East of England talking on the theme of 'fiddly jobs' – working (illegally) while claiming social security benefits. It shows how people developing survival strategies in particular localities hit by unemployment can draw upon globally circulating discourses, in this case (ironically, one might say) the hegemonic neo-liberal economic discourse.

> Phil: There's enough around. All you have to do is to go into any pub or club, that's where the work is. The person you mentioned he probably just sits around watching the telly. To get a job round here you've got to go around and ask people.
>
> Danny: Most of it is who you know. You've got no chance of getting a job in the Job Centre. . . . You go out to the pub. People who go to the pub go to work.
>
> Stephen: he [the 'hirer and firer'] just shows his face in 'The Rose Tree' or 'The Gate' and people jump and ask him for work. When I was working there I've seen him just drive off in his van around the pubs and he'll come back with another 20 men to work, an hour later. No-one asks any questions. It's a matter of us being cheaper. It's definitely easier than having a lot of

lads taken on permanently. It would cost them more to put them on the books or pay them off. It's just the flexibility. You're just there for when the jobs come up, and he (the 'hirer and firer') will come and get you when you're needed. You need to be on the dole to be able to do that. Otherwise you'd be sitting there for half the year with no work and no money at all.

(MacDonald 1994)

Jordan (1996) argues that the 'socially excluded' develop their own often effective social capital and social networks to survive, and that their survival strategies are a perfectly rational (and in no reasonable sense criminal, even where they break the law) response to the conditions they find themselves in, including unemployment as a large-scale effect of economic globalization and re-structuring which they have no control over and which is no fault of their own. Their strategies are he suggests based upon a lay perception of how the new form of capitalism works which is widely recognized but outside official public discourse.

In the extract there is an account of how 'fiddly jobs' and the procurement of black labour work, and the strategy which unemployed people adopt of registering as unemployed ('being on the dole') in order to receive unemployment benefit and frequenting pubs and clubs to find work. Stephen gives an *explanation* of the economic logic behind 'fiddly jobs' that reflects the perception of how the new capitalism works which Jordan refers to: it's a matter of 'us being cheaper', and 'the flexibility'. This is a fascinating appropriation of a major *theme* of neo-liberal and globalist economic discourse ('flexibility') by people who can be regarded as victims of neo-liberal strategies, in their explanation (and, as I'll indicate, legitimization) of a system (black labour) which is illegal and officially condemned by authorities responsible for introducing and implementing neo-liberal strategies, yet a widespread effect of the implementation of those strategies. We can see Stephen as saying (or implying) the 'unsayable': if you want 'flexibility' – as neo-liberals do – 'fiddly jobs' make sense. Stephen's explanation of the economic logic is embedded in an argument which *legitimizes* the strategy of 'being on the dole' while doing 'fiddly jobs': 'you're just there for when the jobs come up', so 'you need to be on the dole', otherwise (because of the chanciness of 'fiddly jobs') you could end up without work or money. A final point to notice is that the strategy is summed up by Danny in the form of a sort of contemporary *proverb*: 'People who go to the pub go to work.'

This example shows not the sort of strategies for struggling against the negative effects of globalism and neo-liberalism such as unemployment which I referred to above, but a strategy of adaptation and accommodation to the realities of unemployment (and of survival, as I said earlier), which includes accepting and taking on the theme of 'flexibility' from neo-liberal economic discourse, and appropriating it within a technically illegal but rational and reasonable strategy for getting work and money.

Global cartographies

My next example is based upon an ethnographic study by Gille (2000), and one aim as I said earlier is to suggest through analysis of extracts from her data how a more systematic and detailed treatment of discourse might contribute to the sort of 'global ethnography' she is carrying out. Gille's study is of a local political struggle over the building of a hazardous waste incinerator in Hungary, in which both sides sought to draw upon global forces and resources. This is an interesting example of how local actors actively take advantage of new possibilities created by changing relations of scale in developing and pursuing their own strategies for change on a local level.

The village of Garé in southern Hungary had experienced a process of decline since around 1960 connected with the introduction of cooperative agriculture. The government's policy was to 'emaciate' small rural communities to encourage people to migrate to the cities where there was a shortage of labour, by measures such as amalgamating agricultural cooperatives and reducing the number of villages with their own local councils. Garé was fused with the neighbouring village of Szalánta, in earlier times a smaller and less important village, which took over its administration. From 1978, the Budapest Chemical Works (BCW) began dumping highly toxic chemical waste in the vicinity of Garé, and when the village regained its independence after 1989, it was faced with a large dump of hazardous waste which was damaging the soil and causing health problems.

The village wanted the waste to be disposed of, but the state was unable to force BCW to act. Garé's leadership took the initiative and approached BCW with the proposal to build an incinerator (a move perceived by many of its inhabitants as also a way of turning the tables economically on Szalánta). Meanwhile BCW became a minority shareholder with a French state firm EMC Services in a new venture called Hungaropec, producing a partnership which would have been unthinkable before 1989 between an industrial firm, a relatively large Western company and a small village. One thing the example shows is how local actors can now bypass the national level (and the state) and form links or networks across national boundaries.

The wider context for this case was changes in the global waste incineration industry. The production of hazardous industrial waste keeps increasing year by year, and incineration is a cost-effective way of disposing of it. But incineration itself causes damage to health and environment, and pressure has built up, especially in more prosperous Western countries, to control the growth of the incineration industry. Many companies have responded by exporting the disposal of waste to areas of the world where regulations are less stringent, including Central and Eastern Europe. The village of Szalánta opposed the Garé incinerator on health and environmental grounds, and became the centre of an alliance against it which included local villages and towns and the Hungarian Greens, as well as competitors of Hungaropec in the waste incineration industry.

Gille observes that 'it is not only funds, people, and information that cross borders in [the] greening of civil society, but also discourses'. The political struggle around the Garé incinerator is in part a discursive struggle. Gille notes that this is not just a matter of either side drawing selectively from available Western discourses (though this is precisely what they do), but also an active process on both sides of engaging in 'cognitive cartography', being 'cognitive mapmakers', and producing their own representations of the world, of the relationship between East and West and between local and global. This discursive process is, she suggests, 'right in the centre of the political action'. As is typically the case in 'global ethnography' however, while she recognizes the importance of discourse in this political struggle, she does not carry out any form of textual analysis. I want to indicate how textual analysis can help to clarify the discursive character of the political struggle.

One can see 'cognitive cartography' working as a textual process in a brochure produced by Hungaropec. Its cover visually conveys the story which the company wants to tell ('We have a global solution to a local problem'): a bird's-eye view of an ECM incinerator in France is superimposed upon a map of the district which is filled with barrels of waste. The first two paragraphs (in Gille's translation) are as follows:

> In the vicinity of Garé, there was a significant amount of industrial waste deposited in accordance with the designation of location and prescriptions of the authorities. The long-term presence of these wastes may endanger the soil, the flora and fauna, agricultural production, the ground- and drinking-water supplies, and indirectly people's health. For this reason it is justified and necessary to eliminate and neutralize the wastes stored here, and to re-establish the cleanliness of the environment in the long run.
>
> Hungary, like her Eastern neighbours, was characterized by the dumping of the hazardous by-products of industry, that is by 'sweeping the problem under the rug' due to the incorrect industrial policy of the past decades, while in Western European countries with a developed industry and with an ever higher concern about the environment the most widely accepted solution has been the utilization of industrial wastes by incineration, which is already applied in numerous densely populated areas of Western Europe (Switzerland, the Ruhr, the vicinity of Lyon, Strasbourg, etc.).
>
> (Gille 2000: 252–3)

The cartographic process Gille calls 'cognitive' is also discursive, a matter of how discourses of spatial and scalar relations are developed and deployed as elements of the strategies of the two sides, and these discourses are concretely developed or 'textured' (Fairclough 2003) in texts like this one. The discourse in this case opposes East to West, associates the East with the past and with economic and ecological failure ('incorrect industrial policy', 'sweeping the problem' (of waste) 'under the rug'), and associates the West with economic and ecological success ('developed industry', 'concern about the environment', and a 'solution' to the problem of waste). By implication the West can provide solutions to the problems which the East has inherited as a legacy of past failure – specifically, there is a Western solution to the local problem of Garé, the solution of incineration, which is the 'most widely accepted solution' in Western Europe.

The first paragraph is an *argument* which legitimizes the disposal of the waste dumped in the area of Garé, with the opening sentence stating the facts (first premise), the second sentence claiming that the waste is potentially dangerous (second premise) and the third sentence very explicitly ('For this reason it is justified and necessary') deriving a conclusion from these premises. The statement of the facts in the first sentence is in the form of a passive sentence (a sentence in the *passive voice* with the verb is 'was . . . deposited') without an *agent*, so there is no direct attribution of responsibility (Fairclough 2003: 145–50). But the prepositional-phrase *adjunct* ('in accordance with the designation of location and prescriptions of the authorities') includes a *nominalization* ('the designation of location and prescriptions of the authorities') of what might otherwise have been a sentence (e.g. 'the authorities designated a location and prescribed ways of disposing of the waste') which includes an agent, 'the authorities', so there is an indirect (and vague) attribution of responsibility to them. The absence of direct attribution of responsibility, the vagueness of 'the authorities', and the abstract and opaque nominalization are noteworthy given BCW's own involvement in and responsibility for dumping the waste, which could also reflect badly on the successor company Hungaropec. We might say that BCW's responsibility is hidden beneath this obfuscating language. The second sentence is interesting in terms of its *modality* (Fairclough 2003: 165–71), given the claims that have been made about actual damage to the environment and health; this is a very cautious claim ('may endanger') with weak *epistemic modality* ('possibility') about possible 'long-term' future 'danger' (not even 'damage').

The second paragraph consists of a single complex sentence divided into two contrastively related parts: the temporal conjunction 'while' combines the sense of 'at the same time as' and the sense of 'on the other hand'. This is where the opposition between East (first part of the sentence) and West (second part of the sentence) is textured or textually constituted. The opposition includes an opposition between what are represented as the failed and denigrated practice of 'dumping' and the successful and virtuous practice of 'incineration'. As this formulation suggests, *evaluation* is a significant feature of this paragraph (Fairclough 2003: 171–90). The part of the sentence that describes waste-disposal in the East includes several expressions which *connote* ('dumping', 'sweeping the problem under the rug') or denote ('incorrect') negative values. Conversely, the part of the sentence that describes waste-disposal in the West involves several positive *value assumptions* which more implicitly convey a positive evaluation of policies: having a 'developed industry', having 'an ever higher concern about the environment', 'utilizing' industrial wastes (rather than just disposing of them) and having a solution which has been extensively 'applied' are all implicit 'goods' (Fairclough 2003: 55–8). We can see a process of value transfer going on here: by positioning 'incineration' within a context of positive evaluations, the authors also imply that it is a 'good', and more specifically that it fits in with 'an ever higher concern about the environment', i.e. that it is an environmentally friendly solution. This is of course highly controversial, as the Garé case indicates.

Both sides in this dispute selectively recontextualize 'Western' discourse. In the case of the Hungaropec text, we can identify in the second paragraph a narrative of the failures of past economic and environmentalist policies which is familiar from the discourse of 'transition', as well as a trace of a somewhat tame environmentalist discourse ('concern about the environment' is rather low-key). The opponents of the incinerator on the other hand represent the West (including the EU) as off-loading their own problems of waste disposal on the East by encouraging the development of the incineration industry and exporting some of its own hazardous waste to the East for incineration. Rather than representing the proposed incinerator as a Western solution to local problems attributable to the failures of the Eastern past, there is a *narrative* of continuity between current policies and the policies of the past, including the decision in favour of a permanent dump at Garé which was made by a socialist government in 1980:

> A decision made by the State Committee of Planning in 1980 cannot be put into effect against the will of the region's taxpaying citizens . . . Once already there was a bad decision made without us; let's not let another bad decision be made again [but] a decision based on consensus.
>
> (Gille 2000: 257)

In this quotation from a pamphlet produced by the Green Circle of the Hungarian city of Pécs there is an implication that current proposals amount to implementing the 1980 decision and that the current decision-making process is not much different from and just as undemocratic as before 1990. An opposition is set up between undemocratic decision-making on the one hand and 'the will of the region's taxpaying citizens' and 'a decision based on consensus' on the other. The selective appropriation of Western discourses by the opponents of the incinerator includes Western Green discourses appertaining to waste and incineration which represent incineration itself as a menace to public health and the environment, as well as discourses of 'ecological colonization' and 'environmental racism' (the charge of 'environmental racism' is made with reference to the heterogeneous population of the area, which includes Croats, Germans and Romanis). It also includes the European democratic discourse illustrated in the extract. Gille notes in this connection that 'democracy and especially local autonomy are the key arguments of the Greens [and] the only positive connotation of ''Europe'' that they acknowledge. This value preference may even take precedence over their environmental principles.'

This example illustrates deterritorialization and 'glocalization'. For the residents of Garé, local memories and resentments about the past and the village's loss of status, memories of the 'good old days' and the wish to restore the village's standing, were combined with the presence of a Hungaropec office in the village, the attempt of the company to portray itself as 'one of the villagers', and its use of media (locally organized exhibitions, a local newspaper which the company set up) to popularize the plan for an incinerator. In this way the lives of people in this small village have been 'glocalized', and this is discursively rationalized as the village's 'insertion into the bloodstream of Europe'. For the people opposing the incinerator, concerns about agriculture and tourism and distaste for the 'to-the-future-via-waste-business' path of transition and the dirty business of incineration ('dirty' also in a moral sense – they consider that Garé was 'bribed') were combined with the (mediated) global connections and discourses which the national and regional Greens brought to the campaign against the incinerator, including Western discourses which understood being European in terms of 'environmentalism', democratic values which emphasized that the 'will' of local people should determine the direction of change, and resistance to racism.

We can begin to see elements of the dialectic of particularism and universalism which I referred to earlier and the effects of contemporary globalization on the forms it takes, though these will be clearer in my next example. There is a crucial discursive 'moment' in the dialectic between particularism and universalism: when local and particular events and struggles are construed in terms of recontextualized discourses which are dominant or at least salient at a 'higher' scale, this constitutes a step towards the universalization of such events and struggles – for instance, construing the concrete and particular events and actions of this struggle as instances of 'the will of citizens' or 'ecological colonization' is itself a form of cartography, for it maps the particular onto the universal and the universal onto the particular. It is for instance construing this particular project to build an incinerator as 'another instance' of 'ecological colonization' and thus universalizing the particular in a way which can yield local strategic advantage.

The character of the alliances on each side of the struggle is also of interest in this respect. On the side of supporters of the incinerator, there is a novel and on the face of it incongruous alliance between a tiny village with just over 300 inhabitants, the Hungarian industrial company (BCW) responsible for polluting it, and a relatively powerful Western company (EMC Services). On the side of the opponents, 'the composition of the public which participated in the Garé case was unusual. An elected mayor was the key organizer of a large social coalition of local NGOs, community groups, economic groups (agricultural, tourism and other local and regional associations and chambers), professional NGOs (like a public interest environmental law firm, EMLA, which undertook the legal representation) and eventually, political parties as well' (UNECE 2000). Such networks of disparate groups, organizations and agencies are increasingly characteristic of such struggles, and they link not only different local groups and interests but also different scales (local, regional, national, European – not only EMC, but also European Greens through their links with local and regional Greens), and are a significant mechanism in contemporary forms of the dialectic of particular and universal.

Globalization of a local environmentalist campaign: Ma Ta Phut

My final example concerns a campaign against the construction of a coal-powered power station in the industrial district of Ma Ta Phut (sometimes also called in English 'Map Ta Phut') in Thailand. Ma Ta Phut is an industrial zone in Rayong province about 140 miles from the capital Bangkok. Originally a fishing and agricultural community, it was designated by the government in the 1970s as the site for Thailand's petrochemical and heavy industries, and there are now over 100 factories. These produce large quantities of hazardous waste much of which is not properly disposed of, and industrial accidents and pollution have had serious effects on the environment and the health of the local population. A joint press release by Greenpeace Southeast Asia, Campaign for Alternative Industry Network and Global Community Monitor in October 2005 about a report they had jointly produced ('Thailand's Air : Toxic Cocktail – Exposing Unsustainable Industries and the case of community-right-to-know') claimed that 'air test results prove people in Rayong province are breathing toxic chemicals from industry that are 60 to over 3,000 times higher than health standards in developed nations' and that 'Ma Ta Phut's toxic cocktail threatens the nation's health'.

Work on the power station began in 2003 and it is due to be completed in 2006. It is being built by a consortium called BLCP Power. The shareholders in that company are the Thai groups Banpu and Loxley, and the UK utility Power-Gen. Each of these three companies has a 30 per cent stake. The remaining 10 per cent is held by mining group, RTZ-CRA, which supplies the plant with Australian coal. PowerGen act as plant operators. The finance is being provided by the Japanese Bank for International Cooperation, the Asian Development Bank, and a range of Thai and foreign private banks including the ANZ Bank of Australia.

Much of the information available in English about opposition to the power station comes from Greenpeace, which is, according to the Greenpeace International website (as of 10 February 2006), a 'global organization' which 'focuses on the most crucial worldwide threats to our planet's biodiversity and environment'. I want to begin by considering how Greenpeace represents the campaign against the power station, looking at a Greenpeace Australia 'briefing' issued in October 2005 (for reasons of space I have omitted some parts which mainly elaborate on Australian exports of coal – omissions are indicated as '(. . .)').

Map Ta Phut: a new market for Australian coal

How Australian coal and Australian banks fuel climate change and impact on local communities in Thailand

Despite the reality of climate change being already upon us, Australia is increasing exports of climate changing coal and, with the financial assistance of Australian banks like ANZ, addicting more developing countries to the fuel. In 2006, exports of Australian coal will begin to the new Map Ta Phut ('*ma ta put*') power plant in Thailand. These will be the first regular shipments of Australian coal to Thailand, opening a new market for Australian coal producers and further cementing coal dependency in Southeast Asia. Greenpeace is working with groups near Map Ta Phut and in the Hunter Valley to protest against the project from both ends and protect communities and the climate. (. . .)

Map Ta Phut coal-fired power station

The Map Ta Phut power plant, currently being built south of Bangkok, is one of the largest Independent Power Producer investments in Southeast Asia, and the largest in Thailand. The first of Map Ta Phut's two 717MW units is due to begin producing electricity in October 2006, and the second in February 2007. The coal will be supplied by Rio Tinto from mines in the Hunter Valley, Queensland and Indonesia. The plant will consume over 4 million tonnes of coal and produce over 8 million tonnes of greenhouse pollution a year. (. . .)

Community opposition to coal and Map Ta Phut

Coal-fired power plants have faced strong community opposition in Thailand. Two large planned power plants – Hin Krut and Bo Nok – were stopped in May 2002. Map Ta Phut is also strongly opposed by local communities. The power plant is the culmination of years of dispossession of local people. The industrial estate in which it will be built – also called Map Ta Phut – was compulsorily acquired 25 years ago after many community members refused to sell their land. There was a long campaign against the decision during which community members were harassed. The estate now houses 60 industrial plants including Thailand's largest petrochemical plants.

The Map Ta Phut power plant will make conditions for the local communities even worse.

At an April 2005 protest outside CLP's Annual General Meeting in Hong Kong, community leader Charoen Detkhum, a fruit and vegetable farmer from the district, said *'the construction of BLCP [Map Ta Phut] has caused water pollution, the land reclamation causes coastal erosion and damages to the marine environment severely affecting the local fishery, livelihood and health of local communities'*.

Thailand is already suffering from climate change

Thailand is in the grip of a drought affecting 63 of the country's 76 provinces and blamed by some scientists on climate change.

Rising sea levels could impact on Bangkok and other low-lying coastal areas. Communities already suffering from the effects of climate change have joined with Map Ta Phut communities to oppose the new coal plant.

Piyaphum Kanchanacharoen, a farmer from north east Thailand, joined Charoen Detkhum at the CLP AGM protest and told of how climate change is already impacting his livelihood: *'production from the farm has decreased significantly . . . there is not enough water to do farming. Cows have no fresh grass to eat and no milk produced from them'*.

Sustainable alternatives to Map Ta Phut

While Thailand's greenhouse emissions are small compared to industrialised countries, CO_2 emissions doubled from 1990 to 2001. Moreover, Thailand's energy intensity and carbon intensity levels increased over the past 15 years – it now takes more energy to produce a unit of wealth. If Thailand continues to rely on fossil fuels, this can only worsen.

Alternatives do exist. The Thai Ministry of Energy estimates that Thailand has about 14,000MW of renewable energy resources, including modern biomass, solar, wind and small hydro resources, compared to a total installed capacity of 23,000MW10. Currently only 622MW is exploited.

A clean energy revolution

With government and investor support, clean energy resources such as wind, solar, bioenergy and energy efficiency have the potential to power the globe without causing climate change. They can replace Australia's export coal industry and speed up Thailand's development in an ecologically and socially sustainable manner.

(Greenpeace Australia 2005)

The first obvious point is that Greenpeace represents the issue of the Ma Ta Phut power station as linked to the issue of Australian coal exports (Australia is the biggest exporter of coal in the world), and both of these as linked to the issue of 'climate change'. If you look at the Greenpeace International website you will find a list of several campaigning activities under 'What we do' (including 'Save our seas' and 'Protecting forests', and 'Stopping climate change'), and the Ma Ta Phut campaign is included under 'Stopping climate change'. We can see the involvement of Greenpeace and other trans-national campaign groups as contributing to the universalization of this particular campaign through representing it in terms of the environmentalist discourse of 'climate change', and we might say subsuming it within that discourse so that the specific features of this particular case are backgrounded. The struggle 'finds its place' within a global classification of environmental issues, and a global campaigning agenda.

A second connected point is that Greenpeace represents itself as 'working with' local groups, as part of a coalition, and as fulfilling a coordinating role between different campaigns, in this case the campaign against the power station and the Australian campaign against coal exports ('Greenpeace is working with groups near Map Ta Phut and in the Hunter Valley to protest against the project from both ends and protect communities and the climate'). Notice the expressions which are *coordinated* together at the end of this sentence ('protest against the project', 'protect communities', '[protect] the climate'). They are brought into a *relation of equivalence*, and *classified* as co-existing elements of Greenpeace's campaigning activity: the relation of equivalence textures together the particular (the protest against the power station) and the universal (protecting communities, protecting the climate).

A third point is that a relationship is textured between two targets of trans-national campaigning organizations such as Greenpeace, threats to the environment (climate change in this case) and, by implication, global capitalism. The text focuses on the responsibility of Australian industry and finance for regional climate change ('How Australian coal and Australian banks fuel climate change'), and it represents their activities metaphorically through the *metaphor* of drug-dealing, 'addicting more developing countries' to coal and creating 'coal dependency'. It also represents the amount of coal which will be consumed as directly correlating with the amount of pollution: 'The plant will consume over 4 million tonnes of coal and produce over 8 million tonnes of greenhouse pollution a year.' There seems to be an *intertextual* allusion here to conventional representations in economic discourse of the equation between the raw materials consumed and the power produced, but with an environmentalist inflection which represents the 'product' as pollution.

The fourth point is that the plan to construct the power station and local opposition to it are located within a *narrative* which links the establishment and growth of the industrial estate to a history of local opposition and resistance, as well as opposition elsewhere in the country to coal-fired power stations (the first paragraph of the section 'Community opposition to coal and Map Ta Phut'). This paragraph also includes a recontextualized statement by a community leader and farmer from the Ma Ta Phut area about the economic, environmental and health effects of the industrial estate, and there is another recontextualized statement in the following section by a farmer on the effects of climate change on farming. Both are factual statements which give concrete and specific information about effects. They are both focused upon the particular and they do not universalize it; it is the Greenpeace text which maps the particular onto the universal by framing the statements in terms of the discourse of community politics (there is 'community opposition') and the discourse of climate change.

There is another point about the section on climate change which concerns *modality*. The headline ('Thailand is already suffering from climate change') makes a categorical assertion about climate change in Thailand which contrasts with the opening sentence, which claims that drought is blamed on climate change 'by some scientists'. The third sentence has a subject ('Communities already suffering from the effects of climate change') which includes an embedded non-finite clause ('suffering from the effects of climate change') that triggers the *assumption* that there are communities already suffering from climate change. Piyaphum Kanchanacharoen's statement is represented as a statement about 'how climate change is already impacting his livelihood' (though as I have pointed out he does not himself mention climate change), which again implies that climate change does impact his livelihood, and assumes that climate change is a fact. So there is a contradiction between climate change being asserted or assumed as fact, and being offered by 'some scientists' as a hypothetical explanation. This is quite typical of media coverage of environmental issues and communications by campaigning groups designed to be picked up by the media: the caution and circumspection that characterizes most scientific assessments gets lost in reports based upon them (Solin 2001). A final point is that the text connects the local issue and the global problem of climate change to the availability of an alternative strategy to develop 'clean energy resources'.

Overall, what is most striking about the text is the connections it makes, the 'cartographic' work it does to use Gille's metaphor. The map which is textured shows relations between global environmental crisis and global capitalism, between the specific local problem of the Ma Ta Phut power station and climate change in Thailand and climate change on a global scale ('the reality of climate change being already upon us'), between campaigns in different places (Thailand

and Australia), between the problems produced by existing energy strategies and the solution offered by an alternative strategy.

The coalition between local community groups around Ma Ta Phut and regional and global organizations has resulted in practical assistance for local campaigners, including the gathering of scientific evidence of pollution. A 'Thailand bucket brigade workshop' was held in Ma Ta Phut with the support of Greenpeace Southeast Asia and Campaign Alternative Industry Network and coordinated by Denny Larson from Global Community Monitor (GCM), USA, who created the 'bucket brigade' in 1995 (Global Community Monitor 2004). A 'bucket brigade' is a group of community residents who monitor the air around suspect industrial sites using a simple and cheap instrument (the 'bucket') for identifying and collecting 100 airborne chemicals, as well as collecting water and soil samples for analysis, and carrying out health surveys or collecting health records. Setting up a local 'bucket brigade' introduces a new technology and a new expert discourse which link Ma Ta Phut to the many other places across the globe where they have been introduced, and in this way contributes to universalizing the particular struggle.

The involvement of Greenpeace also opens up the possibility of the projection of particular issues and struggles through global media to a global public, which may transform them into global issues, through its high-profile media-oriented style of campaigning which often includes its 'flagship' *Rainbow Warrior*. Here is a press release by Greenpeace about a protest in Ma Ta Phut (Greenpeace International 2005):

Stop climate killing coal plants in Thailand: Greenpeace

Map Ta Phut, Thailand – with its flagship the Rainbow Warrior looking on, Greenpeace activists today climbed the loading crane of the BLCP coal plant at Map Ta Phut in Thailand and unfurled banners demanding the plant's immediate closure, calling on the Thai government to phase out coal power and to commit to renewable energy.

'The catastrophic droughts across Thailand this year cost the country US \$193 million – climate change is causing severe hardship here and across the Southeast Asia region and plants like BLCP are the main culprits,' said Greenpeace Southeast Asia's Energy spokesperson Tara Buakamsri from Map Ta Phut.

Greenpeace believes that the Thai government will not be able to deliver on its promise of an 8 per cent renewable energy target by 2011 as long as it continues to give the go-ahead to new coal-fired plants like BLCP.

'Climate change is a reality but so too are the solutions,' said Jean-François Fauconnier of Greenpeace International aboard the Rainbow Warrior.

'Wind, solar and modern biomass power are already big business not only in Europe but also in China. The potential in Thailand is equally huge.

'International financial institutions like the Asian Development Bank and the Japan Bank for International Cooperation should stop financing coal. They continuously talk up their support for renewables yet we've seen very little in the way of funds being re-directed towards alternatives. No more talk, it's time for action.'

The activity is part of an international protest by Greenpeace against new coal power plants. In Germany activists have been protesting since Monday on top of a cooling tower of the RWE energy company, Europe's biggest CO_2 polluter.

Greenpeace's flagship the Rainbow Warrior is in Bangkok on the Thailand leg of its 10-week Asia Energy Revolution Tour, exposing the impacts of climate change and promoting the uptake of renewable energy like wind and modern biomass. The tour started in Australia and will end in Thailand.

Greenpeace is an independent campaigning organization that uses non-violent creative confrontation to expose global environmental problems to drive solutions that are essential to a green and peaceful future.

This is a specifically Greenpeace action in support of Greenpeace 'demands' ('the plant's immediate closure', for 'the Thai government to phase out coal power and to commit to renewable energy') and the only campaigners mentioned are Greenpeace activists. The report again in various ways transcends the particularity of the controversy over and resistance to the Ma Ta Phut power station: it situates it within the wider issue of the effects of climate change (whose reality is assumed) not only in Thailand but also 'across the Southeast Asia region', and in relation to the 'alternative' of 'renewable energy' ('renewables'); and the protest action is represented as 'part of an international protest by Greenpeace against new power plants', and part of the Rainbow Warrior's 'Asia Energy Revolution Tour'. The particular case is used to add to the bigger picture and the bigger campaign, but in the process it is represented in a way which backgrounds its local character and roots, and we might say that it becomes just a 'token' of a 'type' of struggle.

The Ma Ta Phut case illustrates several interconnected tendencies: for a range of different general issues and problems to converge around particular local issues and struggles; for local community organizations and campaigns to cooperate increasingly on a regional scale; and for a range of different trans-national campaigning groups to become involved in particular local struggles. All of these tendencies are relevant to the dialectic of particular and universal, since they all contribute to embedding particular struggles within more general ones, to making available more general discursive and other resources for pursuing them, yet at the same time contributing to the possible reduction of their particular local content and force.

I have already illustrated these tendencies to a degree above, but let me add some more detail and illustration. An example of increasing cooperation on a regional scale is the 'People's Declaration Against Coal' which was signed in December 2005 in Thailand by Greenpeace and over twenty community organizations from Australia, the Philippines, Indonesia, Thailand and Hong Kong. The opening sentence is: 'We, the members of the communities hosting and threatened by coal-fired power plants in Asia, have come together today to claim our rights to clean air, water, soil and living space in our planet.' The Declaration claims that 'the use of coal for energy results in grave environmental, health and social problems the impacts of which fall most seriously on poor communities' especially in producing large quantities of 'the climate changing greenhouse gas called carbon dioxide', and that 'climate change is the most serious environmental threat facing the planet today'. Another example of regional cooperation is a lobby of the Executive Directors of the Asian Development Bank (ADB), which helped to finance the Ma Ta Phut power station, by community leaders from Thailand and the Philippines in December 2005 'to raise their concerns about ADB's involvement in coal-fired power plants' and urge them to stop supporting them. The Thai community leaders referred to the existing power station at Mae Moh as well as the one under construction at Ma Ta Phut.

With respect to trans-national campaigning groups, it is not only Greenpeace that has become involved in the Ma Ta Phut case, but also for instance the Blacksmith Institute (which monitors internationally cases of pollution and their environmental and health impact), Bankwatch (which monitors the activities of banks and financial institutions), the Campaign for Alternative Industry Network and Global Community Monitor. Their involvement is itself indicative of the range of general issues which arise in this particular case. These also include for instance water: Thailand has experienced major problems with drought, and there is a shortage of water as well as concern about the pollution of water. The power station bears upon both, because it is expected to add to water pollution, but also to the existing problem that water which is needed for farming and household uses is being diverted for industrial uses. A report on Global News Wire's Asia Africa Intelligence service in August 2005 reported that the Thai National Human Rights Commission had launched an inquiry into the government's solution to the Eastern water crisis 'after receiving complaints from locals that the scheme was violating their right to natural resources', referring to a government scheme under which 'large amounts of water are to be drawn from major rivers and irrigation dams to feed industrial estates'. The 'complaints' are reformulated as follows: 'The scheme sparked concerns among farmers and local residents that there would be insufficient water for agricultural and household uses.' Concrete and particular complaints about insufficient water are translated in the discourse of human rights into a 'violation' of the 'right to natural resources', another example of the universalization of the particular issue.

Conclusion

The examples I have discussed in this chapter have led us from the strategies of local agents in particular places for adapting to and gaining from change or averting negative effects of change, to the activities and strategies of trans-national activist organizations. The movement from the one to the other is not fortuitous, because contemporary globalization affects what I have referred to as the dialectic of the particular and the universal through a globalization of resources for local situated action by various means, including mediation and the mass media and the internet, and, paradoxical as it may seem, through drawing local strategists and trans-national activists together in the process of 'globalization from below'. The impetus for globalization from below comes from situated action in particular places, but through the dialectic of place and space these places are 'glocalized', so that resources for situated action are less and less purely local and increasingly global.

These tendencies have become increasingly clear in the chapter. My first example involved a local appropriation of a global discourse (specifically the theme of 'flexibility') which the people involved most probably picked up through the mass media. My second example showed both sides in a dispute over building a hazardous waste incinerator in Hungary entering into complex alliances with agencies at different scales and selectively drawing in different ways upon European discourses in developing their strategies. It was in my third example that we saw a coalition between local campaigners against the Ma Ta Phut power station and a trans-national activist organization (Greenpeace) as well as other local campaigns and East Asian regional organizations, in which the trans-national organization was clearly instrumental in construing the particular struggle in terms of a universal discourse of contesting 'climate change'.

Finally let me note the main features I have referred to in analysing extracts from texts: themes associated with discourses, explanation and legitimization, modality, evaluation and value assumptions, nominalization, passive voice, classification and relations of equivalence, metaphor, intertextual allusion and narrative.

7   Globalization, war and terrorism

In this chapter my focus will shift rather sharply, to violence, conflict and war, and particularly the 'war on terror'. In the Introduction I gave a brief rationale for including these themes in a book on globalization. President G.W. Bush, with the support of allies of the USA, declared the 'war on terror' in the wake of the attacks on the World Trade Center in New York and the Pentagon in Washington in September 2001. But rather than interpreting the 'war on terror' simply as a result of these attacks, we can interpret the attacks and their consequences as an important moment in a longer-term process of change in US military and security strategy, a gradual shift from 'soft' power (the capacity to shape opinion, interests and identities in favour of globalism) to 'hard' power (the massive use of economic and military force to compel compliance) in response to pressures on 'globalism' which began to build up from the mid-1990s (Steger 2005, Saul 2005, Pieterse 2004).

These pressures included economic crises in Asia and Latin America which led to widespread doubts about whether globalization in its globalist form was working, coupled with growing concern about the negative effects of this form of globalization (the increasing gap between rich and poor, the international debt crisis, the inequities of world trade), and an emerging international movement in opposition to it. The shift from 'soft' power to 'hard' power was already apparent during the Clinton administration, but it intensified with the rise to power of 'neo-conservatism' in the USA, particularly when G.W. Bush became President. Neo-conservatism has a continuing commitment to neo-liberalism and 'globalism', but combines with a willingness to use the USA's economic and military power, unilaterally if necessary, to preserve US global hegemony, which is seen as associated with successful pursuit of the 'globalist' agenda. The clearest expression of this strategic change is the US National Security Strategy of 2002 (Chomsky 2003). One aspect of these developments is that the view that globalization spells the end of the nation-state has been decisively rebutted in practice.

I shall begin the chapter by returning to the theme of continuity and change in globalist strategy and discourse (discussed in Chapter 3) and interpreting the strategic shift from 'soft' to 'hard' power and the associated discourse of the 'war on terror' as a change in the 'nexus' of strategies and discourses which globalism is a part of, and in that sense a further inflection in the trajectory of globalism itself. (On the concept of 'nexus' see Scollon and Scollon 2004, though my use of it is rather different from theirs.) I shall then review a number of central themes of the discourse of the 'war on terror', drawing particularly on Jackson (2005). The next section will focus on the US National Security Strategy, and more specifically I shall analyse an essay on the strategy by Condoleezza Rice, National Security Advisor and since 2005 Secretary of State in G.W. Bush's administration. Finally I shall discuss speeches by another important contributor to the change in security and military strategy and the discourse of the 'war on terror', the British Prime Minister Tony Blair.

Globalism, security strategy and the 'war on terror'

In Chapter 3, I discussed the continuity and change (or continuity through change) of globalist strategy and discourse with respect to the globalist response to the economic crisis of the late 1990s, and the convergence between globalism and the new strategy and discourse of development, with respect to the convergence of or 'nexus' between globalism and the strategy and discourse of the 'knowledge-based economy' (KBE). We can see the shift from 'soft power' to 'hard power' and the emergence of the discourse of the 'war or terror' as a further move in complexity of what can best be described as the emerging nexus of strategies (economic, political, development, security) and associated 'nodal' discourses (around each of which many other discourses cluster) including the discourses of globalism, the KBE, development and the 'war on terror'. This further move appertains specifically to mechanisms for disseminating and implementing the nexus of strategies, establishing military force as a means for imposing them where necessary.

The *selection* of the discourse of the 'war on terror' (recall the discussion of variation, selection and retention of discourses in Chapters 2 and 3) can be seen as largely motivated by the urgent need for the US government to legitimize the shift to 'hard power' in the face of considerable domestic and international opposition. It has also been effective in legitimizing a series of measures which have diminished legal and democratic rights: conditions of detention and mistreatment (including torture) of prisoners in violation of the Geneva Convention, the extended detention of terrorist suspects without trial, the 'extraordinary rendition' in secret of suspects to countries where legal rights are poorly respected or torture is routinely practised, the curtailment of freedom of speech, new methods of surveillance which have reduced the rights and privacy of citizens, and a more or less permanent state of emergency and state of alert in certain countries which is eating into the democratic fabric of people's lives (Ali and Barsamian 2005, Giroux 2004, Todorov 2005).

The *retention* or institutionalization of the discourse has been secured through many official mechanisms including anti-terrorist and security legislation and changes in regulations (such as those governing international travel), as well as through its effective dissemination across social fields and institutions and across national boundaries. It has been *operationalized* and implemented through for instance changes in military, security and intelligence apparatuses and modes of operation, and changes in procedures and practices in areas like covert surveillance, banking and international travel. The *dissemination* and *legitimization* of the discourse of the 'war on terror' has depended heavily upon the mass media and especially the global media industries. I have already touched upon the mediation of terrorism in Chapter 5, with particular respect to the question of 'distant suffering', referring to Chouliaraki's analysis of television coverage of the attacks on New York and Washington, and the beginnings of the discourse of 'war on terror'.

Terrorism itself has been described as an essentially communicational act in which 'the immediate human victims of violence are chosen randomly (targets of opportunity) or selectively (symbolic or representative targets) from a target population, and serve as message generators' (Schmid 1983). It depends on the compliance of global media networks to 'generate' the 'message' and to heighten awareness and induce fear. Terrorists operate with sophisticated media strategies: the al-Qaida attacks on New York and Washington were timed to reach the evening news bulletins (Lewis 2005). But counter-terrorism and the 'war on terror' also depend on the compliance of global media networks to 'generate messages', and operate with and depend upon sophisticated media strategies.

In Chapter 1, I distinguished five main ways in which discourse figures in processes of globalization on the basis of a review of some of the academic literature on globalization (readers can find a summary at the end of that chapter). My comments above on the legitimizing effects of the discourse of the 'war on terror' suggest that one motive for its selection is that it is rhetorically effective. But I think the discourse also has powerful ideological effects, in the sense that the declared objective of fighting and defeating terrorism can serve to obscure other objectives, including the pursuit of globalism by other means, the preservation and consolidation of US hegemony, opening up of new markets especially for American corporations, achieving American control over international oil supplies. And as I have indicated the discourse also has real constructive effects – it is operationalized and implemented in systems and institutions and ways of acting. There really *is* a war on terror.

And of course there really *is* terrorism, and there was terrorism before the 'war on terror' (Bjørgo 2005). Terrorism can be regarded as only one part of a more general and long-term shift in the character of violence and war, towards 'irregular warfare', which is linked to the growing invincibility of the big armies in open combat, and the consequent need of those who seek to oppose them to resort to irregular means. Irregular warfare includes terrorism, but also guerrilla warfare, jungle warfare, insurgency and counter-insurgency, espionage, underground forces and special forces (Saul 2005). As this list indicates, regular military forces have adapted their own strategies to deal with irregular warfare, using their increasing technological sophistication, and engaging in or sponsoring irregular warfare (including what can reasonably be called terrorism – see below) themselves.

Nevertheless, although terrorism is and has been a reality, we can say that constructive effects of the discourse of the 'war on terror' include 'terrorism' itself (Silke 2005): first, in the sense that it construes 'terrorism' in a particular way which includes and lumps together certain disparate forms of 'irregular' violence while excluding others (I shall go into details below) and second, in the sense that the operationalization and implementation of the discourse include military and other forms of action against 'terrorism' in this sense as a real 'object' and a unitary phenomenon, despite its disparate character, and in so doing help to construct it as a real 'object'. Thirdly, there is the sense that a significant part of contemporary 'terrorism' can be seen as produced by and as the effect of the war on terror. Putting the point differently, the war on terror was launched because according to the discourse of the 'war on terror' terrorism was a sufficiently potent and dangerous enemy to justify such a massive commitment of money and effort and blood. Arguably it wasn't, but now as an effect of the war and a reaction to the war, it increasingly is.

One question which is being increasingly asked is whether this strategic change corresponds to a new phase of imperialism (Ali and Barsamian 2005, Chomsky 2003, Pieterse 2004, Roy 2004). The US National Security Strategy is clear in its rejection of a return to a bipolar or multi-polar world, and in its commitment to preventing the development of any challenges to America's position as the world's sole 'super-power'. This strategy was being developed behind the scenes from shortly after the end of the Cold War – a Defence Policy Guidance which was leaked in 1992 and drafted by Paul Wolfowitz (who held office in the first G.W. Bush administration and is now President of the World Bank) included the statement that 'our strategy must now refocus on precluding the emergence of any future global competitor' (Pieterse 2005: 18). The USA is now clearly perceived by many people across the world as an imperial power, and its own increasing militarism and unilateralism has led to an increase in opposition, some of it violent, not only to its military dominance but also to its economic dominance and the strategy of 'globalism'. The attacks of 11 September 2001 were only the most dramatic expression of this development.

The discourse of the 'war on terror' would appear to have achieved global hegemony in the sense that it has won widespread acceptance throughout the world, as well as being extensively recontextualized, institutionalized and operationalized.

But the Iraq War has led to major challenges both to the discourse and to the strategy of America and its allies, through the discrediting of the reasons which were given for the invasion of Iraq and the subsequent failure of the USA and Britain to fulfil the promises they made about post-war Iraq, and their inability to achieve basic objectives such as a stable democratic political system. The strategy and discourse have been contested by alternative strategies (such as reviving the role of the United Nations as the main protagonist in solving problems of international security) and alternative discourses. Their hegemony has been seriously shaken, though not broken.

Main themes of the discourse of the 'war on terror'

I shall now give a general characterization of the discourse of the 'war on terror' in terms of a number of central *themes*, drawing particularly on Jackson (2005). Each of these themes has a cluster of arguments, narratives and discourses associated with it. They can be formulated as claims, rather like the claims in Steger's characterization of the discourse of globalism (see Chapter 3). They are:

- This is a new era, posing new threats, which requires new responses.
- America and its allies (and indeed 'civilization') face unprecedented risks and dangers which call for exceptional measures.
- Those who pose these risks and dangers are the forces of 'evil'.
- America and its allies are the forces of 'good', and their actions are informed by moral values.

A new era

In the wake of the attacks on New York and Washington in September 2001, it became a commonplace that 'things will never be the same again'. At first glance this is puzzling: terrorist attacks were not new and the horrific loss of innocent lives was not new – why then (in the words of US Attorney General John Ashcroft) was it that 'on September 11, the wheel of history turned, and the world will never be the same again' (25 October 2001)? One can point to the fact (as many did) that this was the first external attack on American soil since Pearl Harbor, and the symbolic significance of the attack being centred upon the World Trade Center, an icon of globalist capitalism and of the leading role of the USA within it. Here for instance is one of Bush's accounts (Bush 2001b):

> On September 11th, the enemies of freedom committed an act of war against our country. Americans have known wars – but for the past 136 years, they have been wars on foreign soil, except for one Sunday in 1941. Americans

have known the casualties of war – but not at the center of a great city on a peaceful morning. Americans have known surprise attacks – but never before on thousands of civilians. All of this was brought upon us in a single day – and night fell on a different world, a world where freedom itself is under attack.

(20 September 2001)

Bush is implicitly arguing from cause to effect: because of the nature of the 'act of war' (on American soil, in an urban centre, a surprise attack on civilians), there is now 'a different world'. Yet the *argument* is *fallacious*. This attack was by its very nature a serious act of terrorism and a morally indefensible indiscriminate assault on innocent civilians. But nothing about the nature or circumstances of the attack make it inherently epoch-making or epoch-changing. There have been many previous terrorist attacks on American targets, and al-Qaida has been targeting America since 1991, so despite repeated claims about a 'new threat' and 'new dangers', the attack of September 2001 could perfectly well be seen as an event (though still an exceptionally dramatic and bloody one) in an established process. This attack became epoch-changing only because it was self-consciously represented in this way by politicians and officials with the power, partly through their capacity to shape the global media agenda, to make it so. This was an important *legitimizing* move: if we are in a new era, 'a different world', if the 'wheel of history' has turned, then old truths and assumptions may no longer apply, we can expect things to be radically different, and this expectation can give politicians the latitude to make them radically different.

Risks, dangers and exceptional measures

What makes this a new era in military and security terms is the unprecedented risks and dangers which face the 'civilized world', and which are constituted by 'terrorism'. Here again is Attorney General John Ashcroft (Ashcroft 2001):

The men and women of justice and law enforcement are called on to combat a terrorist threat that is both immediate and vast; a threat that resides here, at home, but whose supporters, patrons and sympathizers form a multinational network of evil. The attacks of September 11 were acts of terrorism against America orchestrated and carried out by individuals living within our borders. Today's terrorists enjoy the benefits of our free society even as they commit themselves to our destruction. They live in our communities – plotting, planning and waiting to kill Americans again. They have crossed the Rubicon of terror with the use of biological agents . . . terrorists . . . are now poisoning our communities with Anthrax.

The panic about Anthrax poisoning was effective, if briefly, in contributing to a climate of public fear in the USA which helped to legitimize both military intervention abroad and a virtual state of emergency domestically, including 'exceptional' measures notably contained in Patriot Act (2001) – a title which suggests that any dissent is unpatriotic. The Act increased the powers of surveillance of government agents, including access to personal (bank, medical, educational, etc.) records, electronic surveillance (including email), tapping telephone calls, detention of immigrants who are suspected of supporting terrorism without charge, deportation of immigrants who raise money for designated or suspected terrorist organizations, and powers for the Secretary of State to designate any foreign or domestic group as 'terrorist' without appeal (Giroux 2004: 8–9). These powers have been widely seen as a major attack on civil liberties.

But the sort of language that Ashcroft uses also contributes to generating a climate of fear. The *narrative* of terrorism which Ashcroft constructs is not new in the USA: in the McCarthyite period of the 1950s, communism was represented in much the same terms as a sinister domestic conspiracy of people ('the enemy within') waiting to strike, taking advantage of America's 'free society' and backed by an international network ('a multinational network of evil'). Ashcroft speaks of 'a terrorist threat that is both immediate and vast', which strikes me as a scare-mongering *overstatement*. The threat from terrorism is not 'vast' in comparative terms (e.g. if we compare the relatively few people who have died or been injured in terrorist attacks with the number who are murdered or die in road accidents), and there is little evidence in the four years since 2001 of it being 'immediate' for people living in America. There is also overstatement in the claim that 'they live in our communities – plotting, planning and waiting to kill Americans again', which exaggerates the 'internal threat' in an alarmist and indeed paranoid way. And the few claimed instances of traces of Anthrax in the mail by no stretch of the imagination amount to terrorists 'poisoning our communities with Anthrax'. Ashcroft's speech is typical of many exaggerated claims by influential public figures, which one can interpret as attempts to induce fear in order to legitimize policies and actions which would otherwise be unpalatable for many Americans.

The forces of evil

President Bush in one of his first statements on the 11 September attacks stated that: 'Today, our nation saw evil, the very worst of human nature', and referred to the attacks as 'evil acts'. Bush has also christened the 'rogue states' which are claimed or implied to support terrorism the 'axis of evil', evoking the 'axis' of powers which the USA, Britain and their allies fought against in the Second World War, and echoing Ronald Regan's representation of the Soviet Union and its allies as the 'evil empire'. Representing the enemy as 'evil' has a history in the USA, but it also reflects the unprecedented influence of fundamentalist

Christianity on the Bush presidency – the contemporary emergence of religious fundamentalism is by no means solely an Islamic phenomenon, as it is often represented. The religious dimension of the discourse of the 'war on terror' is even clearer in Bush's use of the Biblical expression 'the evil one' (the Devil) in referring both to Osama bin Laden and the terrorists ('the evil ones have roused a mighty nation, and they will pay a serious price', 29 November 2001).

Branding the enemy as 'evil' can be an effective way of legitimizing extreme measures. One cannot negotiate with 'evil'. One can only seek to eradicate it, and acting on the side of 'good' is a guarantee that whatever measures are taken, however unpalatable and with whatever unfortunate consequences, are for the best. It is pointless to try to understand 'evil', or to seek explanations if not justifications for it. It makes no sense to treat 'the evil ones' as rational human beings who act on the basis of reason to achieve objectives (however much one might disagree with them). Politics and diplomacy are irrelevant, violence can only be met with violence, the only possible response to the evil of terrorism is war. Historical analysis is also irrelevant – no past wrongs or injustices can explain 'evil' (Jackson 2005: 66–70).

Moral values and the forces of good

Blair claimed at the time of the Kosovo War that 'this is a just war, based not on any territorial ambitions but on values' (1999, see my discussion of his speeches below). From the Gulf War of 1991 through the Kosovo War of 1999 to the Afghan War of 2001 and the Iraq War of 2003, the claim that the forces of intervention were the forces of good has been tied in with the claim that they were acting on the basis of moral values. Bush (Bush 2003) indeed has recently situated these more recent interventions in a long-term narrative of the USA as a morally driven force for good:

> As a people dedicated to civil rights, we are driven to defend the human rights of others. We are the nation that liberated continents and concentration camps. We are the nation of the Marshall Plan, the Berlin Airlift and the Peace Corps. We are the nation that ended the oppression of Afghan women, and we are the nation that closed the torture chambers of Iraq.
>
> (21 May 2003)

Characteristically, allies (e.g. in the Second World War) are 'forgotten'.

Blair has developed a 'third way' position, on an international scale, that the pursuit of national self-interest and internationally common self-interest is best served by the furtherance of moral values through action on the part of the 'international community'. The approach is neatly summed up in his claim that 'values and interests merge'. But especially after the Iraq War this claim seems like an attempt to provide moral legitimacy for the pursuit of particular national interests. Indeed, it is difficult to see that how the Iraq War has on balance led to an increase in moral good: it has removed from power a vicious and brutal dictator who was opposed by many of us over twenty years ago when he had American and British support, but it has led to death, injury and destitution for many Iraqi civilians, the torture of Iraqis by the 'forces of good', the threat of civil war and an increase in international terrorism.

The National Security Strategy

The US National Security Strategy (2002) is germane to globalization in two central and interconnected respects. The first appertains to what we might call military globalization: the strategy asserts the global military hegemony of the USA, and also asserts that the USA will deter any other country from a military build-up which might challenge this hegemony. This amounts to a bid for permanent military hegemony. The second appertains to economic and political globalization: the USA will use its 'unparalleled military strength' and 'great economic and political influence' to 'create a balance of power that favors human freedom: conditions in which all nations and all societies can choose for themselves the rewards and challenges of political and economic liberty'. This will necessitate 'fighting terrorists and tyrants'. Favouring 'human freedom' amounts to allowing all nations to choose 'economic liberty' (which presupposes that this is the choice all nations will make if they are allowed to). As this formulation begins to indicate, and as the document as a whole makes clear, the strategy includes a commitment to the globalist agenda of spreading neo-liberal 'free markets and free trade' across the world, and the assumption that democracy is their inherent corollary. The 'war on terror' is construed as a war without time limit which is the necessary consequence of the objective of creating 'a balance of power that favors freedom', and its success is represented as depending upon the continuing hegemony of the USA.

Here is an extract from Rice's essay (Rice 2002, reprinted in Stelzer 2004), with omissions indicated by bracketed dots (. . .):

> Perhaps most fundamentally, 9/11 crystallized our vulnerability. It also threw into sharp relief the nature of the threats we face today. Today's threats come less from massing armies than from small, shadowy bands of terrorists – less from strong states than from weak or failed states. And after 9/11, there is no longer any doubt that today America faces an existential threat to our security (. . .)
>
> President Bush's new National Security Strategy offers a bold vision for protecting our nation that captures today's new realities and new opportunities.

It calls on America to use our position of unparalleled strength and influence to create a balance of power that favours freedom. (. . .) This strategy has three pillars:

- We will defend the peace by opposing and preventing violence by terrorists and outlaw regimes.
- We will preserve the peace by fostering an era of good relations among the world's great powers.
- We will extend the peace by seeking to extend the benefits of freedom and prosperity across the globe.

Defending our nation from its enemies is the first and fundamental commitment of the federal government. And as the world's most powerful nation, the United States has a special responsibility to help make the world more secure. (. . .)

We will break up terror networks, hold to account nations that harbour terrorists, and confront aggressive tyrants holding or seeking nuclear, chemical or biological weapons that might be passed onto terrorist allies. These are different faces of the same evil (. . .) The only path to safety is to confront both terrorists and tyrants . . .

(. . .) as a matter of common sense, the United States must be prepared to take action, where necessary, before threats have fully materialized.

Pre-emption is not a new concept. There has never been a moral or legal requirement that a country wait to be attacked before it can address existential threats. (. . .)

To support all these means of defending the peace, the United States will build and maintain twenty-first century military forces that are beyond challenge.

We will seek to dissuade any potential adversary from pursuing a military build-up in the hope of surpassing, or equalling, the power of the United States and our allies. (. . .)

Today, there is an increasing awareness – on every continent – of a paradigm of progress, founded on political and economic liberty. The United States, our NATO allies, our neighbours in the Western Hemisphere, Japan, and our other friends and allies in Asia and Africa all share a broad commitment to democracy, the rule of law, a market-based economy, and open trade.

In addition, since September 11 all the world's great powers see themselves as falling on the same side of a profound divide between the forces of chaos and order, and they are acting accordingly. (. . .)

This confluence of common interests and increasingly common values creates a moment of enormous opportunities. Instead of repeating the historic pattern where great power rivalry exacerbates local conflicts, we can use great power cooperation to solve conflicts (. . .)

The United States will fight poverty, disease and oppression because it is the right thing to do – and the smart thing to do. We have seen how poor states can become weak or even failed states, vulnerable to hijacking by terrorist networks (. . .)

We will seek to bring every nation into an expanding circle of development. Earlier this year the President proposed a 50 per cent increase in US development assistance. But he also made it clear that new money means new terms. The new resources will only be available to countries that work to govern justly, invest in the health and education of their people, and encourage economic liberty.

(. . .) what the President has called the non-negotiable demands of human dignity – free speech, equal justice, respect for women, religious tolerance, and limits on the power of the State.

These principles are universal (. . .) From Cairo and Ramallah to Tehran and Tashkent, the President has made clear that values must be a vital part of our relationship with other countries. (. . .) We reject the condescending view that freedom will not grow in the soil of the Middle East – or that Muslims somehow do not share in the desire to be free. The celebrations we saw on the streets of Kabul proved otherwise. (. . .)

We do not seek to impose democracy on others, we seek only to help create conditions in which people can claim a freer future for themselves. We recognize as well that there is no 'one size fits all' answer. (. . .)

Germany, Indonesia, Japan and the Philippines, South Africa, South Korea, Taiwan and Turkey show that freedom manifests itself differently around the globe – and that new liberties can find an honoured place amid ancient traditions.

Rice claims that '9/11 crystallized' the 'vulnerability' of America, and made clear the 'existential threat' to its 'security', coming not from 'massing armies' or the 'great powers' (between which there is now 'cooperation', no longer 'rivalry') but from 'terrorists' and 'weak or failed states' ('vulnerable to hijacking by terrorist networks') and 'outlaw regimes' and 'tyrants'. The claims that there is a threat to American security and that America must consequentially protect itself are crucial *premises* in the *argument* for an interventionist, preventive and unilateralist military strategy. The USA is indeed vulnerable to 'irregular warfare' as a series of attacks on American military and official personnel outside the USA over a number of years have shown. Imperial powers always have been. But the claim of an 'existential threat' to the security of by far the most powerful country on earth is surely an *overstatement* – except in the sense that we are all subject to 'existential threat' in the age of nuclear and biological weapons. One can see the rhetorical motivation for the overstatement: establishing that the USA is subject to a threat which is both serious and exceptional is crucial to legitimize its aggressive military action abroad and the constant state of alert and curtailment of civil and democratic rights at home.

'Terrorists' and 'tyrants' are 'different faces of the same evil' which will both be 'confronted'. The world is implicitly divided into good and evil (another, over-lapping, division which is often drawn is between 'civilization' and 'barbarity'), an example of the important textual process of constructing (or 'texturing') *classifi-cations*, a binary division in this case (Fairclough 2003). It is taken for granted that America is on the side of good (and 'civilization') – this is implicit in America undertaking to defend, preserve and extend 'the peace', recognizing its 'special responsibility', acting upon the basis of 'values' and 'ideals', and so forth. This Manichean divide does not allow for intermediate categories, grey areas, or the actual complexities of the world – people or countries are either good or they are evil, one of the two.

And as I argued above the substitution of religious categories ('good' and 'evil') for political categories obviates any need to analyse or explain the division, to go into its history, to seek to understand the reasons and objectives of those who are represented as threatening America, to treat them as rational human beings which of course they are, or to consider how America's own actions and policies over many years relate to the perceived 'existential threat'. With respect to the ration-ality of al-Qaida and other terrorist organizations, it is well known that what initi-ally sparked its campaign against America was the establishment of American bases in Saudi Arabia at the time of the Gulf War. Terrorism is a resort of the weak to fight the strong, and much of the support for terrorism since the early 1990s has come from people who see the USA as having failed to bring its influence to bear to achieve a just peace in the Middle East, as having pursued its own imperial ambitions, and given unconditional support to Israel. One may not see these reasons as justifying terrorism, but they are reasons.

The classification (binary division) of the world into 'us' versus 'them', those who are allies or share the same values and commitments with the USA or at least cooperate with it on the one hand, and 'terrorists and tyrants' on the other, leaves no space for those who oppose US policies in political rather than violent ways or have legitimate grievances against the use of American power. There are indeed real terrorists and tyrants, and which reasonable person could disagree that they should be opposed? But in a discourse which works in simple binary oppositions, where there are no third (or fourth) categories, there is a tendency for all those who use forms of 'irregular' force to be categorized as 'terrorists' or 'tyrants', and for opponents of American strategy and policies who do not use force to be somehow lumped together with 'terrorists' or 'tyrants' as not being prepared (or having the 'guts') to stand up to them or even sympathizing with them. There is a dangerous polarization in this discourse between those who are 'with us' and those that are 'against us', and any form of what is labelled 'anti-Americanism' (confusing opposition to American government policies with opposition to America itself, and to American people – many of whom oppose the government – in general) quickly slides into accusations of being 'soft on terrorism'.

Yet 'terrorism' is, as I have indicated, now being used in an opportunistic way as a catch-all category to brand and condemn a wide variety of forms of the use of force, while excluding others which arguably do constitute terrorism. What is 'terrorism'? Definitions of 'terrorism' are by their nature contentious, but let us accept for the sake of the argument the definition in the UK Terrorism Act of 2000, which is quite close to everyday usage of the word 'terrorism'. Terrorism is 'the use or threat of action' (including serious violence against a person or people, serious risk to the health or safety of the public, and serious damage to property) 'designed to influence the government or to intimidate the public for the purpose of advancing a political, religious or ideological cause'. 'The government' here means the British government, but we can generalize the definition by substituting 'governments'.

Let me raise with reference to this definition two of a number of contentious issues. The first is whether a distinction is drawn between 'terrorism' and 'resistance': does irregular warfare in pursuit of 'the right to self-determination, freedom, and independence, as derived from the Charter of the United Nations, of people forcibly deprived of that right . . . particularly peoples under colonial or racist regimes and foreign occupation' (UN Resolution 42/159, 1987) constitute 'terrorism'? The nature of the action may well be very similar to that referred to in the Terrorism Act, and although it may be primarily 'designed' to damage military targets it may also be designed to 'influence' governments or even 'intimidate' sections of the public. This was true of military action against apartheid in South Africa, which was clearly recognized as 'resistance' and not 'terrorism' by the UN. Yet the actions of Palestinians in the context of Israeli occupation of their territories, or Chechen fighters in the context of Russian military offensives in what Chechens regard as their country, and of Iraqis opposed to the occupation of their country against US military targets (as well as civilian targets) are normally referred to as 'terrorism' in the context of the war on terror. By implication they are 'the same as' the 11 September attacks, or the bombings in Madrid and London, which I would have no hesitation in calling 'terrorism'.

The second issue is whether there is a category of 'state terrorism'. Since the definition from the Terrorism Act does not specify the sort of agencies or agents responsible, it would appear to allow for the possibility that the responsible agents may be states. Again, the Palestinian situation could be a case in point: do certain actions on the part of the Israeli government and military constitute 'terrorism'? Some of their actions do seem to be serious violence against people (in many cases civilians) and property designed to intimidate the Palestinian government and public to advance a political cause. And what about the USA itself? Does its open support for 'counter-terrorism' in Latin America and other areas, and for the violent overthrow of governments (e.g. in Chile and Nicaragua) constitute state sponsorship for terrorism? There are good arguments for saying that it does, and indeed for claiming that US support for 'irregular warfare', particularly against the Russians in Afghanistan, was itself largely responsible for building up the Islamic groups it now opposes as terrorist (Chomsky 2003, Honderich 2003). Yet states are now commonly excluded from what is referred to as 'terrorism'.

Let me come back to the analysis of Rice's essay. The National Strategy includes what Rice calls a strategy of 'pre-emption'. There is a certain sleight of hand here, for 'pre-emption' is first set up as equivalent to (in a *relation of equivalence* with) and implicitly defined as 'taking action before threats have fully materialized', which occurs in the previous sentence, then as equivalent to a country not waiting 'to be attacked before it can address existential threats', which occurs in the following sentence. So Rice is sliding from threats that have not 'fully material- ized' (does this mean some doubt about whether they exist?) to a scenario where there are real 'existential threats'.

America will 'confront aggressive tyrants holding or seeking nuclear, chemical or biological weapons that might be passed onto terrorist allies'. There is an *assumption* or presupposition that such scenarios actually exist (that there are such tyrants holding or seeking such weapons with terrorist allies that they might pass them onto), which is certainly questionable. And this undertaking, or threat, leaves a great deal of latitude for interpretation. Who counts as an 'aggres- sive tyrant' and on what grounds? How consistent has the USA been in applying this descriptor? What counts as evidence of 'holding' such weapons? How is it established that a government is 'seeking' such weapons, or that they have 'ter- rorist allies', or whether the weapons 'might' be passed on to these 'allies'? The controversy surrounding the Iraq War and the claims that were made to justify it (which largely proved to be false or exaggerated or ungrounded) provides a vivid illustration of what a minefield such a policy is. A central question is: who decides on these matters, and how can people know whether the justifications provided in public are the real reasons, rather than geopolitical factors to do with American control of certain regions and related economic factors such as access to major supplies of oil?

Rice's description of the strategy as 'pre-emption' is misleading: 'pre-emptive' war where there is a clear and present danger of attack may be justifiable under international law, but the policy that the USA has adopted is 'preventive' war (Chomsky 2003), war which is justified by what officials judge (for whatever motives) hypothetically to be a possible danger at some point in the future. This leaves America free to attack any country it claims to be a potential threat to its security or 'the peace' internationally, which has no justification in inter- national law. Does such an aggressive unilateralist strategy really fulfil America's 'special responsibility to help make the world more secure'? Many commentators consider that it does precisely the opposite.

Rice declares that 'to support all these means of defending the peace, the United States will build and maintain twenty-first century military forces that are beyond challenge'. There is a superficially rational argument here: if there are such potential threats to 'the peace' from 'terrorists and tyrants', then 'the peace' can only be defended by the overwhelming military superiority of those who oppose them. But the argument is fallacious: why should it be the military forces of a single state that are 'beyond challenge', and indeed permanently, so that 'any potential adversary' (who can determine whether a country is a 'potential' adversary, and on what grounds?) will be 'dissuaded' from seeking military equality or superiority? Why not a military force controlled by the United Nations, or an alliance of 'great powers'? Moreover, is not America's bid for unchallengeable military superiority itself responsible in large part for potential threats to 'the peace'? And responsible for the weak who feel threatened by American hegemony and so resort to irregular warfare including terrorism, and for countries which judge that they may come to be regarded as 'potential adversaries' and so resort to defensive military build-ups? There is indeed evidence that America's aggressive unilateralism is leading to a new international arms race.

Merging terrorism and tyranny as 'different faces of the same evil' has allowed the USA and its allies to justify military attacks on states (Afghanistan, then Iraq) and the threat of such attacks (e.g. against Iran and Syria) in terms of the 'war on terror'. And this has allowed them to partly compensate for the vacuity of 'war on terror': how can a war be conducted against such a nebulous and abstract enemy as 'terror' or 'terrorism', or indeed against 'terrorists', who do not constitute an identifiable group and do not occupy specific locations, who are geographically and socially dispersed and fragmented and, most crucially, largely invisible and undetectable until they actually plan or commit acts of terrorism? The 'war on terrorism' is analogous to other metaphorical 'wars' such as 'the war on drugs', and war is just as unlikely to eradicate terrorism as the use of drugs. Eradicating terrorism would call for other means than 'war' – legal means in some cases, and political resolution of conflicts and problems such as those of the Middle East whose enduring irresolution has fed terrorism. States run by 'tyrants' on the other hand are palpable and credible targets for military attack. However, the legitimizing assumption of an inherent affinity between political tyranny or dictatorship and terrorism is fallacious, as the case of Iraq has shown. So also is the assumption that terrorists would use 'weapons of mass destruction' if they were supplied with them: if we assume that terrorism is a form of violence used to achieve political ends, it is difficult to see how such political ends could be achieved by wiping out whole populations.

The National Strategy has two interconnected legitimizing objectives: 'security' (the security of the USA itself in the first instance, but also international security) and 'freedom'. Their interconnection is established near the beginning of the extract. The National Security Strategy 'offers a bold vision for protecting our nation that captures today's new realities and new opportunities. It calls on America to use our position of unparalleled strength and influence to create a balance of power that favours freedom.' The 'three pillars' of the strategy ('defend', 'preserve' and 'extend the peace') bring together 'opposing and preventing violence' and 'seeking to extend the benefits of freedom and prosperity across the globe'. This is *interdiscursively hybrid*, mixing military and security discourse ('protecting our nation', 'balance of power', 'opposing and preventing violence') with political economic discourse ('new opportunities', 'freedom', 'the benefits of freedom and prosperity'), with the strategy offering 'a bold vision', which evokes the discourse of marketing rather than that of defence policy. 'Security' and 'freedom' (in the neo-liberal sense that grounds all freedoms in market freedom) are inextricably merged together. Rice claims that there is 'an increasing awareness' of 'a paradigm of progress, founded on political and economic liberty', and 'a broad commitment to democracy, the rule of law, a market-based economy, and open trade'. The choice of the word 'paradigm' is noteworthy: we can take this as an allusion to the strategy of 'globalism', though there are acknowledgements and apparent concessions to the criticisms and fears that this strategy has provoked: a 'recognition' that 'there is no "one size fits all" answer', that 'freedom manifests itself differently around the globe', and that 'new liberties can find an honoured place amid ancient traditions'. But as I argued in Chapter 3 in discussing the globalist strategy, such concessions to its failures and the fears and criticisms these have led to do not amount to any fundamental change in the strategy.

Rice claims that 'we do not seek to impose democracy on others, we seek only to help create conditions in which people can claim a freer future for themselves'. A covert *equivalence* is set up here between 'democracy' and 'a freer future' (Fairclough 2003). Globalist discourse represents 'democracy' as an inherent accompaniment to 'freedom' in the neo-liberal sense, and in this case they are construed as one and the same thing. In the context of the sequel to the Iraq War, it is difficult to take Rice's claim seriously: in September 2003, before any Iraqi authorities had been constituted, Paul Bremer (the US Administrator of the Coalition Provisional Authority) authorized a series of measures to transform Iraq into a 'free market' economy, including privatization of businesses, full ownership rights for foreign companies, the right for foreign investors to repatriate their profits, and elimination of trade barriers. Lucrative contracts for the 'reconstruction' of Iraq have been awarded to US companies, including Halliburton, of which Vice-President Cheney was formerly the CEO.

Rice claims that America is committed to 'fight poverty, disease and oppression', even if the motivation for doing so is in part moral ('it is the right thing to do') and in part self-interested (it is also 'the smart thing to do', since 'poor states can become weak or even failed states, vulnerable to hijacking by terrorist networks'). But American aid is conditional ('new money means new terms'). It is available only to 'countries that work to govern justly, invest in the health and education of their people, and encourage economic liberty'. 'Governing justly', 'investing in health and education' and 'encouraging economic liberty' are textured in a *relation of equivalence* as co-members of the same class of 'goods', and we can take 'encouraging economic liberty' as a coded way of requiring adherence to the globalist agenda. So development aid to the poorest countries in the world is no longer given on the basis of need. It comes with political preconditions, essentially the precondition that such countries must follow the American path. This is an illustration of the change identified by Duffield (2001) in development strategy and discourse which I discussed in Chapter 3, towards a more interventionist approach (imposing change as a precondition for aid) and a convergence between development policy and security policy, as underdeveloped countries are increasingly seen as dangerous countries.

Tony Blair: international security and war

The construction and legitimization of the strategy of 'hard power' and the discourse of the 'war on terror' is mainly an American accomplishment, but not exclusively so. For instance, the British Prime Minister Tony Blair has been addressing the question of change in international security strategy in a series of speeches since the Kosovo War in 1999 (Fairclough 2005c). Blair's highly influential speech in Chicago at the time of the Kosovo War (Blair 1999) foreshadows the nexus of strategies I discussed earlier in its classification of the main dimensions of globalization: 'But globalization is not just economic. It is also a political and security phenomenon.' This elevation of 'security' to one of the three main dimensions of globalization differs from more usual classifications (which often include 'cultural' but exclude 'security'), and facilitates the interconnection of security with economic and political strategies.

Blair's version of this strategic nexus is based upon a new 'doctrine' of 'international community':

> We are witnessing the beginnings of a new doctrine of international community. By this I mean the explicit recognition that today more than ever before we are mutually dependent, that national interest is to a significant extent governed by international collaboration and that we need a clear and coherent debate as to the direction this doctrine takes us in each field of international endeavour. Just as within domestic politics, the notion of community – the belief that partnership and co-operation are essential to advance self-interest – is coming into its own; so it needs to find its own international echo. Global financial markets, the global environment, global security and disarmament

issues: none of these can be solved without intense international co-operation.

And 'the principles of international community also apply to international security'. Blair sketches out the 'decade of experience' that 'we' now have since the end of the Cold War, noting that 'our armed forces have been busier than ever – delivering humanitarian aid, deterring attacks on defenceless people, backing up UN resolutions and occasionally engaging in major wars as we did in the Gulf in 1991 and are currently doing in the Balkans'.

But what is the 'international community'? Who are 'we'? The *pronoun 'we'* is used in its 'inclusive' sense (meaning 'all of us'), and when for instance Blair says in the indented extract above that 'we are mutually dependent' it would seem to include all nation-states. But elsewhere, when he alludes to humanitarian and military actions, 'we' is used more restrictively. The 'armed forces' are not the armed forces of the 'international community', but of the more limited set of countries that take part in such actions, and in the case of the Kosovo War of NATO.

The issue of who 'we' are is particularly important when it comes to providing a rationale for interventions in the internal affairs of sovereign states. Blair's primary rationale in this speech is moral, but with the characteristically 'third way' twist that acting on the basis of 'our values' also happens to be the best way of acting in our national interests (a conflation which we also find in Rice's essay). 'Our actions' he claims are now:

> guided by a more subtle blend of mutual self interest and moral purpose in defending the values we cherish. In the end values and interests merge. If we can establish and spread the values of liberty, the rule of law, human rights and an open society then that is in our national interests too. The spread of our values makes us safer.

This is how Blair legitimizes the Kosovo War – in terms of considerations of self-interest (the threat to security and stability from Milosevic's policies) and moral considerations (the 'evil of ethnic cleansing', abuses of human rights), which 'merged' in this case. Notice that values are not only to be 'defended' and 'established' but also 'spread', which is evocative of nineteenth-century justifications of empire and imperialism in terms of their civilizing mission. The values which Blair lists include 'an open society', which is a coded way of implying the globalist objective of economic liberalization and free trade. It also includes the relatively new concept of 'human rights', a concept of universal rights which has the virtue of transcending limitations imposed in the name of national sovereignty, but is also increasingly appealed to in legitimizing military actions such as the Iraq War.

What is the status of these values? They are according to Blair 'our values', the values of the international community, and in a speech in January 2003 (delivered at a Foreign Office Conference) Blair asserts that they are 'universal values', and supports this assertion with the claim that 'Given a chance, the world over, people want them.' One quibble is that claiming that values are 'universal' suggests that they are universally held rather than that 'people' (all people? some people?) 'want them'. But the main problem is that it is by no means obvious that everyone 'wants', let alone is actually committed to, the set of values Blair lists. We have seen that there is plenty of opposition to 'an open society' in the globalist sense in which Blair uses the term. There is probably a large measure of global assent to the value of human rights, but many people are suspicious of it because of what it is used to legitimize. There is also no doubt substantial global commitment to the value of the rule of law, though this does not mean that this or any other value will always be interpreted in the same way. Blair's choice of the word 'liberty' rather than 'freedom' is noteworthy, because it is more strongly associated with the 'economic freedom' which neo-liberals advocate, and therefore evokes neo-liberal discourse. While there is large-scale global assent to the value of freedom, many people would be more suspicious of 'liberty'. So, overall, the claim that these values are universal looks suspect, especially as regards 'an open society', which leaves us again wondering who the 'we' is in 'our values'.

Yet this is a crucial claim for advocates of intervention on moral grounds to plausibly legitimize their actions. Blair himself acknowledges the contentious nature of the claim in a speech in 2003 (Blair 2003), asserting that these values:

> have to be pursued alongside another value: justice, the belief in opportunity for all. Without justice, the values I describe can be portrayed as 'Western values'; globalization becomes a battering ram for Western commerce and culture; the order we want is seen by much of the world as 'their' order not 'ours'.

Blair is winningly frank about problems with his claims about universal values, but his solution is not convincing. True, 'justice' is an obvious omission from the list of values discussed above, but Blair's interpretation of it as equality of opportunity ('opportunity for all') shows again how far a list of supposedly shared value terms is from a shared set of values. 'Justice' means a great deal more than equality of opportunity for many people and indeed governments around the world. It means redistribution of wealth and resources to create the equality of resources which is actually a precondition for equality of opportunity. It means adequate provision for the social welfare of those don't succeed as well as those who do, and so forth.

In the aftermath of the attacks of September 2001 and the declaration of the war on terror, there is a convergence in Blair's speeches between this moral discourse and the discourse of the war on terror. Near the beginning of his speech at the George Bush senior Presidential Library, Washington, in April 2002 (Blair 2002), Blair again advocates what he here calls 'an enlightened self-interest' which 'puts fighting for our values right at the heart of the policies necessary to protect our nations'. Later on, he states that:

> My basic argument is that in today's interdependent world, we need an integrated approach, a doctrine of international community as I put it before, based on the values we believe in (. . .) I am arguing that the values we believe in are worth fighting for; they are in the ascendant and we have a common interest in standing up for them. We shouldn't be shy of giving our actions not just the force of self-interest but moral force.
>
> And in reality, at a certain point these forces merge. When we defend our countries as you did after September 11, we aren't just defending territory. We are defending what our nations believe in: freedom, democracy, justice, tolerance and respect towards others.

One contrast with the 1999 speech in terms of *collocations* (Fairclough 2003) is that the emphasis is on 'defending' (rather than 'extending' or 'spreading') values ('fighting for', 'standing up for' as well as 'defending' them in the extract above) in the face of a terrorist attack which threatens both security and values: 'Osama bin Laden's philosophy is not just a security threat to us. It's an assault on our hearts and minds.' Another contrast is that, while 'moral' considerations' are still prominent, considerations of 'stability' loom larger in making the case for intervention. And a third contrast is that while the new 'doctrine' of 'international community' is reiterated, there is an emphasis on 'international alliances' and an 'international coalition': 'A series of interlocking alliances with a common agenda on issues of security, trade and stability should replace old rivalries'. International 'alliances' are very different from international 'community' because they entail exclusions (some countries are in, some countries are out).

Blair like the American leaders formulates the threat both as terrorism and as certain countries possessing or developing weapons of mass destruction, and advocates 'regime change':

> we must be prepared to act where terrorism or Weapons of Mass Destruction threaten us. The fight against international terrorism is right. We should pursue it vigorously. Not just in Afghanistan but elsewhere. Not just by military means but by disrupting the finances of terrorism (. . .) If necessary the action should be military and again, if necessary and justified, it should involve regime change.

'Terrorism and (or) Weapons of Mass Destruction' became a *high-frequency collocation* (Fairclough 2003) in Blair's discourse, in the sense that the two expressions ('terrorism', 'Weapons of Mass Destruction') were frequently conjoined, and 'terrorism' occurred less frequently alone. He also now presents an international community based on shared values as an objective rather than assuming that it actually exists: 'In all these areas, we seek one integrated, international community, sharing the same values, working to the same goals.' This is reminiscent of the globalist strategy for spreading neo-liberal capitalism across the globe.

The claim that international security strategy is based on 'values' and the appeal to 'universal principles' are also used as legitimizations by American leaders, and can be seen in Rice's essay on the National Security Strategy. But it is Blair who has most forcefully made a moral case for the strategic shift to 'hard power'. We can see him as having played an important and distinctive and until recently successful part in the international alliance around this strategy, as the principal spokesman for the moral case in favour of a more interventionist international security strategy.

Conclusion

In this chapter I have argued that the strategy of 'hard power' which has displaced that of 'soft power' and its 'nodal' discourse of the 'war on terror' constitute part of an increasingly complex 'nexus' which includes the strategies of globalism and the KBE and the new strategy for development, and their associated nodal discourses. This is a further stage in the continuity-through-change of globalism. Focusing on the discourse of the 'war on terror', I have identified four main 'themes' which characterize it: that this is a new era, posing new threats, which requires new responses; that America and its allies face unprecedented risks and dangers which call for exceptional measures; that those who pose these risks and dangers are the forces of 'evil'; and that America and its allies are the forces of 'good', and their actions are informed by moral values.

I have discussed and analysed two examples which illustrate the strategy of 'hard power' and the discourse of the 'war on terror'. The first is an essay on US National Security Strategy by Condoleezza Rice, National Security Advisor and since 2005 Secretary of State in G.W. Bush's administration. The second is extracts from speeches by the British Prime Minister Tony Blair on international security and his new 'doctrine of international community' delivered between the time of the Kosovo War (April 1999) and the build-up to the Iraq War (January 2003). I have referred to various textual features including argumentation and argumentative fallacies, legitimization, narratives, assumptions or presuppositions, interdiscursive hybridity (the mixing of discourses), choices of vocabulary, patterns of collocation, the meaning of key words (such as 'terrorism' and 'justice'), overstatement, classification (including binary classification e.g. 'good' v. 'evil'), relations of equivalence, and the shifting meaning of the pronoun 'we'.

I have taken a sceptical view of the discourse of the 'war on terror'. There has certainly been an intensification in wars initiated by the USA in varying alliances, and war has to some extent been waged against what most people would be willing to call terrorists, but the objectives of these wars have, in my view and that of many others, not been simply to defeat terrorists or terrorism, or even those who support or might conceivably support them. Their objectives have also, and I think primarily, been to preserve, consolidate and extend the power of 'the West', and especially the international hegemony of the USA, and this objective has been seen as entailing the pursuit of the globalist objective to establish economic liberalization, open markets and free trade in as many parts of the world as possible. The discourse of the 'war on terror' has quite effectively disguised these objectives, and legitimized actions taken in pursuit of them. These wars can be seen as having had morally good consequences in removing brutal and oppressive leaders and regimes (Saddam Hussein, Milosevic, the Taliban), but this has not been their primary objective, and they have also produced morally bad consequences, including death and injury to many innocent people and serious material damage to the countries concerned. So the legitimization of these wars on moral grounds within the discourse of the 'war on terror' is, on a generous interpretation perhaps sincere but misguided, or on a less generous one just a smokescreen.

Although the discourse of the 'war on terror' has represented 'terrorism' in highly questionable ways to suit the strategic objectives I have referred to, terrorism (including state-sponsored terrorism) is a real phenomenon, and a morally unacceptable way of pursuing political aims which should be punished, though in my view through the institutions of national and international law and where necessary interventions under the auspices of the United Nations, and should be prevented as far as is possible. Yet far from defeating real terrorism as their advocates claimed they would, it appears that the recent wars have actually strengthened it. If the main objective were actually to punish terrorists and reduce terrorism as much as possible, very different means would need to be used, including the prosecution of terrorist suspects in courts of law and much greater diplomatic and political efforts to achieve a political settlement of the Palestinian question.

Conclusion

The tradition of critical research in the social sciences focuses upon what are widely seen as the big issues and problems which people face in their lives in order to arrive at an understanding of the present which can illuminate possibilities for a better future and inform struggles to achieve it. In my choice of globalization as a topic and the approach I have adopted to it, I have sought to work within this tradition of research. Contemporary processes of 'globalization' are relevant to many of the perceived issues and problems of the present for reasons I have indicated in the course of the book. For instance, the most influential strategy for discourse of globalization, globalism, is widely perceived as having many socially damaging effects and contributing to many of the most pressing contemporary social problems, which include a gap between rich and poor which has been widening now for over two decades, and the steady erosion of the support and social welfare that people in many parts of the world receive from states. Globalization in its globalist, neo-liberal form has brought new opportunities and gains for some people, but has made the lives of many others more difficult.

In approaching the topic of globalization, I have aimed to add to existing understanding by focusing on discourse. As I indicated in Chapter 1, the significance of discourse is widely acknowledged in the literature on globalization, but most research includes little systematic attention to or analysis of discourse. Yet as I have argued discourse is crucial to understanding globalization, and a better understanding of its role is important. I have aimed to link understanding of the present to possibilities for a better future and strategies for achieving it by both emphasizing from a discourse analytical perspective that globalism is flawed and contradictory and that its dominance is dependent upon contingent factors which can change, and presenting globalism as no more than one strategy among many, even if it is currently the most powerful one. Certain aspects of globalization may be inevitable and irreversible, but there is nothing inevitable or irreversible about the strategy of globalism. Globalization can be steered in less damaging, more democratic and more socially just and equitable directions.

I shall now conclude by summarizing the main arguments of the book.

Globalization and discourse

I have argued that globalization is a reality: a complex, interconnected but partly autonomous set of processes affecting many dimensions of social life (economic, political, social, cultural, environmental, military and so forth) which constitute changes in the spatial organization of social activity and interaction, social relations and relations of power, producing ever more intensive, extensive and rapid interconnections, interdependencies and flows on a global scale and between the global scale and other (macro-regional, national, local, etc.) scales. Globalization is not, as it is often represented, a phenomenon which developed in the last decades of the twentieth century. It has a much longer history, but there has been a distinctive contemporary surge in globalization associated especially with innovations in communications and information technology.

I have argued that we cannot adequately understand or analyse globalization as a reality without taking language – discourse – into account. If we think about what is globalized, what the 'flows' consist of, this includes discourses, ways of representing, construing and imagining aspects of social processes. And if we think of the changes in social activity, interaction, interconnection associated with globalization, these entail new forms of communication, or genres. So we can say (using a somewhat rough-and-ready distinction) that both the contents and the forms of globalization have a partly discursive character.

Strategies for and discourses of globalization

Human beings engage in social activity in a preconstructed social world which is largely beyond their control. They have to come to terms with it, accept that they can only act within certain parameters and constraints. Yet human beings are agentive, strategic and reflexive beings, and the preconstructed social world is a socially, humanly, constructed world, the outcome of past and continuing human agency, strategy and reflexivity. Wherever people engage in social activity, they reflexively produce representations of it and of their own place within it; these representations may (given certain social conditions) be consolidated and stabilized as diverse shared discourses, and they may include imaginaries for possible alternative forms of social activity, and may (always subject to particular social conditions) come to be parts of strategies for social change. In short, in analysing any social activity or social processes, we need to be mindful of both its preconstructed *structural* characteristics, and of the *strategic* action of groups of people to change it in particular directions, which inherently includes discourses which represent and imagine and narrate the social activity or process in question in particular ways.

This applies in the case of globalization. We are faced with a preconstructed social world with certain globalized properties and globalizing tendencies which we must largely come to terms with. My description of globalization above referred to it as a set of real processes which have produced and continue to produce structural characteristics of the world we live in. But the social world we are faced with also includes strategic action on the part of various groups of agents and agencies to inflect or re-direct existing processes of globalization in particular directions, and the various strategies include discourses of globalization (such as the 'globalist' discourse I have focused upon in the book).

There is a great deal of confusion between real globalization and discourses of globalization, and understandably so, because they are both a part of the world we are faced with, and discourses of globalization make competing claims about what the real character of globalization is. But despite the difficulty in doing so, it is vital to distinguish between realities and strategically motivated discourses if we want to achieve a better understanding and better analyses of globalization. As I suggested in the Introduction, making this distinction amounts to determining the relative 'practical adequacy' of different discourses, how good their representations of real globalization are, asking for instance whether what a particular discourse suggests about what will happen if we act in a certain way actually does happen.

One more specific reason why we must distinguish between realities and strategically motivated discourses is that the relationship between them is crucial for the analysis of globalization – and we obviously can't explore the relationship between two entities which we are unable to distinguish. The relationship is crucial because the way in which globalization develops depends upon a dialectical relation between existing structures and tendencies and successful strategies and, as part of that, successful discourses. This is how the social (re)construction of the social world comes about, and how discourses contribute to the construction (of non-discursive elements or 'moments') of the social world, i.e. have causal effects upon the social world. However, what I've called real globalization is far too complex to be comprehended by any strategy, and strategies are targeted just on particular aspects of it. A major concern in this book has been the identification and analysis of discourses which are associated with successful or hegemonic strategies for inflecting and directing aspects of globalization in particular ways, in particular the globalist discourse of globalization and other discourses it has converged with (the discourses of the KBE, development and the 'war on terror').

Relations between discourse and other 'moments' of globalization

In Chapter 1 I discussed the various positions taken in the academic literature about globalization on discourse as an element or moment of globalization, distinguishing four main positions: objectivist, rhetoricist, ideologist and social constructivist.

On the basis of these positions, I argued that we can distinguish five main claims about the relationship of discourse to other elements or 'moments' of globalization:

- Discourse can represent globalization, giving people information about it and contributing to their understanding of it.
- Discourse can misrepresent and mystify globalization, giving a confusing and misleading impression of it.
- Discourse can be used rhetorically to project a particular view of globalization which can justify or legitimize the actions, policies or strategies of particular (usually powerful) social agencies and agents.
- Discourse can contribute to the constitution, dissemination and reproduction of ideologies, which can also be seen as forms of mystification, but have a crucial systemic function in sustaining a particular form of globalization and the (unequal and unjust) power relations which are built into it.
- Discourse can generate imaginary representations of how the world will be or should be within strategies for change which, if they achieve hegemony, can be operationalized to transform these imaginaries into realities.

These are often treated as alternatives we have to choose between, but they are not: discourse can have these effects separately or in combination in particular texts and bodies of text. What is missing from the existing literature on globalization is a systematic approach to theorizing and analysing discourse as a moment of globalization which can show these various effects of discourse and the relationship between them, and help explain them.

Cultural political economy and discourse

My theoretical and analytical framework is based upon a particular version of critical discourse analysis (CDA) which I outlined in Chapter 2, but I have adopted a 'trans-disciplinary' approach which involves embedding this version of CDA into a form of 'cultural' political economy. I argued that this allows us on the one hand to approach the theme of globalization in a way which can ensure systematic attention to discourse as a facet of globalization, but on the other hand it helps avert the danger of a de-contextualized focus on discourse which overlooks the fact that discourse can only be effective in the social construction of globalization subject to certain conditions.

Cultural political economy asserts, like conventional political economy, that economic processes and systems are politically embedded and subject to political conditions, but it also claims that they are culturally conditioned and embedded. It emphasizes the socially constructed character of economies, states, forms of government and management and other economic and political 'objects', and argues that the processes of their social construction inherently have a partly discursive character. In approaching processes of social construction, cultural political economy works with the dialectical view of the relationship between structures and strategies which I referred to above, and it takes strategies to include discourses and narratives which represent economic activities and systems, narrate past and present problems and failures, and imagine and prescribe possible alternatives. It addresses the issue of what mechanisms and conditions govern the selection of particular strategically motivated discourses over others, their retention or institutionalization, and their operationalization as changes in forms of social activity and interaction, institutions, forms of governance, cultural values and identities, aspects of physical reality and so forth. If we see globalization as changes in scales and relations between scales as I suggested in Chapter 4, then its strategic dimension includes strategies to construct new scales, and new relations between scales, and to 're-scale' particular spatial entities (such as nation-states or urban areas). Such strategies can be seen as part of the search for a new 'fix' between a regime of capital accumulation and a mode of social regulation, which I discussed in Chapter 3 in the case of the emerging 'fix' between the 'knowledge-based' economy (KBE) and neo-liberal forms of social regulation.

This cultural political economy approach is, like CDA itself, the outcome of a trans-disciplinary dialogue between disciplines and theories, and in the version which has been developed by Jessop (2002, 2004, Jessop and Sum 2001) which I have mainly drawn upon, categories of CDA have been integrated into the theoretical framework. Part of what I have been doing in this book is continuing the dialogue by embedding a more elaborated version of CDA within the cultural political economy approach.

Critical discourse analysis

This version of CDA differentiates three levels of abstraction in social analysis (the levels of social events, social practices and social structures) each of which has a semiotic moment which is dialectically related to other moments. Texts constitute the semiotic moment of social events. Orders of discourse are the semiotic moment of social practices, and languages of social structures. Texts are the outcome of dialectical relations between the causal power of more or less stabilized orders of discourse (and, at the most abstract level, languages) and the causal power of social agents to act and produce potentially innovative 'objects' (in this case, texts) with given resources and within particular constraints. Orders of discourse are constituted as relatively stabilized configurations of different discourses, different genres and different styles. Social agents draw upon (rather than simply instantiate) orders of discourse in producing texts, but in potentially innovative ways with potentially innovative outcomes. The categories of 'discourse', 'genre' and 'style' figure in the analysis of texts as well as the analysis of orders of discourse, because one analytical question about texts is whether and how (conventionally or innovatively) they combine different discourses, different genres and different styles. Texts are 'interdiscursively hybrid' in so far as they combine them in innovative ways. Innovative production of texts is the source of variation in discourses, genres and styles, producing new hybrid discourses, genres and styles which may (subject to the conditions I alluded to above) be selected and retained, and incorporated into orders of discourse.

The approach is firmly relational: new discourses, genres and styles are produced in texts by articulating together existing discourses, genres and styles in new relations; new orders of discourse articulate existing and new discourses, genres and styles together in new relations. And such changes in orders of discourse are the semiotic moment of changes in relations between social practices, social institutions and organizations, social fields and social scales. Let us take for instance the view of globalization as changes in scale and relations between scales which I drew upon in Chapter 4. The semiotic moment of the construction of a new scale is the construction of a new semiotic order which is constituted by a new articulation of orders of discourse in particular relations within a particular space (be it the globe, Europe, a nation-state, or an urban region). The semiotic moment of a change in relations between scales is the construction of a new semiotic order which articulates orders of discourse at different scales in particular relations, e.g. the local scale, the national scale and the European scale. The semiotic moment of the re-scaling of some spatial entity is the construction of a new semiotic order in which its orders of discourse are articulated in particular relations with those of other scales (e.g. Romanian orders of discourse with European orders of discourse).

Re-scaling of a spatial entity such as a nation-state (I discussed the case of Romania in Chapter 4) involves the recontextualization within that entity of social practices, forms of institution and organization, forms of governance, strategies, orders of discourse, discourses, genres and styles which are institutionalized and operative elsewhere. Recontextualization is often 'led' by discourses, in the sense that people are initially faced with representations of and imaginaries for new practices, institutions, identities and so forth. The process of recontextualization is an active process of appropriation within new contexts, where circumstances, histories, trajectories, strategic positions and struggles within these contexts shape the ways in which recontextualized elements are appropriated and the outcomes of recontextualization. Recontextualized discourses may or may not be operationalized (enacted in new practices and forms of social activity, inculcated in new identities, materialized in physical changes), or they may be operationalized in diverse and largely unpredictable and unmanageable ways, depending upon such properties of the contextualizing context. Processes of operationalization (enactment, inculcation, materialization) are dialectical processes in which discourses become internalized in other social elements, and in part they are 'intra-semiotic' processes in that discourses are also enacted as genres and inculcated as styles.

Textual analysis

I have argued that one important contribution which CDA can make to social research on globalization (or indeed on any aspect of social change) is analysis of texts, and I have analysed quite a number of texts in the course of the book. As I explained in Chapter 2, providing an introduction to textual analysis is beyond the scope of this book, and readers are referred to Fairclough (2003) which does provide such an introduction. The textual analysis I have carried out has referred to a diverse range of features of texts, and I have not been able to analyse particular linguistic or pragmatic features (such as nominalization, modality, or 'genre chains') in the sort of depth one would expect in a methodologically oriented monograph or journal article.

But readers may find it useful to have a summary of the main features of texts which I have referred to, which I shall divide into two groups. First, I have referred to a set of features which broadly relate to the intertextuality and interdiscursive hybridity of texts:

- genres, discourses and styles which are drawn on in texts;
- interdiscursive hybridity or 'mixing' of genres, discourses or styles;
- genre chains;
- nodal discourses and other discourses which cluster around them;
- themes associated with particular discourses;
- intertextuality and intertextual allusions.

Second, I shall simply list alphabetically linguistic features of texts in a broad sense, with some related features grouped together:

- argumentation, particular argumentative genres, fallacious arguments, explanation and legitimization;
- assumptions, presuppositions and implications;
- classification as a process in texts, and relations of equivalence;
- contradictions;
- control of the floor in interaction;
- dialogicality and polemic;
- direct address to audiences;
- evaluation in texts, and value assumptions;
- inference;
- metaphor;
- modality;

- narratives and particular narrative forms such as conversational narratives;
- nominalization;
- overstatement;
- paralinguistic features and body language;
- passive voice;
- pronouns: inclusive/exclusive 'we' and the shifting meaning of the pronoun 'we'; formal and informal second-person pronouns;
- representation of social agents and their actions (process types), and of spatial and temporal relations;
- rhetorical and persuasive features of texts;
- vocabulary, choices of vocabulary, patterns of collocation, the meaning of key words;
- wordplay.

Discourses of globalization

I have argued that there are diverse strategies for globalization associated with diverse discourses of globalization. Selection of these strategies and discourses is the outcome of hegemonic struggles which take place on different scales – on the global scale, on the macro-regional scale (for instance on the European scale), at the national scale, at local, urban and regional scales, and at the scale of specific institutions and organizations. Globalism is the globally dominant strategy and discourse, and it has achieved dominance at other scales though by no means universally, but its hegemonic position is not guaranteed. It constantly has to be re-established by adjusting the strategy and discourse to changing circumstances, and it is open to challenge from other strategies and discourses. Hegemony is always provisional.

I have suggested that globalist discourse is a 'nodal' discourse around which many other discourses cluster. Although its continuity has been maintained over a considerable period of time, this has been through adaptation to changing circumstances and challenges which has involved changes in the cluster of discourses. In addition to the category of 'nodal' discourse (or 'master' discourse, Jessop 2004), I have worked with the category of 'nexus of discourses'. Perhaps the best way of relating the two is to see a nexus as a relation between nodal discourses, and I have referred specifically to the emerging and developing nexus between the nodal discourses of globalism, the knowledge-based economy, development and the 'war on terror'. The same set of questions arises for a nexus of discourses as for particular discourses. How and under what conditions are they selected at different scales, retained or institutionalized, and operationalized as changes in forms of activity and interaction, practices, institutions, identities, and so forth, as well as changes in the physical world?

Recontextualization and re-scaling

Chapter 4 focused on the 're-scaling' of a nation-state, Romania. I used this case study to argue that the re-scaling of spatial entities such as nation-states can be a complex process with uneven, contradictory and unpredictable outcomes. This is because re-scaling involves the recontextualization of strategies and discourses, and recontextualization is an active process of appropriation in which the extent and nature of the selection, retention (institutionalization), operationalization and implementation of strategies and discourses depends upon economic, political, social and/or cultural characteristics of the recontextualizing context.

I focused on two cases which involve change in the relations between the Romanian national scale and the European (EU) scale, the Bologna strategy for higher education reform, and EU strategy for combating social exclusion and achieving greater social inclusion. In both cases, Romania's status as a future EU member means that these EU strategies and associated discourses virtually selected themselves rather than being selected at the national scale. In the case of the social exclusion/inclusion strategy, I argued that it is based upon assumptions about social reality which are wrong in the case of Romania. This has led to contradictions and confusions in policies for operationalization and implementation which are evident in the official documentation. In the case of the Bologna strategy and discourse, there are major tensions between the sort of institutions, practices, social relations, professional and collegial relations which the Bologna strategy and discourse presupposes and those that actually exist in Romania, so that it is difficult to predict or manage with any precision the actual outcomes of reform. So the re-scaling of Romania is taking place, but in a rather chaotic way, with various obstacles, complexities and contradictions. Change in structures, institutions, practices, people and (orders of) discourse is happening, but in an uneven and unstable way.

Mediation

In Chapter 5 I discussed the influence of mass media and mediation on processes of globalization. In part I was extending the analysis of the re-scaling of Romania in Chapter 4 with a discussion of mediatization of politics and political branding and of the mediation of gender identity in the Romanian version of *Cosmopolitan*, and partly I was addressing the contribution of mass media to the construction of a global scale, specifically a global public, with respect to representations of 'distant suffering' and particularly the attacks on New York and Washington in September 2001.

My arguments about mass media and mediation can be summed up in five main points. First, that the mass media are a crucial element in the global dissemination of information and news and reactions to and interpretations of them, new strategies, discourses, ideas and practices, new norms and values in economic activities, political systems and processes, social institutions, organizations, and the conduct of ordinary life, changes in attitudes, sentiments and identities and so forth. Media 'messages' about virtually all aspects of social life now circulate globally. Second, these 'messages' are mediated, and that means that whatever aspects of social life are represented in the mass media pass through the particular semiotic codes, conventions, norms and practices of specific media, and their forms and meanings are transformed in the process. CDA can contribute to the analysis of these codes, conventions, norms and practices. Third, the global dominance of trans-national media corporations, and their close connection with centres of power in politics, government and business, mean that the latter can use the mass media as vehicles for disseminating their own 'messages' in the furtherance of their own strategies. Fourth, the impact of mass media and mediation cannot however be taken for granted because it depends upon the recontextualization of media 'messages' in many diverse recontextualizing contexts whose specific structural, historical, institutional, social and cultural characteristics and circumstances shape the reception and impact of media 'messages'. Fifth, the globalization of the mass media has contributed to the construction of a global public, global public opinion, and even perhaps the beginnings of a global 'cosmopolitan public sphere' in which debate, action and mobilization on a global basis are generated, though this is still a limited and emergent phenomenon for several reasons, including the continuing centrality of the national scale for the press and broadcasting. CDA can productively be used to show how the mass media construe and contribute to constructing certain events as global events and audiences as a global public.

Globalization from below

The actual trajectory of globalization can be seen as shaped by a dialectic between two strategic forces, 'globalization from above' and 'globalization from below'. Globalization from above is driven by the strategies of powerful agents and agencies such as those which have adopted the strategy of globalism. Globalization from below is driven by the strategies of individuals or groups in specific places to adapt to and gain from change, or defend themselves against it.

Contemporary globalization affects the forms taken by what I have called the dialectic of the particular and the universal in these situated strategies of groups and individuals. Its effects include the effects of media and mediation in bringing general or universal resources (and discourses) into particular struggles, and the development of new forms of alliance or coalition around local struggles which cut across different scales, and in some cases involve new forms of trans-national activism. The strategies and discourses of local agents in situated local action and struggle increasingly draw upon strategies and discourses which are established and successful at other, 'higher', scales (global, macro-regional, national, etc.), and in some cases this 'glocalization' takes organizational forms in which local action and struggle are undertaken by an alliance of local agents and regional, national, macro-regional and even global agencies. This was illustrated in Chapter 6 in the case of resistance to the construction of a coal-fired power station at Ma Ta Phut in Thailand, where the trans-national activist organization Greenpeace was in alliance with local campaigners. Construing local and particular issues and struggles in terms of global discourses such as the environmentalist discourse of 'climate change' can be strategically empowering, but it can on the other hand background the particularity and local specificity of issues and struggles.

Globalization and the 'war on terror'

I have taken a sceptical view of the discourse of the 'war on terror' and made clear my opposition to actual military actions that have been taken, arguing that the discourse has been an effective way of legitimizing military actions with other objectives and a smokescreen for these objectives, and that military action has strengthened real terrorism (as opposed to opportunistic construals of 'terrorism') rather than weakened it.

I have argued that the discourse of the 'war on terror' is best understood as part of the shift in the international security strategy of the USA which is linked to the strategy of globalism. There has been a strategic shift from 'soft power' to 'hard power', partly in response to the challenges to globalism which arose in the late 1990s and as a means of pursuing the strategy of globalism by other means. This has involved a change in the nexus of strategies and nodal discourses which has brought security strategy into a closer relationship with globalist strategy as well as the strategies for development and for the KBE, and has brought together the discourses of globalism, the KBE, development and the 'war on terror'. The 'war on terror' is from this perspective a further stage in the continuity-through-change of globalism.

Globalization and language

I want to conclude by reiterating what I said at the beginning of the book about its limitations. 'Globalization and language' is a very big topic and it could be approached in many ways. I have in no sense exhausted the topic. Rather, I have chosen one particular approach which has very selectively brought certain aspects of language as a part of globalization into focus. Various factors have contributed to my choice of approach, apart from fortuitous ones (the reading I happen to have done, the people I happen to have met). The first is my commitment to critical social research, which has inclined me towards a focus on relations of power in efforts to strategically direct or incline globalization in particular directions – hence my attention to globalism. The second is my background in critical discourse analysis, which has predisposed me towards the particular view of the relationship between discourse and other elements of globalization which I have argued for. The third is my long-term commitment to using CDA in trans-disciplinary social research, which in this book takes the particular form of adopting an approach which embeds CDA within a form of cultural political economy. So many other books might have been written on the topic, but I hope you have enjoyed this one.

References

Ali, T. and Barsamian, D. (2005) *Speaking of Empire and Resistance. Conversations with Tariq Ali*, New York: The New Press.

Anăstăsoaie, V., Könczei, C., Magyari-Vincze, E. and Pecican, O. (2003) *Breaking the Wall. Representing Anthropology and Anthropological Representations in Post-communist Eastern Europe*, Cluj-Napoca: EFES.

Ashcroft, John (2001) Prepared remarks for the US mayors' conference, October 25, reprinted in R. Jackson *Writing the War on Terrorism. Language, Politics and Counter-Terrorism*, Manchester: Manchester University Press (2005).

Barnett, C. (2003) *Culture and Democracy. Media, Space and Representation*, Edinburgh: Edinburgh University Press.

Bauman, Z. (1998) *Globalization: The Human Consequences*, Cambridge: Polity.

bin Mohamad, Mahathir *Renewing Asia's Foundations of Growth*. East Asia Economic Summit (2002). Online. Available HTTP: http:www.larouchpub.com/other/2002/2940. mahathir.html (accessed 3 October 2005).

Bjørgo, T. (2005) *Root Causes of Terrorism. Myths, Reality and Ways Forward*, London: Routledge.

Blair, Tony (1999) *Doctrine of the International Community*, Chicago, 22 April. Online. Available HTTP: http:www.number-10.gov.uk/output/Page1297.asp (accessed 10 October 1999).

Blair, Tony (2002) Speech in the George Bush Senior Presidential Library, Washington, April 10. Online. Available HTTP: http:www.number-10.gov.uk/output/Page1712.asp (accessed 7 December 2003).

Blair, Tony (2003) Speech at the Foreign Office Conference, London, 21 January. Online. Available HTTP: http:www.number-10.gov.uk/output/Page1765.asp (accessed 7 December 2003).

Blumler, J. and Gurevitch, M. (1995) *The Crisis of Public Communication*, London: Routledge.

Boltanski, L. (1999) *Distant Suffering. Politics, Morality and the Media*, Cambridge: Cambridge University Press.

Bourdieu, P. and Wacquant, L. (1992) *An Invitation to Reflexive Sociology*, Cambridge: Polity Press.

Bourdieu, P. and Wacquant, L. (2001) 'NewLiberal speak: notes on the new planetary vulgate', *Radical Philosophy* 105: 2–5.

Boyer, R. (1990) *The Regulation School. A Critical Introduction*, New York: Columbia University Press.

Boyer, R. and Hollingsworth, R. (1997) 'From national embeddedness to spatial and institutional nestedness', in R. Hollingsworth and R. Boyer (eds) *Contemporary Capitalism: the Embeddedness of Capitalist Institutions*, Cambridge: Cambridge University Press, 433–84.

Burawoy, M., Blum, J., George, S., Gille, Z., Gowan, T., Haney, L., Klawiter, M., Lopez, S., O'Riain, S. and Thayer, M. (2000) *Global Ethnography: Forces, Connections and Imaginations in a Postmodern World*, Berkeley: University of California Press.

Burawoy, M. and Verdery, K. (1999) *Uncertain Transition: Ethnographies of Change in the Postsocialist World,* New York: Rowan and Littlefield.

Bush, G.W. (2001a) *Address to the Nation, 11 September 2001*. Online. Available HTTP: http://www.whitehouse.gov/news/releases/2001/09/20010911–16.html (accessed 16 September 2005).

Bush, G.W. (2001b) *Address to a Joint Session of Congress and to the American People*. Online. Available HTTP: http://www.whitehouse.gov/news/releases/2001/09/20010920-8.html (accessed 16 September 2005).

Bush, G.W. (2003) Remarks in Commencement Address to US Coast Guard Academy. Online. Available HTTP: http://www.whitehouse.gov/news/releases/2003/o5/20030521-2.html (accessed 16 September 2005).

Butler J. (1996) 'Gender as performance', in P. Osborne (ed.) *A Critical Sense: Interviews with Intellectuals*, London: Routledge, 102–24.

Callinicos, A. (2003) *An Anti-Capitalist Manifesto*. Cambridge: Polity Press.

Cameron, A. and Palan, R. (2004) *The Imagined Economies of Globalization*, London: Sage.

Chelcea, L. and Mateescu, O. (eds) (2004) *Economia informală în România*, Bucharest: Paidela.

Chiribucă, D. (2004) *Tranziţia postcomunista şi reconstrucţia modernităţii în România*, Iaşi: Editura Dacia.

Chomsky, N. (2003) *Hegemony or Survival: America's Quest for Global Dominance,* New York: Metropolitan Books.

Chouliaraki, L. (2004) 'Watching September 11. The politics of pity', *Discourse & Society* 15.2–3: 185–98.

Chouliaraki, L. (2005) 'Spectacular ethics: on the television footage of the Iraq war', *Journal of Language and Politics* 4.1: 143–59.

Chouliaraki, L. (2006) *The Spectatorship of Suffering*, London: Sage.

Chouliaraki, L. and Fairclough, N. (1999) *Discourse in Late Modernity*, Edinburgh: Edinburgh University Press.

Clutterbuck, D. and Megginson, D. (1999) *Mentoring Executives and Directors*, London: Butterworth.

Coaching and Mentoring Website (2005) *What are Coaching and Mentoring?* Online. Available HTTP: http:www.coachingnetwork.org.uk/ResourceCentre/WhatAreCoaching AndMentoring.htm (accessed 5 December 2005).

Collinge, C. (1999) 'Self-organization of society by scale: a spatial reworking of regulation theory', *Environment and Planning* 17(5): 557–74.

Comisia Anti-Sărăcie si Promovare a Incluziunii Sociale (Romanian Commission against Poverty and for Promotion of Social Inclusion) (2001) *National Action Plan Against Poverty and for Social Inclusion*. Online. Available HTTP: http://www.capsis.ro/pagini/ro/pnainc.php (accessed 6 February 2005).

Commission of the European Communities (2005) *Communication from the European Commission on the Social Agenda*. Online. Available HTTP: http://europa.eu.int/comm/employment_social_policy_agenda/spa-en.pdf (accessed 4 December 2005).

Cosmopolitan (2005) 'Ghidul Cosmo al marilor decizii (Cosmo guide to big decisions)', *Cosmopolitan (Romanian edition)* April 2005: 90–4.

Council of the European Union (2000) *Presidency Conclusions, Lisbon Council Meeting.* Online. Available HTTP: http://ue.eu.int/ueDocs/cms_Data/docs/pressData/en/ec/00100–r1.eno.htm (accessed 4 November 2005).

Cruse, A. (2000) *Meaning in Language. An Introduction to Semantics and Pragmatics*, Oxford: Oxford University Press.

Dăianu, D. (2000) *Încotro se îndreaptă ţarile postcomuniste?* Bucharest: Polirom.

Dăianu, D. (2004) *Pariul României. Economia noastră: reformă şi integrare*, Bucharest: Compania.

Dale, R. (2005) *Knowledge Economy and Lifelong Learning (KnELL) as a New Social/Educational Sector in Europe*, paper delivered at the Workshop on Critical Semiotic Analysis of the Knowledge-Based Economy, Institute of Advanced Studies, University of Lancaster.

Delanty, G. (2000) *Citizenship in a Global Age. Society, Culture and Politics*, Buckingham: Open University Press.

Delanty, G. and Rumford, C. (2005) *Rethinking Europe. Social Theory and the Implications of Europeanization*, London: Routledge.

DeMartino, G. (2000) *Global Economy, Global Justice. Theoretical Objections and Policy Alternatives to Neoliberalism*, London: Routledge.

Department of Trade and Industry (1998) *Our Competitive Future (UK Competitiveness White Paper)*. Online. Available HTTP: http://www.dti.gov.uk/comp/competitive/ (accessed 24 September 2005).

Driver, S. and Martell, L. (1998) *New Labour: Politics after Thatcherism*, Cambridge: Polity Press.

Duffield, M. (2001) *Global Governance and the New Wars. The Merging of Development and Security*, London: Zed Books.

Eagleton, T. (1991) *Ideology*, London: Verso.

ECLAC (2002) *Globalization and Development*. Online. Available HTTP: http://www.eclac.cl/cgi-bin/getProd.asp?xml=/publicaciones/xml/5/10035/P10035.xml&xsi=/tpi-i/p9f.xslebase=/tpl/top-bottom.xslt (accessed 12 October 2005).

Edwards, J. and Martin, J. (2004) 'Introduction: approaches to tragedy', *Discourse & Society* 15: 2–3 (Special issue, 'Interpreting tragedy: the language of September 11 2001'): 147–54.

Eizenstat, S. (1999) The threat to a more open global system. Online. Available HTTP: http://bogota.usembassy.gov/wwwse909.shtml (accessed 23 September 2005).

ENQA (2005) *Standards and Guidelines for Quality Assurance in the European Higher Education Area*, report to meeting of Ministers of Education at Bergen. Online. Available HTTP: http://www.enqa.net/files/BergenReport210205.pdf (accessed 7 September 2005).

Fairclough, N. (1992) *Discourse and Social Change*, Cambridge: Polity Press.

Fairclough, N. (1995) *Media Discourse*, London: Edward Arnold.

Fairclough, N. (2000a) 'Discourse, social theory and social research: the discourse of welfare reform', *Journal of Sociolinguistics* 4.2: 163–95.

Fairclough, N. (2000b) *New Labour, New Language?* London: Routledge.

Fairclough, N. (2001) 'The dialectics of discourse', *Textus* 14, 231–42.

Fairclough, N. (2003) *Analysing Discourse: Textual Analysis for Social Research*, London: Routledge.

Fairclough, N. (2005a) 'Critical discourse analysis, organizational discourse, and organizational change', *Organization Studies* 26: 915–39.

Fairclough, N. (2005b) 'Critical discourse analysis', *Marges Linguistiques* 9: 76–94.

Fairclough, N. (2005c) 'Blair's contribution to elaborating a new doctrine of "international community"', *Journal of Language and Politics* 4.1: 41–63.

Fairclough, N. (forthcoming) 'Discourse in processes of social change: "transition" in Central and Eastern Europe', to appear in Shi-xu (ed.) *Multiculturalism and Discourse Research*, Hong Kong: Hong Kong University Press.

Fairclough, N., Jessop, B. and Sayer, A. (2004) 'Critical realism and semiosis', in J. Joseph and J. Roberts (eds) *Realism, Discourse and Deconstruction*, London: Routledge, 23–42.

Fairclough, N. and Thomas, P. (2004) 'The globalization of discourse and the discourse of globalization', in D. Grant, C. Harvey, C. Oswick and L. Putnam (eds) *The Sage Handbook of Organizational Discourse*, London: Sage.

Fairclough, N. and Wodak, R. (1997) 'Critical discourse analysis', in T. van Dijk (ed.) *Discourse as Social Interaction*, London: Sage, 258–84.

Fairclough, N. and Wodak, R. (Working paper) 'Higher education and the knowledge-based economy: recontextualizing the Bologna strategy in Austria and Romania'.

Falk, R. (1999) *Predatory Globalization. A Critique*, Cambridge: Polity Press.

Flowerdew, J. (2004) 'The discursive construction of a world-class city', *Discourse & Society* 15.5: 579–605.

Franklin, B. (1994) *Packaging Politics. Political Communications in Britain's Media Democracy*, London: Edward Arnold.

Friedman, T. (2000) *The Lexus and the Olive Tree*, New York: First Anchor Books.

Gallagher, T. (2004) *Theft of a Nation. Romania since Communism*, London: C. Hurst & Co.

Gergen, K. (1999) *An Invitation to Social Construction*, London: Sage.

Giddens, A. (1981) *A Contemporary Critique of Historical Materialism*, volume 1, 'Power, property and the state', London: Macmillan.

Giddens, A. (1991) *Modernity and Self-Identity. Self and Society in the Late Modern Age*, Cambridge: Polity Press.

Gille, Z. (2000) 'Cognitive cartography in a European wasteland: multinational capital and Greens vie for village alliance', in M. Burawoy *et al.*

Giroux, H. (2004) *The Terror of Neoliberalism. Authoritarianism and the Eclipse of Democracy*, Boulder, CO: Paradigm Publishers.

Global Community Monitor (2004) *Thailand Bucket Brigade Workshop Summary*. Online. Available HTTP: http://www.gcmonitor.org/workshop_map_ta_phut.html (accessed 16 February 2006).

Gould, P. (1998) *The Unfinished Revolution: How the Modernisers saved the Labour Party*, London: Little, Brown and Co.

Gramsci, A. (1971) *Selections from the Prison Notebooks*, London: Lawrence & Wishart.

Gray, J. (1999) *False Dawn: The Delusions of Global Capitalism*, London: Granta Books.

Greenpeace Australia (2005) *Map Ta Phut: A New Market for Australian Coal*. Online. Available HTTP: http://www.greenpeace.org.au/climate/pdfs/MapTaPhut.briefing.pdf (accessed 16 February 2006).

Greenpeace International (2005) *Stop Climate Killing Coal Plants in Thailand*. Online. Available HTTP: http:www.greenpeace.org/international/press/releases/stop-climate-killing coal-plan (accessed 16 February 2006).

Halliday, M. (1994) *Introduction to Functional Grammar*, second edition, London: Edward Arnold.

Hamelink, C. (1994) *The Politics of World Communication. A Human Rights Perspective*, London: Sage.

Harvey, D. (1990) *The Condition of Postmodernity. An Enquiry into the Origins of Cultural Change*, Oxford: Blackwell.

Harvey, D. (1996) *Justice, Nature and the Geography of Difference*, Oxford: Blackwell.

Harvey, D. (2001) *Spaces of Capital*, Edinburgh: Edinburgh University Press.

Harvey, D. (2003) *The New Imperialism*. Oxford: Oxford University Press.

Harvey, D. (2005) *A Brief History of Neoliberalism*, Oxford: Oxford University Press.

Hável, Vaclav (1997) Fulbright Prize Address. Online. Available HTTP: http://www.fulbrightalumni.org/olc/pub/FBA/fulbright_prize/havel_address.html (accessed 4 November 2005).

Hay, C. and Marsh, D. (2000) 'Introduction: demystifying globalization', in C. Hay and D. Marsh (eds) *Demystifying Globalization*, London: Palgrave, 1–17.

Hay, C. and Rosamond, B. (2002) 'Globalization, European integration and the discursive construction of economic imperatives', *Journal of European Public Policy* 9.2: 147–67.

Heintz, M. (2005) *Etica muncii la Românii de azi*, Bucharest: Curtea Veche.

Held, D., McGrew, A., Goldblatt, D. and Perraton, J. (1999) *Global Transformations: Politics, Economics and Culture*, Cambridge: Polity Press.

Holmes, L. (1997) *Post-communism. An Introduction*, Cambridge: Polity Press.

Honderich, T. (2003) *After the Terror*, expanded, revised edition, Edinburgh: Edinburgh University Press.

Ieţcu, I. (2004) *Dialogicality and Ethical Perspective in Romanian Intellectual Discourse after 1989. A Study of H.R. Patapievici*, PhD Thesis, Lancaster University.

Jackson, R. (2005) *Writing the War on Terrorism. Language, Politics and Counter-terrorism*, Manchester: Manchester University Press.

Jessop B. (1999) 'Reflections on the (il)logics of globalization', in K. Olds, P. Dicken, P.F. Kelly, L. Kong and H.W.C. Yeung (eds) *Globalization and the Asia Pacific: Contested Territories*, New York: Sage, 81–100.

Jessop, B. (2002) *The Future of the Capitalist State*. Cambridge: Polity Press.

Jessop, B. (2004) 'Critical semiotic analysis and cultural political economy', *Critical Discourse Studies* 1.2: 159–74.

Jessop, B. and Sum, N-L. (2001) 'Pre-disciplinary and post-disciplinary perspectives in political economy', *New Political Economy* 6: 89–101.

Jordan, B. (1996) *A Theory of Poverty and Social Exclusion*, Cambridge: Polity Press.

Larrain, J. (1979) *The Concept of Ideology*, London: Hutchinson.

Lavigne, M. (1999) *The Economics of Transition*, second edition, New York: St Martin's Press.

Levitas, R. (1998) *The Inclusive Society? Social Exclusion and New Labour*, London: Macmillan.

Lewis, G. (2005) *Language Wars. The Role of Media and Culture in Global Terror and Political Violence*, London: Pluto Press.

McChesney R., Wood, E.M. and Foster, J.B. (1998) *Capitalism and the Information Age. The Political Economy of the Global Communication Revolution*, New York: Monthly Review Press.

McLuhan, M. and Fiore, Q. (1967) *The Medium is the Message*, Harmondsworth: Penguin.

MacDonald, R. (1994) 'Fiddly jobs, undeclared working and the something for nothing society', *Work Employment and Society* 8.4: 84–106.

Machin, D. and Thornborrow, J. (2003) 'Branding and discourse: the case of Cosmopolitan', *Discourse and Society* 14.4: 453–71.

Matei, S. (2004) *Boierii mintii*, Bucharest: Compania.

Meadows, D.H., Meadows, D.L., Rauders, J. and Behrens, W. (1972) *The Limits to Growth*, New York: University Books.

Ministerul Integrării Europene (Romanian Ministry for European Integration) (2002) Planul National de Dezvoltare 2004–2006 (National Development Plan 2004–2006). Online. Available HTTP: http://www.mie.ro/Pdr/Romana/mdp_ro/dezvoltare/pnd2004/download/cuprins.htm (accessed 14 February 2005).

Ministry of Communications and Information Technology (Romania) *'Outsourcingul'* (2005) Press release, 22 November.

Miroiu, M. (1999) *Societatea Retro,* Bucharest: Editura Trei.

Miroiu, M. (2004) *Drumul câtre autonomie,* Bucharest: Polirom.

Mouffe, C. (2005) *On the Political*, London: Routledge.

Mungiu-Pippidi, A. (2002) *Politica după comunism. Structură, cultură şi psihologie politică,* Bucharest: Humanitas.

Mungiu-Pippidi, A. and Ioniţă, S. (2002) *Politici publice. Teorie şi practică,* Bucharest: Polirom.

Muntigl, P., Weiss, G. and Wodak, R. (2000) *European Union Discourses on Un/employment. An Interdisciplinary Approach to Employment Policy-making and Organizational Change,* Amsterdam: John Benjamins.

Mureşan, L. (2004) *Monitoring Professional Development in an Educational NGO,* Bucharest: Punct.

Negrine, R. (1996) *The Communication of Politics*, London: Sage.

Newman, B. (1999) *The Mass Marketing of Politics: Democracy in an Age of Manufactured Images*, London: Sage.

Ong, A. and Collier, S. (2005) *Global Assemblages. Technology, Politics and Ethics as Anthropological Problems*, Oxford: Blackwell.

Outhwaite, W. and Ray, L. (2005) *Social Theory and Postcommunism*, Oxford: Blackwell.

Pasti, V. (2003) *Ultima inegalitate. Relațiile de gen în România*, Bucharest: Polirom.

Pickles, J. and Smith, A. (1998) *The Political Economy of Transition*, London: Routledge.

Pieterse, J. (2004) *Globalization or Empire?* London: Routledge.

Polanyi, K. (1944) *The Great Transformation. The Political and Economic Origins of our Time*, Boston: Beacon Press.

Preoteasa, I. (2002) 'Intellectuals and the public sphere in post-communist Romania: a discourse analytical perspective', *Discourse and Society* 13: 269–92.

Przeworski. A. (1992) 'The neoliberal fallacy', *Journal of Democracy* 3.3: 67–84.

Pride, R. (2001) 'Wales: can a country be a brand?', in F. Gilmore (ed.) *Warriors on the High Wire. The Balancing Act of Brand Leadership in the Twenty-First Century*, London: Harper Collins, 163–75.

Ramonet, I. (1999) *La Tyrannie de la communication*, Paris: Galilée.

Rice, Condoleeza (2002) 'The president's national security strategy', Walter Wristin Lecture for the Manhattan Institute, 1 October 2002, reprinted in I. Stelzer (ed.) *Neoconservatism*, London: Atlantic Books, 81–7.

Ricoeur, P. (1981) *Hermeneutics and the Human Sciences. Essays on Language, Action and Interpretation*, edited and translated by J.B. Thompson, Cambridge: Cambridge University Press.

Ricoeur, P. (1986) *Lectures on Ideology and Utopia*, New York: Columbia University Press.

Robertson, R. (1992) *Globalization,* London: Sage.

Robertson, S. (2002) 'Changing governance/changing equality? Understanding the politics of public-private-partnerships in education in Europe', Working Paper, Bristol: Department of Education, University of Bristol.

Room, G. (ed.) (1995) *Beyond the Threshold: The Measurement and Analysis of Social Exclusion*, Bristol: The Policy Press.

Roper, S. (2000) *Romania. The Unfinished Revolution*, Amsterdam: Harwood Academic Publishers.

Rose, N. (1999) *The Powers of Freedom: Reframing Political Thought*, Cambridge: Cambridge University Press.

Roy, A. (2004) *The Ordinary Person's Guide to Empire*, London: Harper Perennial.

Saul, J. R. (2005) *The Collapse of Globalism and the Reinvention of the World*, London: Atlantic Books.

Sayer, A. (2000) *Realism and Social Science,* London: Sage.

Schiller, H. (1969) *Mass Communications and American Empire*, New York: Augustus M. Kelley.

Schmid, A. (1983) *Political Terrorism*, New Brunswick, NJ: Transaction Press.

Scollon, R. and Scollon, S. (2004) *Nexus Analysis. Discourse and the Emerging Internet*, London: Routledge.

Sen, A. (1999) *Development as Freedom*, Oxford: Oxford University Press.

Shore, C. and Wright, S. (2000) 'Coercive accountability: the rise of audit culture in higher education', in Strathern (ed.) 2000: 57–89.

Silke, A. (2005) 'Fire of Iolaus: the role of state countermeasures in causing terrorism and what needs to be done', in Bjørgo 2005: 241–55.

Silver, H. and Miller, S. (2002) 'Social exclusion: the European approach to social disadvantage', *Indicators* 2.2: 5–21.

Silverstone, R. (1999) *Why Study the Media?* London: Sage.

Simai, M. (2001) *The Age of Global Transformations: The Human Dimension*, Budapest: Akadémia Kiadó.

Smith, N. (1992) 'Geography, difference and the politics of scale', in J. Doherty, E. Graham and M. Malek (eds) *Postmodernism and the Social Sciences*, London: Macmillan, 57–79.

Solin, A. (2001) *Tracing Texts: Intertextuality in Environmental Discourse (Pragmatics, Ideology and Contacts Monographs 2)*, Helsinki: Department of English, University of Helsinki.

Sparks, C. (1998) *Communism, Capitalism and the Mass Media*, London: Sage.

Stănculescu, M. and Berevoescu, I. (2004) *Sărac lipit, caut altă viață! Fenomenul sărăciei extreme și al zonelor sărace în România 2001*, Bucharest: Nemira.

Stark, D. and Bruszt, L. (1998) *Postsocialist Pathways. Transforming Politics and Property in East Central Europe*, Cambridge: Cambridge University Press.

Steger. M. (2005) *Globalism: Market Ideology meets Terrorism*, Lanham: Rowman and Littlefield.

Stelzer, I. (ed.) (2004) *Neo-Conservatism*, London: Atlantic Books.

Stiglitz, J. (2002) *Globalization and its Discontents*, London: Penguin Books.

Strathern, M. (ed.) (2000) *Audit Cultures. Anthropological Studies in Accountability, Ethics and the Academy*, London: Routledge.

Swyngedouw, E. (1997) 'Neither global nor local: glocalization and the politics of scale', in K.R. Cox (ed.) *Spaces of Globalization*, New York: Guildford, 137–66.

Szacki, J. (1994) *Liberalism after Communism*, translated by C.A. Kisiel, Budapest: Central European University Press.

Tarrow, S. (2005) *The New Transnational Activism*, Cambridge: Cambridge University Press.

Thompson, J. (1984) *Studies in the Theory of Ideology*, Cambridge: Polity Press.

Thompson, J. (1995) *The Media and Modernity*, Cambridge: Polity Press.

Todorov, T. (2005) *The New World Disorder*, translated by Andrew Brown, Cambridge: Polity Press.

Tomlinson, J. (1999) *Globalization and Culture*, Cambridge; Polity Press.

University of Bucharest (2004) Manual of Quality Control. Online. Available HTTP: http://www.unibuc.ro/ro/ (accessed 6 February 2005).

van Eemeren, F. and Grootendorst, R. (1992) *Argumentation, Communication and Fallacies*, Hillsdale, NJ: Lawrence Erlbaum Associates.

van Eemeren, F. and Grootendorst, R. (2004) *A Systemic Theory of Argumentation. The Pragma-Dialectical Approach*, Cambridge: Cambridge University Press.

van Ginneken, J. (1998) *Understanding Global News. A Critical Introduction*, London: Sage.

Van Leeuwen, T. (1995) 'Representing social action', *Discourse and Society* 6.1: 81–106.

Verschueren, J. (1999) *Understanding Pragmatics*, London: Arnold.

Virilio, P. (1997) *Open Sky*, London: Verso.

Wapner, P. (1996) *Environmental Activism and World Civic Politics*, Albany NY: State University of New York Press.

UNECE (United Nations Economic Commission for Europe) (2000) *Public Participation in Making Local Environmental Decisions: Good Practice Handbook* (http://www.unece.org).

Wernick, A. (1991) *Promotional Culture*, London: Sage.

Wilkin, P. (2001) *The Political Economy of Global Communication: An Introduction*, London: Pluto Press.

Williams, R. (1977) *Marxism and Literature*, Oxford: Oxford University Press.

Williams, R. (1989) *Resources of Hope*, London: Verso.

Wodak, R. (2000) 'From conflict to consensus? The co-construction of a policy paper', in P. Muntigl *et al.* 73–114.

Zamfir, C. (2004) *O analiză critică a tranziţiei*, Bucharest: Polirom.

Index

Other titles from the author
New Labour, New Language?

'This is a real book, not written by a spin doctor. Read it and worry. Read it and hope.'

Ted Honderich, *The Guardian*

It's time to 'bin the spin'!

Is New Labour's 'new politics for a new Britain' just rhetoric, just empty words?

This is a book about the politics of New Labour that focuses on language. Norman Fairclough gets behind the rhetoric to uncover the real meaning. Examining a wide range of political speeches and texts, from Tony Blair's speech following the death of Diana to the 1997 Labour Party manifesto, *New Labour, New Language?* blows open the whole debate on the nature of the political discourse of New Labour and the 'Third Way'.

ISBN10: 0-415-21826-8 (hbk)
ISBN10: 0-415-21827-6 (pbk)

ISBN13: 978-0-415-21826-9 (hbk)
ISBN13: 978-0-415-21827-6 (pbk)

Other titles from the author

Analysing Discourse

Textual Analysis for Social Research

Analysing Discourse is an accessible introductory textbook for all students and researchers working with real language data.

Drawing on a range of social theorists from Bourdieu to Habermas, as well as his own research, Fairclough's book presents a form of language analysis with a consistently social perspective. His approach is illustrated by and investigated through a range of real texts, from written texts, to a TV debate about the monarchy and a radio broadcast about the Lockerbie bombing. The student-friendly book also offers accessible summaries, an appendix of example texts, and a glossary of terms and key theorists.

ISBN10: 0-415-25892-8 (hbk)
ISBN10: 0-415-25893-6 (pbk)

ISBN13: 978-0-415-25892-0 (hbk)
ISBN13: 978-0-415-25893-7 (pbk)

Available at all good bookshops
For ordering and further information please visit: www.routledge.com

Related titles from Routledge

Translation & Globalization

Michael Cronin

Translation and Globalization is essential reading for anyone with an interest in translation, or a concern for the future of our world's languages and cultures. This is a critical exploration of the ways in which radical changes to the world economy have affected contemporary translation.

The Internet, new technology, machine translation, and the emergence of a worldwide, multi-million dollar translation industry have dramatically altered the complex relationship between translators, language and power. In this book, Michael Cronin looks at the changing geography of translation practice and offers new ways of understanding the role of the translator in globalized societies and economies. Drawing on examples and case-studies from Europe, Africa, Asia, and the Americas, the author argues that translation is central to debates about language and cultural identity, and shows why consideration of the role of translation and translators is a necessary part of safeguarding and promoting linguistic and cultural diversity.

ISBN10: 0-415-27064-2 (hbk)
ISBN10: 0-415-27065-0 (pbk)

ISBN13: 978-0-415-27064-9 (hbk)
ISBN13: 978-0-415-27065-6 (hbk)

Available at all good bookshops
For ordering and further information please visit:
www.routledge.com

eBooks – at www.eBookstore.tandf.co.uk

A library at your fingertips!

eBooks are electronic versions of printed books. You can store them on your PC/laptop or browse them online.

They have advantages for anyone needing rapid access to a wide variety of published, copyright information.

eBooks can help your research by enabling you to bookmark chapters, annotate text and use instant searches to find specific words or phrases. Several eBook files would fit on even a small laptop or PDA.

NEW: Save money by eSubscribing: cheap, online access to any eBook for as long as you need it.

Annual subscription packages

We now offer special low-cost bulk subscriptions to packages of eBooks in certain subject areas. These are available to libraries or to individuals.

For more information please contact webmaster.ebooks@tandf.co.uk

We're continually developing the eBook concept, so keep up to date by visiting the website.

www.eBookstore.tandf.co.uk